CLOTILDE BREWSTER

ARCHITECTURAL HISTORY OF THE BRITISH ISLES

Series Editor: Dr Timothy Brittain-Catlin, University of Cambridge

British architectural history has a very prominent reputation internationally and sets the standard for publishing and for the development of new ideas and narratives in the field. Covering all periods of architectural history, the series consists of accessible and authoritative studies of specific periods, styles, architects and types of building, and provides fresh insights into fascinating subjects with perpetual appeal. The series is not comprehensive in terms of its selection, but offers the best scholarship in this field, reflecting the richness and quality of British architecture.

Series Advisory Board:

Dr Timothy Brittain-Catlin (Chairman), Director of Studies in Architecture and Design, Gonville & Caius College, University of Cambridge

Professor James W.P. Campbell, Professor of Architecture and Construction History and Seear Fellow in Architecture and History of Art, Queens' College, University of Cambridge

Professor Christine Casey, Professor in Architectural History, Trinity College Dublin

Dr John Goodall, Architectural Editor, *Country Life*

Professor Hilary J. Grainger, Professor Emerita of Architectural History, University of the Arts and Honorary Professor, Durham University

Professor Aonghus MacKechnie, former Head of Heritage Management at Historic Scotland and Visiting Professor, Department of Architecture, University of Strathclyde

Professor Elizabeth McKellar, Emerita Professor of Architectural and Design History, Art History Department, The Open University

Professor Alan Powers, former Professor of Architecture at the University of Greenwich and Chairman of the Twentieth Century Society

The Revd Professor William Whyte, Professor of Social and Architectural History, Fellow and Tutor in History, St John's College, University of Oxford

CLOTILDE BREWSTER

Pioneering Woman Architect

Laura Fitzmaurice

For Garrett, Kieran and Aidan

First published in 2024 by Lund Humphries

Lund Humphries
Huckletree Shoreditch
Alphabeta Building
18 Finsbury Square
London
EC2A 1AH
UK

www.lundhumphries.com

Clotilde Brewster: Pioneering Woman Architect © Laura Fitzmaurice, 2024
All rights reserved

ISBN 978-1-84822-695-1

A Cataloguing-in-Publication record for this book is available from the British Library.

All rights reserved. No part of this publication may be reproduced, stored in a retrieval system or transmitted in any form or by any means, electrical, mechanical or otherwise, without first seeking the permission of the copyright owners and publishers. Every effort has been made to seek permission to reproduce the images in this book. Any omissions are entirely unintentional, and details should be addressed to the publishers.

Laura Fitzmaurice has asserted her right under the Copyright, Designs and Patent Act, 1988, to be identified as the Author of this Work.

Cover: Photograph of Clotilde Brewster taken at her rented rooms at 96 Philbeach Gardens, London SW5, the home of Letitia and Henrietta Cole. Photographer: Mary C.D. Hamilton. Courtesy of The Brewster Archives at San Francesco di Paola.

Copy edited by Pamela Bertram
Designed by Jacqui Cornish
Proofread by Beverley Winkler
Cover design by Crow Books
Set in Adobe Caslon Pro
Printed in Bosnia and Herzegovina

This book is printed on sustainably sourced FSC paper

CONTENTS

Acknowledgments — 6

Introduction — 8

1 Family Background — 11
2 *Genius Loci* – Florence — 19
3 Two Childhood Traumas — 26
4 Lessons with Emanuel La Roche and Mother's Health — 36
5 Rome and the World's Fair — 44
6 Newnham College — 51
7 Lady Pupil in Reginald Blomfield's Office — 54
8 The New Woman and the Problem with Duennas — 67
9 Between Spiritualists and Physicians – Projects for the Hamiltons — 79
10 Socialites and Suffragettes – Projects for the Smyths — 89
11 Roman High Society Meets the Lady Architect – Projects for the Frankensteins — 102
12 The Heiress and the Castle – Project for Contessa Ada Telfener — 118
13 Edwardian Prosperity and Pekes Manor and Estate — 127
14 Home Sweet Home: Stonehill, Chiddingly, East Sussex — 142
15 Moated Grandeur and Shabby Chic: Beckley Park — 155
16 Catalog of Work — 173

Notes — 178
Index — 188
Picture Credits — 192

ACKNOWLEDGMENTS

In 2009, I was hired to design a new side-porch, a new primary bath and renovate a kitchen for a late Victorian-era house for my neighbor in Newton Highlands, Massachusetts. I was surprised when she informed me that her house, and many others in the neighborhood had been designed and built by a woman named Annie Cobb (1830–1911). Fascinated, I then applied and received a research grant from the Boston Society of Architects to document her life and work. She turned out to be the first woman architect in the United States of the pre-professional era. During my research I discovered that she, along with four other American women architects were showcased at the World's Columbian Exposition in Chicago in 1893 in the Woman's Building. Among those women, there was one name I was unfamiliar with – Clotilde Kate Brewster. This sparked a new journey, one which would last for a number of years and involved four trips to Italy, two trips to England, two published articles and now this book. Initially, I planned just to catalog her projects. However, with every letter I translated (her letters to her father were written in French), her story grew increasingly remarkable, inspiring me to create a permanent record of her life. There were many people who helped me along the way.

I owe a tremendous debt to Starr Brewster, grandnephew of Clotilde Brewster – who generously invited me to come and stay at his home San Francesco di Paola in Florence, Italy, in the summer of 2012 to go through boxes of Clotilde's letters to her father. This was the first of a number of such visits and innumerable email exchanges.

My heartfelt gratitude to Eve Leckey, San Francesco di Paola's archivist who put up with my multiple requests, read through my manuscript, made suggestions, and came up with clever chapter titles. And to Eve's friend, Candida Lacey, former publishing director of Myriad Editions, who critiqued my manuscript and accompanied Eve to tour and photograph Pekes Manor.

I am particularly grateful to Clotilde's family: Amanda Feilding, Countess of Wemyss and March, who allowed me to tour her grandmother's last home, Beckley Park, which now houses the Beckley Foundation, and her assistant Vivian Kear who unearthed a treasure trove of Clotilde's drawings in an old dresser drawer and arranged to have them reproduced. Many thanks to the late Jocelyn Feilding and the late Valerie Hibbert-Hingston, Clotilde's grandchildren, for sharing family stories about Clotilde during a lovely afternoon at Valerie's home in the Cotswolds and to her son Mark who kindly arranged the visit. I would also like to thank Clotilde's great-grandchildren, James Hibbert-Hingston whose own collection of letters to Clotilde have been enormously helpful; and Alex Rebanks who shared images of items of Clotilde's he inherited, such as her architect's table and drafting instruments.

Much gratitude to Graeme Taylor who arranged scans of photographs of Clotilde's projects for Mary Hamilton from the Bev and Mary Taylor collection of photographs of Rustington, West Sussex. Thanks also to Clare Snoad of the Rustington Museum for all her help.

I am very grateful to Umberta Telfener, great-granddaughter of Ada Telfener, for hosting a dinner for me in Rome and sharing her family documents; Giulia Ajmone Marsan, biographer of Giuseppe Telfener, for all her help with the chapter on the Castello dell'Oscano; Pierfrancesco de Martino, also a descendant of Ada and Giuseppe, and his wife Lory de Martino for arranging a visit to the Castello and sharing an archival photograph of it; and Patricia Osmond de Martino, for all her help contacting various people and archives in Italy.

I also wish to thank the owners of the properties: Franco Ricotti and Fiammetta Carena, the great granddaughter of Marianna Soderini, for generously giving me a tour of the Palazzo Soderini and sharing related documents and images; Lord Barnard, for sharing images and an historical analysis of Selaby Hall; Kildare Bourke-Borrowes, for all his help and information on Pekes Manor; Fabrizio Temperini for allowing me access to the Castello dell'Oscano, which has been closed to visitors for a number of years and for his generous sharing of photographs; George and Gillian Bretten for welcoming me into their former home, Stonehill and Jamie Hornby, the present owner of Stonehill, for providing documents.

I owe a great deal to Hanni Myers, Lecturer, German Studies Program at Boston College and a close friend who translated letters in German from Clotilde to Eva Hildebrand and letters from Emanuel La Roche to Baroness Clothilde von Stockhausen, among other texts. I also want to thank her for accompanying me to Florence for further research in 2018. A wonderful traveling companion, her energy and sense of humor matches Clotilde's. Other people who were generous with their translation skills were Francesco Castellano, professional linguist, former lecturer in Italian at Boston College and the late Duscha Schmid Weisskopf, former director of Historic Newton.

I want to express my immense gratitude to my family: my sister, Jenny Steigerwald, for accompanying me on three research trips – one to England and two to Italy; and my sons Kieran and Aidan Fitzmaurice – Kieran for his confidence in me and Aidan, who read through the manuscript and made insightful suggestions and edits. Most of all I want to thank my husband Garrett, for his unwavering support and encouragement. He exhibited endless patience when I brought the subject of Clotilde into most if not all of our dinner conversations over the past decade.

Finally, many thanks to the team at Lund Humphries especially my editor Valerie Rose for her assistance throughout the project and the Architectural History of the British Isles Series Editor, Dr Timothy Brittain-Catlin, University of Cambridge, for his excellent advice and suggestions. In addition, I would like to thank my copy-editor Pamela Bertram for all her wonderful work.

INTRODUCTION

LADY ARCHITECT MARRIES That talented lady architect, Miss Clotilde Brewster . . . was wedded this afternoon, at St. John's Church, Smith-square, Westminster . . . The bridegroom was Mr. Percy Feilding, son of the late General Sir Percy Feilding, K.C.B., and cousin of the Marquis of Bath and the Earl of Denbigh.

(*London Evening News and Evening Mail*, 3 May 1904, p.2)

Architecture is a challenging profession even today. But what was it like for a young woman in the late Victorian age, to enter into what was then an inescapably all-male world? Some evidence can be found in the surviving correspondence of Clotilde Brewster (1874–1937), held in family archives and in contemporaneous newspapers such as the *London Evening News* whose marriage notice actually celebrated her role as a woman architect.

Clotilde Brewster's achievements were many: in 1893, while still a teenager, she was chosen to exhibit her work at the World's Columbian Exposition in Chicago. In January 1896, she was the first woman to pass the rigorous, two week-long examinations to enter into the architecture school at the Royal Academy.[1]

She produced a remarkable submission: 'John [Singer] Sargent, then on the committee, often said that he had never seen bolder, more masterly drawings than were handed in by this aspirant'.[2]

His views were shared by others. Robert Weir Schultz wrote, 'Another woman, also articled to a well-known architect, applied for admission to the Schools of the Royal Academy, and her probationary work was, I am informed, the best ever sent in by a student'.[3] In June of 1899, Brewster gave a speech at the International Congress of Women in London, on the subject of architecture as a profession for women. In 1901, The *Lady's Pictorial* published an article on Brewster which featured a photograph of an Arts and Crafts-style cottage she had designed. That same year, at the age of 27, she designed what were her two most prominent projects: the Renaissance Revival-style Palazzo Soderini, which overlooks the Piazza del Popolo in Rome and the neighboring Palazzo Frankenstein.

By any definition, she was a success. After early training in architecture in Florence, Italy, where she was raised, in 1894 Clotilde articled herself to architect Sir Reginald Blomfield in London. The only other women who were training in England at the same time as Clotilde were Ethel Mary Charles (1871–1962) and her sister, Bessie Ada (1869–1932). The Charles sisters were not successful – they had difficulty attracting clients and their output was extremely small. Clotilde, in contrast, found success by aligning herself early on with those at the heart of the women's movement in England who advised and encouraged her. Networking ceaselessly, she courted wealthy women as potential clients. At the beginning of her career, she asked her friends for referrals, offering them a large percentage of the profits should a project be realized.

Though she was intelligent, talented and a trained professional, she was subject to humiliating treatment because she was female. Clients issued her letters of good moral conduct as if she were a scullery maid. Clotilde wrote of one unstable client to her father: 'She then started to tear me to pieces, to accuse me of all sorts of crimes, then heaped praise on me and has just sent me a certificate of good conduct and morals. I want to make a collection of them as in My Papers and present them to passersby so they can countersign'.[4] Clotilde dealt with these clients in a calm and stoic manner. For her Italian projects, she worked intensely with clients but chose to hire local engineers and architects to liaise with city officials and commissions who would have refused to approve any design by a woman and a foreigner. She used the male term 'Architetto' to hide her gender.[5]

Given the era's attitude toward female sexuality, Clotilde rightly believed the smallest indiscretion might damage her reputation and adversely affect her career. Being unmarried, she was obliged to live with an older woman of unblemished reputation who acted as her moral guardian – or as Clotilde mockingly titled it, her 'duenna'. In fact, she had two successive women live in her home and spent more time guarding their morals then they, hers. In order to liberate herself entirely, her only recourse was to marry. Clotilde's criteria in a husband, she wrote her father, was that he must be an architect, physically attractive and of good social standing.[6] In 1904, she married Percy Feilding, who had been her fellow pupil in Blomfield's office. Though far beneath her in talent, the partnership worked. Not only was she allowed her to continue her career unhindered, but she was the architectural designer for many of his projects as well, not least on their own homes in Stonehill in Sussex and Beckley Park, Oxfordshire, which were restorations of older houses. So successful was the restoration of Beckley Park, that it became one of the favorite houses in England of Nancy [Tree] Lancaster, socialite, decorator and owner of Colefax & Fowler, who made a habit of dropping by to show it to friends.[7]

Ultimately, the secret of Clotilde's success was her extraordinary personality. Composer Dame Ethel Smyth wrote an obituary in tribute to Clotilde in 1937,

> Gifted, generous, big in every way, blessedly indifferent to what the world thinks, the staunchest of friends, and a grand listener, she was not only a perpetual source of astonishment and amusement to her friends but, also an intellectual stimulus; for she never uttered an idea – and some of her ideas were startling! – that was not home-grown. When such people are born into this world the mould is broken; and we all know that last Thursday one of the rare things that really matter has gone out of our reach.[8]

To Smyth's appreciation should be added that besides being highly intelligent, Clotilde Brewster, from a young age was energetic, self-confident and a risk-taker, traits then not usually associated with the female sex. Her grand achievement was to be able to successfully negotiate the rigid gender roles of the Victorian and Edwardian era and not be censured or despised for it, but instead, applauded by society.

This biography is not only a social/cultural history, but a contribution to women's history in an important period. Women in the profession of architecture during the Victorian and Edwardian age are virtually unknown; Clotilde Brewster's story is a rare account of elite professional life in Victorian Britain and Europe going into the 20th century. Also included is an in-depth description of a number of her patrons and projects including those with her husband.

Unfortunately, in the 20th century and before, there was a very strong sexual bias in the architecture profession. Thus, it is not unusual for women's participation to have been ignored or actively suppressed. Clotilde Brewster has been largely forgotten by history. Her properties have often been mistakenly reported as belonging to Percy. The work they did on these properties has been solely attributed to him, with her name omitted.

In the case of Stonehill, author Viscountess Wolseley in a 1937 article refers to Percy as a previous owner and states, 'He, being an architect, was able to do much to the restoration of the house.'[9] Architectural historian Sir Nikolaus Pevsner in his guide book for Sussex repeated this mistake when he described Stonehill as 'An idyllic timber-framed Sussex house of the c.15, restored in 1912 when the Sackvilles sold the house to an architect, Percy Feilding.'[10]

Even during Clotilde's lifetime, there were ownership errors regarding her home in Oxfordshire, Beckley Park. A 1925 *Vogue* article about the property stated, 'Beckley remained in the possession of his heirs until it was sold to Mr. Percy Fielding [*sic*], who is its present owner.'[11] This was repeated in articles in *House & Garden* in January 1927[12] and in *Country Life* in March 1929.[13] Incredibly, the 2017 Pevsner *Guide to Oxfordshire: North and West*, Percy is mentioned in connection with Beckley but not Clotilde.[14]

Even when women contributed significantly to architectural projects, their work was frequently attributed to male colleagues or partners. This is especially true when the partners were married to each other. How many people know that Alvar Aalto's design collaborator and wife was architect Aino Aalto? In 1991, the Pritzker committee failed to acknowledge the work of Denise Scott Brown of Venturi, Scott Brown and Associates, when they awarded the $100,000 prize solely to her husband Robert Venturi.

Misogyny in architecture has not disappeared. According to Oliver Wainwright in his article, *Snubbed, Cheated, Erased: The Scandal of Architecture's Invisible Women*, Patty Hopkins, co-founder of Hopkins Architects and wife of architect Michael John Hopkins 'was quite literally erased from history when she was photoshopped out of a group of male hi-tech architects to promote the 2014 BBC series, *The Brits Who Built the Modern World*.'[15]

I have written Clotilde's story because without proper documentation, the legacy of women architects risks being forgotten. Preserving their stories and achievements ensures their place in history for future study and appreciation.

I

FAMILY BACKGROUND

Clotilde's parents, Julia Stockhausen and Henry Bennet Brewster sprang from very different origins. The disparities between the Stockhausen and Brewster families could not have been more extreme: one side came from inherited privilege and wealth and was elegant and polished; the other had humble beginnings in a new land, but was extroverted, self-reliant and entrepreneurial.

On her mother's side, the Stockhausens, Clotilde inherited the aristocratic traditions of Europe, not only the aristocracy's refined manners and taste but also its cultivation of high culture: the study of philosophy, history, the arts and literature, in other words, the acquisition of a classical education that was the hallmark of the patrician classes. This lifelong pursuit was often accomplished through the employment of private tutors, promoted through cultural salons, and passed down through a rigid class system put in place hundreds of years before.

On her father's side, the Brewsters, Clotilde inherited American traits which dated back to the *Mayflower*, when her ancestor Elder William Brewster had arrived on the shores of Massachusetts. In egalitarian New England, qualities such as thrift, hard work and perseverance were admired and seen as paths to success no matter where one started off in life. An ambitious man, through ingenuity and energetic personality, could go far. These qualities were also expected of New England women, but it was only in the late 1830s when the first women's rights movements were formed that ambition in a woman began to be seen as a positive attribute. It took until the latter half of the 20th century for this attitude to be adopted by the general public.

Clotilde's maternal grandfather, Baron Bodo Albrecht von Stockhausen (1810–85), belonged to the old German aristocracy; his noble rank could be traced back to the year 1070 when Dietrich I von Stockhausen was mentioned as being in the service of Duke Otto of Bavaria. By the year 1319 the Stockhausens were granted their feudal lands in Löwenhagen in Lower Saxony. Besides Löwenhagen, Bodo von Stockhausen inherited a number of large family estates in the surrounding area.[1]

After studying at the Universities of Göttingen, Heidelberg and Bonn, Bodo joined the diplomatic service of the Kingdom of Hanover. In 1835, he was sent as an attaché to Paris and later served as ambassador from 1841 to 1851.

In Paris, the income from his estates enabled Stockhausen to have a leisured lifestyle and host regular musical evenings at his home. A lover of music and an accomplished pianist, he soon became the pupil and friend of Frédéric Chopin, the as-yet-unknown Polish composer and pianist, and it was Stockhausen who introduced Chopin to Parisian society. In 1836, Chopin dedicated his Ballade in G minor, Op. 23, to 'Baron de Stockhausen'. That same year, Stockhausen and Chopin visited the Dresden home of Wolf Graf Baudissin, a renowned translator of Shakespeare and Molière. Baudissin hosted a weekly musical and literary salon that welcomed visiting performers, such as the pianist and child prodigy Clara Wieck, the future Clara Schumann. On one of those musical evenings, Stockhausen met Clothilde Gräfin Baudissin (1818–91), Wolf's beautiful and intelligent adopted daughter, who, aged 18, had just come out in society. Bodo soon began to court Clothilde with Baudissin's blessing. They were married in Dresden in July 1837 and went on to have three children: Ernst in 1838, Julia (Clotilde's mother) in 1842 and Elisabeth 'Lisl' in 1847.

In Paris, the newly married Clothilde, a music lover as well, added much to her husband's cultural salon, which was soon frequented by the leading aristocrats of Europe. Chopin attended these events and in 1846 he dedicated his Barcarolle in F major, Op. 60 to Bodo's wife, 'Mme. la Baronne de Stockhausen'.

In 1845, the Stockhausens felt that three-year-old Julia was already showing strong musical abilities and hired Chopin to teach her the piano. The lessons continued until Chopin's death in October 1849. The Stockhausen's younger daughter, Elisabeth, also began her musical education very early, including instruction on musical theory. As the years went by, Elisabeth pursued her musical studies seriously and became known within her circle as a fine singer, inspired pianist and music critic. In 1868, she married the Austrian composer Heinrich von Herzogenberg and became immersed in the musical world of Leipzig, Germany. She later composed music for her own pleasure, some pieces of which were published after her death. Ernst von Stockhausen, Julia's and Elizabeth's older brother, also became a composer.

What was unusual about the Stockhausens was how early they recognized their children's artistic ability and began their training. It seems extraordinary, to have Chopin, the greatest pianist in Europe at that time, teach a young child music. That being said, Julia and her siblings achieved high levels of competency by the time they reached adulthood.

Julia repeated this pattern of early education with her own children. Clotilde was not musically inclined, but she was unusually clever and literate. Letters written by an eight-year-old Clotilde reveal that Julia was already reading to her and her five-year-old brother passages from Plutarch and entire works by Shakespeare. Later, when Clotilde became passionate about architectural design, Julia hired the best professionals available to instruct her.

In 1866 the lives of Clotilde's grandparents were changed dramatically when Hanover was annexed by Prussia in the Austro-Prussian War. Bodo von Stockhausen's diplomatic career came to an abrupt end. Five years later in 1871, Bodo's former colleague, American diplomat John Lothrop Motley, gave a glimpse of Bodo's changed circumstances in a letter to his wife from Dresden, 'We had the pleasure of finding out the Stockhausens. They were out when we called, but they came over the same evening – I mean he and his daughter Julia . . . Stockhausen looks much as usual and was very affectionate. He lives only in his souvenirs, he says. We are going to a family dinner with them to-morrow.' Then Motley continued with a strange statement: 'Julia Stockhausen has been here an hour this morning. She is very bright and intelligent as usual, but hates the world, and they live in great retirement.'[2] Julia's peculiar attitude might have been caused by the consequences of the political events from which her family recently suffered, but it also seems that Motley had picked up on something innate in Julia's character, as later accounts would evidence.

Another description of Julia comes from British composer Ethel Smyth, who met her ten years later

1 Julia Brewster. The Brewster Archives at San Francesco di Paola

in Florence, Italy, after Julia was married and had children: 'Julia was the strangest human being, if human she was, that I or anyone else ever came across, fascinating, enigmatic, unapproachable, with a Schiller-like profile and pale-yellow hair; and though completely under her spell, I knew far less of her at the end of my two Italian winters than at the beginning' (fig.1).[3]

In truth, Julia's aristocratic bearing and great intelligence masked a depressive and reclusive nature. Unlike her daughter Clotilde, who was exceptionally robust, she was plagued by ill health. Turning to books and ideas in search of life's meaning, she would spend her time, according to grandson Harry Brewster, in 'a life-long pursuit of metaphysics and abstract disquisition'.

At the time of Motley's letter, Julia was 29 years old. She was unmarried but had been engaged in correspondence with a young man named Henry Bennet Brewster, or 'Harry' (known later as 'H.B.'), whom she met as a child when her family visited Paris after Bodo's 1852 transfer. She reconnected with him when he came to Dresden for a four-month stay in the fall of 1867. Harry's origins, though, were very far from Julia's aristocratic roots as Harry's father was an American dentist living in Paris. As Christopher Starr Brewster, known as 'C. Starr Brewster' (1799–1870), actually worked for his fortune instead of inheriting it, he was considered a social inferior, and when Harry went on to marry Julia, he married above his station.

Of all her antecedents, Clotilde most resembled her Brewster grandfather, both physically – fair with wide-set eyes, a dimpled chin and flaxen wavy hair – but also in personality. Clever, self-confident and a risk-taker, Brewster's journey from son of a New England tanner to dental surgeon to the royal houses of Europe is the archetypical story of the self-made man.

Both Clotilde and Dr Brewster were original personalities and free-thinkers, valuing the actions of the individual more so than maintaining the status quo. Both believed that through force of will, one could determine one's destiny. This sort of self-determination was especially difficult for women whose roles in society and family were firmly in place, but Clotilde chafed against traditional roles and patterned herself on her grandfather, believing that she was entitled to certain rights because of her American heritage and using it to justify controlling her own future. She rejected the notion that she must submit to parental wishes, and though she had never stepped foot in the United States, dramatically infused her language with American imagery. In 1892 when she was almost 18, she wrote to a friend to announce that she had convinced her parents to allow her to leave home:

FAMILY BACKGROUND   13

I have finally reached it—the objective I've been striving for—freedom. And why should it be any different, 'the land of the free and the home of the brave' is after all my home country, what child of such a country could live in a cage, bound by chains—no—I choose the blue sky and the stars and stripes.[4]

Following a path that has now become an American ideal – pulling yourself up by your own bootstraps by dint of hard work and ingenuity – C. Starr Brewster established a career as a highly sought-after dentist in Paris and became rich beyond his wildest imagination. With no inherited wealth or patronage, he had to make his own way in the world and did not attend university. Brewster, 'an energetic, intelligent and gentlemanly young man', left the family home to clerk in his half-brother Elisha's drugstore in Middlebury, Vermont.[5] During his leisure hours he studied all the literature on dentistry he could obtain. Determined to enter into the profession, he purchased a set of dental tools and practiced on his friends and other willing participants.[6]

By the summer of 1820, Brewster had become skilled enough to start taking patients, and he moved north to Montreal, Quebec. This would be the first of many moves through North America and the Caribbean as a traveling 'Surgeon-Dentist', by which Brewster gained practical experience. Then, in 1823, he settled in South Carolina and opened an office. His business among the well-to-do citizens of Charleston was highly successful – successful enough for him to maintain a second office in New York and to embark on a tour of England and France sometime in 1832 to 1833.

While visiting Paris, Dr Brewster, who was already well known, was urged by the American expatriate community to stay and introduce the superior American methods of dentistry to Europe. Brewster agreed and opened an office on rue de la Paix in 1834.[7] Brewster also became a pioneer in the field of anesthesia, introducing ether to European dentistry in 1847, one year after it was successfully used in a public demonstration in New England.[8] As extraction was the most common dental procedure of the day, the use of ether would revolutionize treatment.

Brewster very rapidly made a fortune as his reputation spread. In 1839, Brewster became the dentist to the 'Citizen King' Louis-Philippe and his family, and he was soon summoned to most of the royal and princely courts of Europe. Brewster's clients included Louis Napoleon and his wife, Eugénie, as well as Tsar Nicholas I of Russia, who in 1842 made him a Knight of the Order of St Stanislas and Dentiste Honoraire of the Russian Court. Other clients included French authors Prosper Mérimée, George Sand, Honoré de Balzac and painter Eugène Delacroix.

In 1848 Dr Brewster decided to settle down at the rather advanced age of 49 and married Anna Maria Bennet (1821–73), the younger sister of a medical colleague and friend, Dr James Henry Bennet. The marriage produced three children: Louis Seabury in 1849; Clotilde's father, Henry Bennet, in 1850; and 'Kate' Mary Catherine in 1857. Soon after Harry's birth, in 1852, Dr Brewster chose to go into semi-retirement; at the time he was 'computed to be worth about $1,500,000', or $44,000,000 when adjusted for inflation.[9] He purchased a large manor house in Versailles called *Hôtel des Princes de Poix*, which was situated less than one mile from the Palace of Versailles.

Though exceedingly wealthy and surrounded by the worldly atmosphere and trappings of the French court, Dr Brewster's New England character essentially remained unchanged. He raised his children in the traditional New England fashion, running a simple household with the same strong Puritan beliefs that had been handed down from generation to generation since the 1600s.

That same year, the Stockhausens moved to Vienna but visited Paris often.[10] According to family tradition, Baron von Stockhausen first came to Dr Brewster as a patient, and they struck up an unlikely friendship. Like Clotilde, Dr Brewster was talkative and exceptionally social; in addition, he quite literally had a captive audience in his patients.

Harry was educated at a Paris-Lycée, which besides providing a classical education, exposed him to rationalist philosophy, promoting the idea that knowledge comes from logical reasoning – as opposed to the religious teaching he received at home. As a teenager he experienced an existential crisis. He would later relate the events to Ethel Smyth: 'When I was fourteen, I went very nearly stone deaf: people had to shout in my ears. And I believe it was due to great anxiety and trouble because I had lost my religion. I had been very intense on the subject for four years and had (heaven help me) converted Zouaves to Protestantism.'[11] In fact, Harry rejected religion as a whole and Clotilde and her brother were not introduced to religious thought or any concept of God.

In the autumn of 1867, Harry's mother, concerned about his poor performance at school, sent him to Dresden to receive private tutoring in preparation for taking his *baccalauréat*, the secondary school leaving examinations that qualified a student to enter university. Anna Maria wanted to get him away from the entertainments of Paris and the company of his many friends, with whom Harry enjoyed a rather light-hearted and somewhat decadent life. Toward this end, she asked her old friend Clothilde von Stockhausen, then living in Dresden, to find suitable tutors and to arrange accommodation for him with a pious family. In this manner, Julia met Harry again; he was almost 17 and she was 25.

Perhaps Harry had every intention of taking his studies seriously, but rather than diligently studying,

2   Henry Bennet Brewster. The Brewster Archives at San Francesco di Paola

he spent much of his time in Dresden frequenting cafes, discussing art and philosophy with Julia, going to the theatre and opera, and sowing his wild oats in nightclubs. His letters home revealed a reluctance to enter a university and take on a profession. His only ambition in life was to be the pursuit of *le vrai, le beau, et le bien* – the true, the beautiful and the good (fig.2).

After four months in Dresden, he returned home, and much to his parents' disappointment failed his exams. A decision was made that he should accompany his brother, Louis, on his trip to

FAMILY BACKGROUND   15

America. Louis intended to settle in New York and establish himself in a career with the help of his banker uncle, Seabury Brewster. The hope was that Harry would be inspired to do the same. Instead, as he wrote to Julia in October 1868 (soon before he left), he intended to spend a year 'travelling, hunting, and dreaming'. During the brothers' trip to the United States, Louis took to life in New York, but Harry viewed America as vulgar and populated with people preoccupied by making money to the exclusion of most everything else.

When Harry returned to Versailles, he retook his examinations and passed. But he was no more willing than before to follow his parents' wishes to take up a useful occupation. His formal schooling thus ended at the age of 16. He began to spend much time with an acquaintance, Henri Cazalis, who would become a lifelong friend. Cazalis was then studying medicine in Versailles and would go on to successfully combine a career as a physician with that of a man of letters. One of his more well-known poems was set to music by Camille Saint Saëns, called 'Danse Macabre'.

Cazalis introduced Harry to the highly cultured circles he frequented – musicians, avant-garde painters and philosophers. Parnassian poets dubbed him the *Hindou du Parnasse contemporain* for his fondness of Eastern thought and he exposed Harry to Hindu, Buddhist and Taoist teachings – philosophies that entirely absorbed Harry's attention for many years to come. Besides spending his time reading and discussing Eastern and European literature, Harry spent these years traveling in Europe, Scandinavia and North Africa.

When France declared war on Prussia in July 1870, Napoleon III's army was vastly outnumbered by Prussia's and within seven weeks, the Second Empire collapsed. Hundreds of thousands of people fled Paris and the surrounding areas, and Harry cut short his travels to join his family in Versailles. Dr Brewster took his wife, daughter and two sons (Louis was visiting from New York), along with the family valuables, to safety in England but returned home with Harry.

On 20 September, the Prussians marched into Versailles. As described in the book *The Cosmopolites*, written by Harry's grandson and namesake, Dr Brewster and Harry were alone in the large house except for two servants: their butler, Dupont, and his wife. Before the end of September came the feared knock on the door. After an inspection of the house, a Prussian captain informed the Brewsters that the whole property would be requisitioned for the use of 16 officers, 40 soldiers and 20 horses. The Brewsters' servants would cook and care for them. If Dr Brewster and his son wanted to stay, the Prussian captain informed them, they would have to live in one small room. As Harry translated what the captain was saying, Christopher Starr became increasingly agitated, 'swearing and waving his American passport at them', insisting that as he was an American, the Prussians had no right to occupy his house. They ignored his declarations and for three months, Dr Brewster had to suffer innumerable indignities, including officers consorting with prostitutes in his own home, everything clearly heard through the door of his room.

Harry would later write of this time:

> Nothing could induce my father to leave his house, so I had to stay with him, he was seventy-one and gouty, and hot-tempered, and he treated the Prussian officers outrageously. My time was spent in explaining 'spread eagle, and the land of the free and the home of the brave' to them and soothing their feelings; they were on the point of arresting him time and again. But all the while I was burning inwardly with a sort of shame-fever at not being able to join my old schoolmates and enlist in the *francs-tireurs*. Often that seemed to me the higher duty; the commonwealth before

the family. Then death came and struck my old father down and there was no one but me to hold his hand. That settled my opinion for life – first think of persons and then of ideas if you have the leisure; ideas can wait.[12]

Dr Brewster died on the 15 December 1870 of a 'ramollissement', a term used for a stroke, and was buried in the cemetery of Notre-Dame at Versailles.[13]

More deaths occurred over the course of the next few years. His closest friend from boyhood, Georges du Buisson, died of consumption in March 1873. In late June, tragedy struck again. Harry had been touring Eastern Europe and had traveled from Constantinople to Vienna to meet his mother and sister; together they went to see the exhibits at the Vienna World's Fair. Suddenly his mother was struck down with cholera during an epidemic.[14] She died and was buried as quickly as possible, typical for victims of the disease. Harry was only 23 years old.

From 1868 up to the point of his mother's death (except for Harry's nine months in America), Julia Stockhausen and Harry wrote to each other continuously in what was dubbed by their grandson, Harry Brewster, as a 'metaphysical courtship'. The main topics of discussion were the philosophy of religion, aesthetics and literature. Harry never included any words of affection. Nor did Julia. They addressed each other very formally as 'Godsister' and 'Godbrother', and except for those four months in Dresden in 1867, had not seen each other face to face.

Then, in August 1873, affected by the recent deaths of both his mother and good friend, Harry sent Julia an unusual letter, unusual in that it contained a dramatic declaration:

> Dear Godsister—it is the last time I am addressing you as such. Either I shall call you differently or it will be the end. We shall have met and quitted, we shall have travelled together for a short while, I shall stay where I am, you will proceed on your way and everything will have been said. What is extremely simple for me is that I don't care for life without you and everything I love and admire is attached to your name—your Christian name. May I call you by it? I don't want to try to persuade you. Apart from secondary considerations you must pronounce yourself either for or against . . . This I must tell you however: whether you answer for or against, you have had, for the time I have known you, and will continue to have, until I have joined the dead of yesterday, my first, my last and unswerving love. Your Godbrother, Henry Brewster.

Harry and Julia were married three months later.

The marriage pact was unusual in that it outlined conditions under which either could freely end the union while maintaining a relationship as Ethel Smyth recorded her memoirs:

> It appeared they had only gone through the marriage ceremony in church in order to avoid wounding the feelings of Julia's family . . . but it was not looked upon as a binding engagement. If either of the couple should weary of married life, or care for someone else, it was understood that the bond was dissoluble, and there was a firm belief on both sides that no such event could possibly destroy, or even essentially interrupt their 'friendship' as they called it, founded as it was on more stable elements than mere marriage ties.[15]

So, Julia and Harry, two people who knew each other intellectually but not emotionally, soon after withdrew to an apartment in Florence to begin their married life together.

3 Cityscape view looking towards cathedral, Florence, Italy.
United States Library of Congress

2

GENIUS LOCI – FLORENCE

For the first ten years of the Brewsters' marriage, Julia and H.B. closed themselves off from the world and devoted themselves to the study of metaphysics, literature and ancient languages. During this time their children were born, Clotilde 'Cloto' in 1874 in Fontainebleau, France and Christopher 'Killy' in 1879. For six months out of every year, for eighteen years, the Brewsters wintered in Florence (fig.3). It was the only permanent home Clotilde would know during her childhood. It is where her aesthetic sensibilities were formed and it significantly influenced design work during her life (fig.4).

As the 19th century progressed, Italy attracted foreign visitors in increasing numbers. They came by steamship and rail, to expand their knowledge of the world and in search of culture. Many wanted to escape from the stresses of modern life. Italy, lacking in natural resources such as coal and iron ore, never experienced the first industrial revolution which had galvanized the economies of Great Britain and the United States and thus avoided all its associated ills – rapid urbanization, the spread of factories, smoke pollution and loss of handmade goods and crafts. A visit to the land of Italy was a retreat into the glorious past and, as noted by novelist Henry James, could awaken one's spirit. 'This Italy of yours on whose threshold I stand, is the home of history, of beauty, of the arts – of all

4   Clotilde Brewster in Florence, about five years of age. The Brewster Archives at San Francesco di Paola

19

that makes life splendid and sweet. Italy for us dull strangers is a magic word, we cross ourselves when we pronounce it.'[1]

Florence, the birthplace of the Renaissance, became a mecca for those foreigners seeking sublime art and architecture. The cultivation of art, in all its forms, was considered conducive to happiness and inspired an almost religious emotion – a visit to Florence was a pilgrimage. Aspiring artists came to study the techniques of the masters; others found lucrative work in painting and sculpture including copying famous works to sell to culture-hungry patrons back home. Scholars established careers as art historians or as dealers in antiques. Still others only wanted to bask in its congenial atmosphere.

The allure of Florence and its relatively inexpensive lifestyle encouraged many foreign visitors to settle permanently. They brought with them all the comforts found at home. There were shops where they could buy familiar goods, churches where they could worship in their own languages and even doctors to treat them in times of illness. Together, they established schools to educate their children. Guidebooks, such as Baedeker, helped ease the transition for newcomers. The Brewsters belonged to both the English and German speaking colonies, but neither to one or the other completely as the language they spoke within the family was French. As a result of their upbringing, H.B. and Julia considered France their cultural home and Clotilde was taught the history of France to the exclusion of American or German.

Considering that language and culture are deeply connected, life in Italy for many foreign residents was, 'like lovely scenery to a blind man', as C. Starr Brewster wrote to H.B.[2] Those who lacked the language skills would never have a deep understanding of the Italian culture or form lasting friendships with Italians. For Clotilde, raised here since infancy, it was the opposite. An Italian noblewoman would later remark that Miss Brewster had 'none of the awkwardness of her compatriots . . . She speaks with a perfect accent not only in English but also French and German as well as our own Italian with a gentle lilt'.[3]

The Brewsters moved in the mid-1870s into an apartment located in the Oltrarno quarter on the southern side of the river. The area consisted of small medieval houses until the 15th and 16th centuries when numerous imposing palaces were built by the aristocracy whose illustrious names they still bear.

Many other, less grand courtyard houses were built in the area by merchants, the ground floor serving as commercial space and the upper floors for domestic use. One of these, called the Palazzo Canigiani (formerly known as the Palazzo Bardi-Larioni) was the Brewster home. It was located on a narrow and sloping road called via de' Bardi, between the river and a hill, and midway between the picturesque Ponte Vecchio and the Ponte alle Grazie. The rear gardens of the palazzo opened up to the river, along the Lungarno Torrigiani, one of the handsome stone quays of the Arno that run the length of Florence.

With its vaulted loggia, massive octagonal pier and Corinthian corbels, the interior courtyard of the Palazzo Canigiani was 'considered to be the most beautiful in Florence'.[4] The windows overlooking the old antique courtyard are medieval in style with a colonnette dividing it into two arched lights and decorated with floral medallions. There is a magnificent stone staircase with balusters in the form of ionic colonettes, at the base of which is an ornate statue of Abundance. On the wall is found a terra-cotta high-relief from the Della Robbia workshop of a Madonna, a homage to Leonardo da Vinci's *La Belle Jardinière* (fig.5).

Colorfully glazed reliefs on the walls of buildings were a popular architectural decoration in Florence since the Renaissance. Adjacent to the Palazzo is the little church of Santa Lucia dei Magnoli, its simple facade enlivened by a 'lunetta' over the

5   Courtyard in the Palazzo Canigiani, home of the Brewsters.
Harvard Fine Arts Library, Digital Images and Slides Collection

entryway, depicting St Lucy flanked by worshiping angels by Luca Della Robbia. Further afield lies the foundling hospital, the Ospedale degli Innocenti, which features Andrea della Robbia's rondels on its loggia. Clotilde measured and drew this building as a teenager and would later use two rondels by the Della Robbia workshop to adorn a converted oast house for a client in Sussex, England.

The Brewster apartment was on the *piano nobile* of the palazzo and extended lengthwise from the front of the palace to the back with a balcony overlooking the gardens.[5] The décor reflected the refined taste of H.B. and Julia. Lining the walls were paintings in gilt frames, mirrors and plates artfully arranged and the occasional tapestry. Rough Italian furniture was placed side by side with elegant inlaid antiques and carved chests. The floors were laid with Persian carpets upon which were placed upholstered sofas and armchairs – a small table made of ivory in H.B.'s bedroom

– family portraits looking down on bookcases filled with carefully chosen books tastefully bound in H.B.'s study. The books reflected the Brewsters' wide philosophical interests – Plato, Aristotle, Upanishads, the Zend-Avesta, Kant, Schopenhauer and Nietzsche.[6] Each room revealed new treasures: A large Japanese vase – a bronze statuette – a drawing by Caravaggio. There were more personal works by sculptor and friend Adolf Hildebrand.

The apartment was spacious and besides the Brewsters, housed a series of maids, the cook, the young Irish governess, Miss Gardiner and the housekeeper, Candida Magnanelli. There was a wood workshop set up perhaps in the apartment but certainly in the building, where the children were given lessons by Italian carpenters named Lorenzo and Angiolo. A young Italian woman named Miss Rossi came to the house every day to help with the children from noon until eight o'clock in the evening. If the weather was good, she would take the children out for long walks in the Cascine Park, a little over a mile away on the north bank of the Arno.

The presence of figures like Lorenzo, Angiolo, Miss Gardiner and Miss Rossi was not always met without protest from the children as evidenced by a letter from Clotilde to her father at age ten. She would have preferred being taught and cared for by him and not outsiders. 'Mother says she wants to hire a tutor for us this winter. I hope that you will give me my lessons and not a tutor. I will learn French, English, arithmetic, geography, history of the old kings and warriors and the history of the cultivation of plants and fields; I will do my best to learn.'[7] But Julia's desires held sway and the children were tutored at home three mornings a week. Otto Lange, the director of the German School, taught Clotilde history and mathematics. Pierrel Oberlé, author of the schoolbook, *Corso teorico pratico di lingua francese ad uso delle scuole italiane*, taught her French and there was a German tutor for both children. Clotilde's grandmother, Clothilde von Stockhausen spent part of each year in Florence, renting her own apartment. She gave Clotilde guitar lessons while the girl's mother taught her to play the piano.

It was her father who first encouraged Clotilde's interest in art. After Christmas 1885, she wrote to him, 'Thank you a thousand times for the little trunk that you sent me; it is charming. I have already put in it everything I need for drawing: in one drawer some models; in the second: box of colors, paper, pencils, charcoal etc. and in the third: my copies.'[8] A few weeks later, 'At the moment I draw regularly every day; I draw from busts and photographs.'[9] She sent him her drawings and received encouraging replies, 'I am very glad that you found my drawings good but don't forget that I chose the best ones. Goodbye dear father.'[10]

In H.B. Brewster's library were books on architecture. Clotilde's favorites were architectural engravings by French architect Eugène Viollet-le-Duc.[11] In 1888 she enthused about another Viollet-le-Duc book, *The Story of a House*, 'You can imagine how happy I am that you are coming back to Florence so soon. We'll have time to read and reread Histoire d'une maison; I have almost finished the chapter on the frame.'[12]

Clotilde's other interest in childhood was farming. In 1887 she wrote to H.B., 'The other day while looking in your bookcase what do you think I saw? Two large volumes entitled: *La maison rustique du 19e siècle* [The Rustic House of the 19th Century]. I said to myself good, here is some architecture, but on opening one of the books I saw that it was not about architecture at all, but about agriculture! You cannot imagine how delighted I was.'[13] She filled entire notebooks with her thoughts on agriculture and in December 1888, subscribed to the *Journal d'agriculture pratique.* As an adult she would put her knowledge into practice at her farm in East Sussex.

Through her letters, she reveals her keen eye and appreciation of art and architecture. She was familiar with the Bargello Museum, the sculptor Donatello and the ornate ceiling of the Badia Fiorenta when she was just 11.

> The drawing room is very beautiful. Above the small Saint John there are laurel branches in bloom in honour of Donatello. We are going to celebrate his birthday soon. And the Madonna over the chimney piece is decorated with a blessed olive branch that Uncle Henry bought on Palm Sunday (on leaving the Bargello) in the church just opposite; the one with the beautiful ceiling.[14]

The following Easter season, a visit to the Certosa di Firenze, a Carthusian monastery which Clotilde knew as the Chartreuse, prompted an inspired account of her day.

> Yesterday we and the Herzogenbergs took an enchanting walk at the Chartreuse. It was charming. The Chartreuse's large chapel (the one which we couldn't see before because they were saying mass) we saw yesterday. It was truly beautiful; the violet colour of the marble slabs harmonises wonderfully with the colour of the wood of the choir. Granny and Aunt Lisl, but especially granny were delighted with the view from the small veranda that the monks show you.

Architecture was never without its setting. In 1887, her grandmother, had found an apartment with magnificent views.[15]

> I'm writing to you from granny's house, sitting on the terrace. You have no idea how beautiful it is. There is not a tree that is not covered with leaves. Before me the reapers are in the midst of scything the grass. On the other side of the garden, they return with pitchforks and the perfume of the hay is exquisite. The sky is blue; there is not a breath of wind; the birds are singing; in brief it is charming.[16]

The veneration of art and architecture was not confined to the foreign visitors. There was a passionate love of art which seeped into the soul of every Italian no matter from what level of society. When the facade of the Florence Cathedral, the Duomo, was finally completed, it coincided with the 500th birthday of Donatello and the transfer of composer Gioachino Rossini's ashes from the Père Lachaise Cemetery in Paris to Florence's Basilica di Santa Croce. The city officials honored these historic events with a series of elaborate celebrations held in 1887: musical performances, an Historical Fancy-Dress Ball, boat races on the Arno, fireworks, illuminations and the Grand Historical Procession – all of which centered around the official unveiling of the facade.

Clotilde wrote of the Grand Historical Procession as if telling a fairy tale. 'Yesterday we went to see the cortege; it was truly magnificent. I have never in my life seen anything nobler and more pompous. Let us start at the beginning of that day when everyone seemed to have forgotten all their troubles and worries and seemed to live only for gaiety and pleasure.'[17] She went on to describe the costumes and decorations in great detail.

Celebratory fireworks were set off on the hill of San Miniato and the city illuminations – when all the great buildings of Florence were outlined with lamps, including the Duomo and other monuments: the Basilica of Santa Croce, the Uffizi Gallery, the campanile of the Cathedral, the Badia, the Palazzo Vecchio and the tower of the Bargello – all of which Clotilde could see from her balcony. Her neighbor, Fosco Tricca (1856–1918), Italian painter and later president of the *Circolo artistico fiorentino*, and whose gallery was on the ground floor of the palazzo, was one of five commission members in charge of creating the illuminations of the monuments, streets, squares and avenues.[18]

Another of Clotilde's neighbors, William Warren Vernon, a British expert on the poet Dante Alighieri, recorded his impressions of the celebrations,

> The Palazzo Vecchio was like a magic castle. All its outlines were marked by lines of fire up to the summit of its quaint machicolated tower. All the people were in the streets, and carriage traffic was suspended, but the next day it was remarked that not a single accident had been reported, and I was assured that, had it been in Rome, there would have been at least a dozen stabbing affrays to be dealt with by the police courts.[19]

The Palazzo Canigiani itself was closely associated with Dante Alighieri (c.1265–1321). Dante attended Holy Mass in the adjacent church of Santa Lucia dei Magnoli on Sundays and feast days. This was the church said to have been frequented by Beatrice, the inspiration for his *La Vita Nuova*. Here, Dante could freely gaze upon his beloved without fear of discovery.

Dante's *La Vita Nuova* was a text much loved by Clotilde's mother, Julia. After her death, Clotilde designed her tomb and on it was inscribed a quote taken from a passage after the death of Dante's Beatrice. '*Non è di cor villan si alto ingegno, Che possa immaginar di lei alquanto*' [No vulgar mind hath grasp of thought so wide, As may her image but in part embrace].[20]

Clotilde spent many leisurely hours on her balcony, especially in the evenings after dinner. Referred to by Clotilde as 'the Arno of a thousand colours', it was sometimes dark and brooding, sometimes silvery blue or jade green, and in the evenings, rose with tints of gold.

Clotilde's views across the Arno from the Palazzo Canigiani were captured in watercolor by another neighbor and friend American Brigadier General Truman Seymour (1824–91). General Seymour had a commanding presence – tall, slender, with piercing black eyes, a thick mane of white hair and a full beard. A career army officer, Truman Seymour was a Civil War hero and a talented watercolorist. In 1877, after retirement from the Army, he and his wife Louisa left for Europe spending a number of years traveling to different countries: England, Germany, France, Spain and Italy. Sadly, he had been plagued by illness throughout his life and had been seriously wounded in the Civil War. He never fully recovered. In 1885, as reported by Clotilde, they moved into a spacious apartment on the top floor of the Palazzo Canigiani after the death of the previous occupant Fosco Tricca's father, Angiolo, a caricaturist and painter of historical scenes who, it later emerged, was author of a number of forgeries.

Visits from friends meant a great deal to General Seymour as for the last five years of his life he was in the critical stage of Bright's disease and was confined to his home. The Seymours' only child had died in infancy and he had become very fond of Clotilde and Christopher.

The General was genuinely delighted when Julia, Clotilde and Christopher returned to the palazzo after their summer absence in November 1890.[21] When he heard Clotilde was to get a velocipede the following summer, he spontaneously went and fetched a book on how to ride a bicycle to give to her. Christopher seemed to be his particular favorite. In June 1891, he wrote to his sister-in-law Emma Weir Casey in Vermont, 'I have a favor to ask of you, or of Casey – that you scrape up some postage stamps for me, U.S. all sizes except 1.2.3 of 5 cents, which are plentiful here: 4.6 and higher are very rare. Chris Brewster is the youngster I want them for, and he is a regular fiend for stamps.'[22]

Before the Brewsters left for Switzerland that summer, Clotilde made sure to visit the General and bid her farewells. That August, he wrote to Christopher:

> From the glimpses we get of repairs being made in your apartments we hope you will surely come back to us next winter: I shall be desolate indeed without you and Clotilde, not to say anything of your dear Mother: we send you each and all our best regards and most sincere wishes for constant good health and happiness. I shall be glad to hear more about your fishing successes whenever you can feel any inclination to write to your old friend – now so lonely that a letter is a blessing.[23]

Truman Seymour died on 30 October 1891, just days before Clotilde, her brother and mother returned to Florence.

Florence (and indeed, the Palazzo Canigiani) was populated by people who were immersed in the making of art or its contemplation. It is not so unusual then, that Clotilde would enter this aesthetic-artist world. From an early age, she acquired a deep understanding of art and architecture. The stimulation of her surroundings, visiting museums and churches, palaces and their gardens, and the process of drawing and woodworking, greatly enhanced her visual and spatial awareness. Most women who enjoyed the privileges of wealth and who were passionate about the arts became painters, a few even became sculptors and some very wealthy ones spent their lives amassing collections but in the 1880s, no one in Clotilde's circle envisioned a woman could be an architect. Though she had no role models, by the end of the decade Clotilde came to desire what no woman of whom she knew had done before – to become a professional architect. It was traumatic events – the devastation by fire of what was to be the family home and the breakdown of her parents' marriage – which would trigger in her this unusual desire and change the course of her life.

3

TWO CHILDHOOD TRAUMAS

An American woman (born in Germany), an acquaintance of Hildebrand, has an extraordinarily ambitious 13-year-old daughter, to whom I was already supposed to give architectural lessons last year. I finally started yesterday and was astonished at the amazingly quick understanding of the little girl. The story is in itself not at all bad, and financially speaking, quite welcome.[1]

(Swiss architect Emanuel La Roche speaking of Clotilde in an 1888 letter to his mother.)

Architectural concepts are difficult to understand by the majority of adults and its study and interpretation is the domain of academics. How is it that a 'little girl' possessed the ability to grasp it so easily? She had an innate talent for the arts, and was highly intelligent, but it was the effect of two tragedies in her early childhood which caused her to become emotionally invested in architecture as a means to reconstruct her past – a world lost with the destruction of what was to be the family home in Avignonet, France and the breakdown of her parents' marriage (fig.6).

Sometime during the year of their son's birth in 1879, the Brewsters began to search for a house of their own, intending to divide their time between the new residence and their apartment in Florence. They had been renting a house for the summer in the town of Claix, near Grenoble situated in the dramatic setting of the Dauphiné Alps. In 1880 they finally found a suitable estate in the area called Château d'Avignonet. Overlooking the Drac River, it was an enchanting mansion built in the early 17th century (1620) by King Henri IV of France for Gabrielle d'Estrées, his favorite mistress.[2] It took two years to fully restore and furnish the château but instead of moving into the new family home that he worked so hard to achieve, H.B. abruptly left for Africa on a five-month lion-hunting expedition in January 1883.

There was more to H.B.'s abrupt departure than was first evident. At the time, British music student Ethel Smyth (1858–1944) (fig.7) was taking a sabbatical from her studies in Germany with Julia Brewster's brother-in-law, composer Heinrich von Herzogenberg. She had arrived in Florence sometime in December 1882 with letters of introduction and thereafter spent a great deal of time first at the home of sculptor and architect Adolf Hildebrand and his wife Irene and then with the Brewsters. Ethel formed warm friendships with both Julia and H.B., but the latter began to feel a strong attraction for their guest. Visiting the Brewster home in the Palazzo Canigiani, Ethel found H.B. pleasant but was put off by his French manner as she wrote in her memoirs.

> My acquaintance with the man destined to become my greatest friend began, it is amusing

6   Clotilde aged about 10 years old.
Architekturmuseum der TUM, Sign. hild-491-1001

to reflect, with a 'little aversion' on my part, although his personality was delightful . . . He seemed to have read all the books, to have thought all thoughts; and last but not least was extremely good looking, clean shaven but for a moustache, a perfect nose and brow, brown eyes set curiously far apart, and fair fluffy hair. It was the face of a dreamer and yet of an acute observer, and his manner was the gentlest, kindest most courteous manner imaginable. But alas! . . . as a thinker I found him detestable! Half American, half English, brought up in France, he was a passionate Latin in the presence of an Anglomaniac . . .³

Before long Ethel changed her mind:

My initial dislike of H.B.'s mentality began to yield to interest as he proceeded to open up a mind hitherto hermetically sealed to the Latin race . . . It was H.B. who first persuaded me to study Flaubert, Baudelaire and Verlaine seriously,

7   Photograph of Ethel Smyth as a young woman. The Brewster Archives at San Francesco di Paola

introduced me to Anatole France, and kindled a flame of enthusiasm for French literature . . .[4]

When Henry Brewster returned to Europe from Africa, he received a telegram informing him that Avignonet had been almost entirely destroyed by fire, the result of the negligence of one of the workmen restoring the château. The newspapers reported losses exceeding 400,000 francs. Insurance would cover only a fraction of the cost.

Ethel Smyth was there when the telegram arrived.

> Just before I left Florence, news came that the Brewsters' château near Grenoble, a grand old pile made habitable by them at great expense, had been burned to the ground. Julia, the superwoman, was overwhelmed, and remained invisible for two or three days, but the bearing of H.B. was a revelation to me; he took it as one might take the loss of an old cigarette-holder.

Ethel Smyth returned home as planned, but came back to Florence early in 1884 for an extended stay and renewed her acquaintance with the Brewsters. When she left this time, H.B. knew for certain that he was in love with her. Ethel returned his feelings.

> My second visit to Florence was fated to supply the test. Harry Brewster and I, two natures to all appearance diametrically opposed, had gradually come to realise that our roots were the same soil – and this I think is the real meaning of the phrase to complete one another – that there was between us one of those links that are part of the Eternity which lies behind and before Time.[5]

In addition, in her memoirs Ethel Smyth falsely gave the impression that her friendship with H.B. was mostly platonic. This was, in all probability, a self-serving attempt to save face in the eyes of the public, who might otherwise view Ethel as a homewrecker. She claimed that it was only in 1895, just over a decade after their first meeting, that they began to have a physical relationship. It was then, during a visit to Paris that she lost her virginity to him as she wrote in her memoirs.[6] In fact, it was as early as 1884 that the two had begun to be intimate as evidenced in their early correspondence.[7]

Even before Ethel's arrival the Brewster marriage was an unhappy one. Many years later in a letter to Ethel, he would describe his initial attraction to her:

> I am a migratory creature, anti-domestic, anti-moral, anti-institutional, anti-prosper and wax fat at home, anti-everything except what savours

of exodus, of departure for far lands; thought of a certain kind, poetry, art, desire, rapture of the body or of the mind. And I struck up a great friendship with a yearner who, for other reasons, in virtue of her perpetual craving, saw things somewhat as I do, as though they were moving and not stationary; one whose view of life often blended perfectly with mine and often contrasted with it so drolely that it was a delight.[8]

H.B. declared that he would not give Ethel up, but Julia refused to condone a triangular relationship – sexual or platonic – as he had hoped. He left for France. Then in November 1885, after a year and a half of total separation, Julia and he met in Milan to sign a separation contract. Ever concerned about her social position and perhaps distraught she was the cause of the Brewsters' marriage breakdown, Ethel broke off all contact with him. For the next six years H.B. led a nomadic existence that included two long stays in New York, partly on family business.

The fire at the Château d'Avignonet followed by the breakdown of the marriage had taken place during the same short period. Associating the two events, Clotilde Brewster, still a young girl, strove to find a means to realize her dream of rebuilding Avignonet and thereby reassemble her family; in her mind, the two goals were inextricably linked. Importantly, these events were to trigger her interest in building, which eventually led to her education and career in architecture.

A sad letter when Clotilde was only ten years old reveals her hope that somehow, she could lead the way to a happy resolution to all the family's problems. In it she first mentions her design for a replacement home. 'Are you never going to rebuild Avignonet? It is the most beautiful place I know. In summer the wind blows, and in winter the snow is deep; is there anything more charming than that? In any case, I'm sending you a plan, what do you think of it?'[9]

Though Clotilde did not know all the reasons until many years later, her father to whom she was enormously attached had gone. He had been a consistent presence in her life from birth until she was eight and, unlike the stereotypical Victorian father, he had been actively involved, giving her lessons, sketching with her, engaging her in discussions and encouraging her to go where her interests and inclinations led. Their personalities were alike in many ways and his leaving had a profoundly negative effect on her.

In addition, Julia never told Clotilde that she and H.B. had permanently separated and in a punitive manner refused his repeated requests to have Clotilde stay with him in France. Clotilde waited in vain for him to come home. Thinking he might arrive in time for her 12th birthday she wrote to him,

> Every time I hear a carriage in the street I run to the window; there is very well a carriage, but no trunk on the seat, no H.B. painted on it and not you in the carriage. Useless to look out the window, I tell myself, yet the next time I set off again, and each time it's the same disappointment.[10]

Clotilde believed that their family home was to be rebuilt. She drew plans, elevations and sections; constructed models; read books on architecture; and discussed her designs with others.

> I'm constructing our house in walnut. I have already sculpted the roof on the Drac side, and I am in the middle of making the side facing the allay. Don't imagine that the roof is polished and clean, no, it's only roughly cut. The roof is not as complicated as we thought. I hope that when you see the house (and that will be soon) it will not displease you too much. I hope that you will be willing to accept it when it's finished.[11]
> (Letter from Clotilde to her father, May 1887 – aged 12)

She composed persuasive arguments to rebuild in the mistaken belief that money was the only obstacle. In the process her interest in architecture and building progressively grew.

> I have just received your letter saying that a wood house costs 275 francs per square foot. This is a horror. But I have an idea! Don't get discouraged. We make the skeleton of the house in beautiful oak timbers or if that is too expensive another type of wood, then we fill between the skeleton with plaster, straw, small stones, lime, mortar and anything else leaving the dark wood timbers exposed. The effect should be very nice, white lime with brown wood. In the interior the rooms will be paneled and the floors cemented . . . It will cost little and look very rustic.[12]

After she began to suspect that the estate was going to be sold, she sank into a state of despair. She conveyed her worries with astonishing clarity to H.B., when she was almost thirteen in a series of daily letters:

> I am delighted that this time you will not stay long in New York, but there is something that is worrying me. Would you by any chance – *I tremble when I think of it* – if you win your lawsuit, establish yourself in Geneva and abandon poor Avignonet for good, who has waited for you these many years with open arms?[13]

Clotilde's visions for a new Avignonet grew increasingly detailed, dominating her dreams and disturbing her sleep.

> During the night I had an idea that I want to share with you. The idea is for Avignonet because all the houses, and all the châteaux that I design – I depict them only at Avignonet, and the beautiful allay where it is found. The idea that prevented me from sleeping is to build the house entirely of wood. You will say, 'There is the danger of fire;' we will insure it at a very high price, and will have a fire pump. The house would be of horizontal beams, one on top of the other, and at the four corners there would be perpendicular posts . . . We would not have architect, or contractor; we would have a carpenter, a blacksmith and some other labourers. The only difficulty would be to take the measure of beams and boards etc. but once this difficulty is overcome, it would be fine.[14]

The summer months were spent with the entire family together, H.B. included, in a rented house in Switzerland. At some point during that time, it was agreed that Clotilde should be tutored by a professional architect.

Julia turned to the Hildebrands for advice, and that fall, Swiss architect Emanuel La Roche was engaged as her *maître d'architecture*. It was still early in his career but he would later go on to design with Emil Faesch the magnificent Basel railway station and other important buildings; he had been invited to Florence in 1887 to collaborate on Heinrich von Geymüller's monumental work *The Architecture of the Renaissance in Tuscany* and in time he would join Adolf Hildebrand's architectural staff.

Clotilde Brewster's path to the profession of architecture depended upon a unique set of circumstances and people. Of these, Irene and Adolf Hildebrand were perhaps the most important; through Clotilde's family's close association with this extraordinary couple, she was able to transfer her fantasy of recreating Avignonet into a real objective – learning to be an architect.

Though only a year older than Hildebrand, Irene was vastly more experienced in life than he. She was the daughter of a wealthy industrialist, Gustave Schäuffelen and his wife, August Syffer, herself a daughter of a physician. In addition, the cultured and beautiful Irene had previously been married to the writer Franz Koppel-Ellfeld. She was well-traveled, had run her own household in Dresden and played a role in its society. Unhappy in her marriage, she left Koppel and moved to Florence, where she began an affair with Adolf Hildebrand, whom she had hired to do her portrait. At that moment, she would later write, her love for Adolf gave her that 'wealth, that plentitude of feeling for which my entire being was yearning'.[15]

Adolf soon purchased San Francesco di Paola, a former convent built by the Fratres Minimi monks in the 16th century and located on the slopes of Bellosguardo Hill overlooking Florence. When the wealthy Irene married Adolf, they created a cultural salon frequented by the elites of Europe. Irene took over the running of San Francesco di Paola, handling the day-to-day business which would have burdened her husband and taken him away from his studio. As Adolf Hildebrand's reputation grew, San Francesco became one of the sites to see when visiting Florence.

Visitors included the Italian aristocrats Count Giuseppe Rasponi and his wife Angelica Pasolini, man of letters Carlo Placci, actress Eleonora Duse, American novelist Henry James and British politician Gerald Balfour. Among the German-speaking world, guests included musicians Richard Wagner and Clara Schumann, composer Franz Liszt, theologian Rudolf Otto, conductor Hermann Levi, painter Wilhelm Füssli and art historian Conrad Fiedler.

Many remembered being in the presence of Adolf as transformative. The poet Isolde Kurz wrote that the air suddenly became infused with oxygen, breathing became easier and the very space itself seemed to expand – 'a magnetic stream coming from him, cosmic as it were, which communicated to all around the sensation of a higher consciousness and order. The dejected would become cheerful, the timid bold, the mournful would take heart'.[16]

German Secessionist sculptor Theodor Georgii who worked as Hildebrand's assistant, wrote after Hildebrand's death: 'His being was radiant; he had an extraordinary temperament, lived and breathed classical harmony, but with a full sense of humour . . . His noble, pure spirit was endlessly stimulating and full of challenges – original, spontaneous, bright as lightning and always generous – he transformed the mundane into something sublime.'[17]

When their second and third daughters, Elisabeth (1878–1958) known as 'Lisl' and Irene (1880–1961) known as 'Zusi', showed artistic promise, Irene and Adolf were delighted. For Adolf, the only thing that counted was talent, no matter if the budding artist was a man or woman. He supported their talents, besides teaching them to draw, model and sculpt, but also to see, to study Greek and Roman sculptures, and those of Donatello, Verrocchio, Michelangelo and the paintings of Renaissance Florence – and most importantly, frequently critiquing their work. He allowed the two girls, then aged 12 and 14, to paint on a wall of his bedroom a Tuscan landscape scene with classical figures.

Zusi showed a preference for sculpture and Hildebrand gave her a studio near to his own where he frequently appeared. Under his tutelage, Zusi became a successful sculptor who exhibited a marble relief of a woman in 1902 at the International Art Exhibition 'Secession' held in Munich.[18] Her own work became so strongly influenced by that of her father, to the point that they were indistinguishable, in fact, an acquaintance of the family wanted to buy her mythological figure 'Flora' (1906) because he thought it was the work of Adolf. Her most public work is the Renaissance-styled Madonna and Child, 'Patrona Bavariae' for the Wittelsbacher fountain in Eichstätt, in 1905, for which she was paid 16,000 Marks.[19]

Zusi married her father's assistant, Theodor Georgii in 1907 and mostly ceased to participate in competitions and exhibitions but continued to sculpt for her own pleasure (fig.8). Her later work

8   Irene 'Zusi' Hildebrand Georgii, bust of Theodor Georgii, 1909, 59 cm, bronze, with marble pedestal. Courtesy of Dr Johannes Wetzel

included freestanding figures and busts of her husband, children and their friends, as well as tomb monuments. After her conversion to Catholicism when she was 36 years old, she primarily created religious works, most of which she donated to churches.[20]

The Hildebrands' second daughter, painter Lisl, aged 12, wrote Clotilde, was already a perfectionist who when drawing, obsessively 'erased and re-erased until nothing was left'.[21]

Lisl lived her entire life at San Francesco di Paola except for 10 years at the start of her marriage to Clotilde's brother, Christopher. The landscape of San Francesco with the backdrop of Florence and its environs would become the inspiration for her paintings.

Her most evocative paintings feature moody dreamlike images reminiscent in style and color of the work of Renaissance artists, whose work she saw in churches and museums, especially those painted on the bases (predella) of Renaissance altarpieces but also influenced by the modern classicism. She created tranquil scenes of peasants in their fields or idealized nude figures in meditation and repose. In other work, her scenes are less intentionally historical, and are more of her time – the literal, real landscape of her picturesque surroundings – but worlds away from the more brutal aspects of the 20th century and the two World Wars (fig.9).

A catalog of her paintings was compiled in 2007 for a retrospective exhibition titled *Natura E Bellezza – Elisabeth Brewster Hildebrand* in Lucca; she produced approximately 150 paintings over the course of her lifetime.

Hildebrand encouraged and shaped Clotilde's talent in much the same way as he had his daughters. She was invited into his studio and considered part of the family. Hildebrand gave young people in his studio great responsibility and opportunities which challenged their abilities. At 16, Clotilde produced a design for Hildebrand for the tomb of his friend, Swiss journalist Heinrich Emil Homberger (1838–90), who is buried in Florence's Cimitero Evangelico agli Allori.[22]

In the Hildebrand archives in Munich, are drawings by Clotilde dating from the 1890s for the remodeling of British statesman Gerald Balfour's villa. Even after moving to England, Clotilde returned to Florence on a regular basis to work with Hildebrand on various architectural projects (fig.10).

9   Elisabeth Brewster Hildebrand, *Meditazione*, oil on wood, 106 × 193 cm, private collection
by courtesy of the Brewster Archives at San Francesco di Paola

10   One of five drawings of the Balfour Villa remodel drafted by Clotilde Brewster, *c.*1894.
Architekturmuseum der TUM, Sign. hild-238-3

11 Adolf Hildebrand, Portrait of Clotilde Brewster, 1889, plaster, 66.99 × 46.67 × 18.73 cm, Los Angeles County Museum of Art, James E. Clark Bequest (M.87.119.18). Photo © Museum Associates/LACMA. This was the study for the more formal marble bust Hildebrand sculpted in 1890

When Clotilde was a teenager, Hildebrand created a high-relief in marble of her with the inscription: CLOTHILDE BREWSTER, ARCHITECTURA ALUMNA, AETATIS SUAE XV, FLORENTIAE MDCCCXC (Clotilde Brewster, student of Architecture, at age 15, Florence 1890) but whether Hildebrand actually thought architecture a suitable profession for women is unknown (fig.11). The Women's Rights Movement only began in Germany around 1890, much later than in Great Britain and America and not something of which the Hildebrand daughters would have been aware at the time.

In 1896, Clotilde was staying at San Francesco and reported to her father: 'As for Lisl, she is in disgrace. The poor girl wastes a few minutes each morning and night curling her hair and her parents cry out that she doesn't take her talent seriously. Her hair must be cut.'[23] It was an idle threat but illustrates the Hildebrands' conviction that first and foremost, one must be true to one's calling. This was a spiritual dictate though and not an earthly one. There is no evidence they wished their daughters to work for financial gain. Zusi, and especially Lisl, never had a strong desire for recognition and never promoted their own work. Whether it was for money or ambition, allowing women to work in parity with men was to risk them being infected by the moral taint associated with public life. It was a persistent notion. In fact, theologian Dietrich Hildebrand would say approvingly of his sister Lisl much later 'Totally unworldly, she never tried to become famous, to advertise her work, or to stoop to the demands that the modern "artistic" world . . . makes upon those who wish to gain recognition in their lifetime.'[24] Ambition was considered unnatural in a woman. Their calling was to selflessly serve others – whether church, family or philanthropic organizations – the common good.

Clotilde, in contrast, was unabashedly ambitious. She not only wanted to immerse herself in the study of architecture but wanted to enter the profession and earn the prestige and rewards associated with high levels of success. In addition, what drove Clotilde's atypical desire was not materialism but a need for financial independence. It was driven in part by a desire to escape from her mother, who as described in the next chapter, was becoming increasingly unstable.

4

LESSONS WITH EMANUEL LA ROCHE AND MOTHER'S HEALTH

In choosing Emanuel La Roche (1863–1922), Adolf Hildebrand could not have found a better *maître d'architecture* for Clotilde. Young, enthusiastic and handsome, La Roche made important contributions to her development as an architect. First and foremost, he took her ambitions seriously. He was a talented teacher and showed a genuine interest in her work and almost as important, her welfare (fig.12).

La Roche had an unusually rich education for an architect. In Basel, he first apprenticed with a master stonemason and carpenter while simultaneously attending lectures given by eminent art historian Jacob Burckhardt. He then went on to study architecture for two years at the Polytechnic Institute in Stuttgart after which he worked for one year in the studio of French sculptor Eugène Dock, who had been a teacher of Auguste Rodin, the founder of modern sculpture.[1] Dock specialized in architectural decoration, caryatids and figurines worked in a variety of media. To complete his education, in 1886–7, La Roche was employed in Mannheim by the classicist architect Leonhard Schäfer where he learned the practical aspects of construction.[2]

La Roche's family was intellectually prominent in the city and actively involved in the arts. His father, Emanuel La Roche-Stockmeyer was the pastor of the Basler Münster, the city's Gothic Cathedral, as well as the curator of the Basel art collection at the Museum on Augustinergasse. The Cathedral would loom large in his son's early professional life as well. As a teenager, La Roche collaborated with his father on its historical study.[3] During his first apprenticeship, he worked on the restoration of the Cathedral towers. In 1888, while living in Florence and working with Adolf Hildebrand, La Roche was commissioned to design the bronze doors for the cathedral's most celebrated feature, the Romanesque St Gallen portal.[4] He wrote to his mother that he possibly would have Hildebrand 'as an excellent collaborator in making the figurative decoration for the doors'.[5]

Thus, Emanuel La Roche, already at the age of 24, had impressive family and artistic credentials when Heinrich von Geymüller invited him down to work on the multi-volume work, 'The Architecture of the Renaissance in Tuscany' in 1887. Art historian Jacob Burckhardt assured his friend Geymüller: 'You will have great support with La

12   Photograph of Emanuel La Roche, Clotilde's architecture teacher. University of Basel Library. NL 96: IV 95. The Eduard Wölfflin Thesaurus Foundation

Roche. For talent and ambition are not always found in the same person. This time, the right man has come to Italy. For many architects who are blessed with money and fortune do not know what to do with Italian art.'6

In the fall of 1888, La Roche was hired to instruct Clotilde. The first lessons involved drafting intersecting geometric shapes which she copied onto cardboard, cut out and glued together. Though abstract in nature, the lessons directly related to forms in the built environment. In one letter, she wrote excitedly to her father how vaults were created from her model of two intersecting half cylinders.

For her next project, La Roche engaged her carpentry skills in a whimsical project. Working from drawings they developed together, Clotilde designed a Renaissance-styled dovecote for her father, an avid pigeon fancier. It was an elaborate construction, made entirely of oak with classical columns and capitals, besides the more practical elements such as dividers and doors for the birds. It would take her almost a year and a half to complete, from drafting board to the finished polish. The project charmed La Roche, for each time he arrived at the Palazzo Canigiani for a lesson, he stopped in her carpentry workshop to see how the work was progressing.

They continued their lessons through the spring of 1889, which included studying and drawing the Classical orders; how to sketch with China ink; formal drafting and free-hand sketching; mechanics; perspective drawing and how to use photography to reconstruct the geometry of a building when unable to measure a structure in its entirety.

The following winter their studies would be interrupted. Encouraged by Adolf Hildebrand who advised him it would be important for his career, La Roche left in November 1889 with a friend, banker Alfred Sarasin, on a seven-month trip to Asia, three months of which he would spend in India recording its architecture and ornament.[7] Clotilde wrote to her father, 'It's a shame I have to interrupt my lessons for so long a time, but he'll give me plenty to do. This is at least some consolation to me.'[8]

La Roche returned in the fall of 1890 where he took up his work again for the Società San Giorgio and the lessons with Clotilde resumed. He took her along to the sites he was documenting.[9] Three times a week, he gave her lessons at the house, the other days, they were out in the field.

In an amusing incident, Clotilde and La Roche were stopped abruptly by the guards of a building they were about to sketch. 'They said I could not draw without a permit certifying that I was a painter, sculptor or architect.' La Roche took her to the city hall to apply for a permit – where they faced another obstacle. As Clotilde wasn't Italian, the city officials told them, she needed a stamped letter from her country's consul officially stating that she could draw. After a false start at the German Consulate, they eventually made their way to the U.S. one – where, without blinking an eye, the American Consul supplied her with a completely false document, certifying that she was a fully fledged architect who had done her studies in New York. They made their way back to the municipality with the letter – and pleased to have outmaneuvered the Italian bureaucracy – Clotilde wrote to H.B. 'The employee was astonished but did not make any kind of difficulty; now I can draw any monument or painting in a museum without paying an entrance fee. We are currently taking the measurements of the *Ospedale*; it's very amusing. We have a tall ladder; I climb up and as I go, I note all measurements while Mr. La Roche writes them down. Tomorrow, we measure the arches and vaults; however, as they are not semi-circular but segmental it will be complicated.'[10]

During the winter of 1890–91 Clotilde and La Roche would measure the masterpieces of the Renaissance such as the Pazzi Chapel (designed by Filippo Brunelleschi); Chiostro dello Scalzo (designed by Giuliano da Sangallo), and the courtyard and loggia of the Palazzo Guicciardini.

That spring when La Roche was temporarily away, Hildebrand arranged for a replacement teacher, his friend and colleague Rudolf Seitz (1842–1910). Seitz was highly talented, but Clotilde missed the young, handsome and energetic Emanuel La Roche. She complained to her father in March 1891, 'Mr. Seitz is very nice, but he looks to me to have burned all his fireworks. He says that after all, he didn't know whether a quiet life in the country might not be better. He doesn't have any ambition or aspirations. He said it himself. That's the trouble.'[11]

La Roche took as much pleasure from their excursions as Clotilde. He wrote to his mother on 30 December 1890, 'The lessons with the little Brewster girl are taking up a lot of my time, but they are richly rewarded, in that this child is so interested – for she is still a child despite her 16 years.'[12] Clotilde was, in fact, socially immature. She had been kept isolated from the outside world by her mother, and allowed no freedom to freely associate with those of her own age. The only playmates of which Julia approved were the Hildebrand children and Clotilde was the eldest of the group by three years.

This behavior echoed the parenting of the previous generation. Baroness Clothilde von Stockhausen never allowed Julia or her sister Lisl to have friends. According to Ethel Smyth when she first met the Baroness: 'This old woman, handsome, gifted, violent as ten devils rolled into one, who looked like a Louis XV marquise, I found very attractive, and hoped she would like me; but unfortunately I was hated at first sight with the vitriolic jealousy of one who had never permitted her children to have friends, or even playmates.'[13] The sight of Ethel Smyth at Lisl's home, 'drove Frau von Stockhausen into convulsions'.[14]

Julia was Spartan in many aspects but very generous in others. Severe in manner and dress, she withheld physical affection from her daughter yet purchased only the finest drafting instruments, carpentry tools and architectural books for her. Julia hired tutors who were exceptionally accomplished educators in their own right and charged fees accordingly. Beyond her children's intellectual development, though, she had little interest in them. Ethel Smyth wrote of her, 'I also noticed that the simplest reactions of human nature seemed incomprehensible to her till she had stated them to herself in terms of metaphysics . . . after that all was clear – now she held the clue!'[15]

When Clotilde's younger brother showed signs of being academically lazy, Julia became extremely distressed – obsessing from morning till night over his lessons – his Latin, his French, his arithmetic, his piano. She was easy to anger and being around her was like walking on eggshells. Clotilde dreamed of escape and confided in Nini [Eva] Hildebrand her desire to 'go into the reading room, to smoke, to not always be at the mercy of others – to be independent and free of family life'.[16]

Clotilde began to rebel, spending more and more time away from home. The more Clotilde tried to pull away, the more control Julia tried to exert over her. Invitations were turned down and Clotilde was not allowed to correspond with anyone without Julia's permission. All the letters Clotilde received were read; all those Clotilde wrote, were read, edited and rewritten according to Julia's standards and wishes – including letters to her own father. Miss Rossi, who had accompanied Clotilde whenever she went out with La Roche, now kept watch inside the house – making sure Clotilde didn't sneak out.

In February 1891 a telegram announced H.B. was intending to visit. In a letter Clotilde wrote in the middle of the night and mailed in secret she expressed her joy at his possible return and quoted a passage from Parnassian poet Leconte de Lisle's *Midday*, a work which H.B. was no doubt entirely familiar with.

> You cannot imagine, picture, conceive the pleasure, the happiness, the joy your telegram has caused me.
>
> *Come! The Sun speaks to you in sublime words;*
> *Absorb yourself forever in its implacable flame;*
> *And return with slow steps toward the minuscule cities,*
> *Your heart dipped seven times in divine oblivion.*[17]
>
> Mother will write to you this evening. She will tell you to come in a few days so that her face has time to recover, but good heavens, her face has healed, or it will be in two or three days in any case, come then, be here on the 25th., I count on you; come I beg you.[18]

H.B. did travel to Florence, stayed for a short time and left abruptly.[19] In another *Poste Secrète* sent in April, Clotilde told her father of the worsening situation at home.

We are getting on each other's nerves (I speak of
mother and myself); we attack each other; we don't
understand each other. I'm sure you'll be the first
to understand this; you have had this experience,
and you packed your bags. You were damn right
. . . She is so nervous that it's hardly bearable.
She takes offense at everything said – but no one
offends and hurts her. I am speaking not of me or
Killy, but of granny, of the Hildebrands. Granny
says that she (granny) is going to go crazy if this
continues. The Hildebrands are forced to agree
with her in everything, to always give in; otherwise,
it infuriates her and she has nervous attacks.[20]

Julia had also been plagued with numerous chronic illnesses throughout her adult life, but now it developed into something new and frightening. 'Mother is very weak; she has a strong cough again; she eats very little; and she has absences of mind that are very odd.'[21] The situation took a dramatic turn for the worse and a week later Clotilde wrote again of what appears in retrospect to be a grand mal seizure,

Mother was very white, mouth closed but she
drooled, with unfocused eyes, and her fists
clenched convulsively. I went to call Candida,
when we returned, she was bluish-red, she twisted
her neck, and gesticulated while drooling and
moaning; after a quarter of an hour she was fully
recovered and did not remember anything . . .
Mother is beside herself, extremely weak.[22]

In the summer Julia, Clotilde and Christopher had planned to meet H.B. in Switzerland as was customary. But now, Clotilde did not want to travel alone with her mother and brother, as she feared Julia might have a seizure during the journey. She begged H.B. to return to Florence and help with the arrangements, as 'travelling with someone of whom you're not sure, it's something else altogether – this is less than pleasant'.[23]

Clotilde, pushed to her limit, had been writing to La Roche of her troubles. The letters were sent through Irene Hildebrand, who was sympathetic to Clotilde's plight, on the one condition that Clotilde burn all his letters immediately after reading them. Eventually, La Roche became concerned enough to write to Irene Hildebrand on 1 April 1891.

I ask myself whether these relations have for a
long time been such that they cannot be mended
and may be harmful to Cloto. Would it not be
better to remove her from her mother's side and
to transplant her to an environment of quite a
different kind, above all to one different from the
present one. Her father could surely step in for he
loves his child and certainly wants the best for her.
He must also have noticed the discord between
mother and daughter. He could find a place for
Cloto in London or Paris; the *École des Beaux Arts*
in Paris would probably be best . . . It would be
such a pity if Cloto came to harm because of the
unhappy situation of her family. If you believe that
Mr. Brewster's intervention is desirable I would of
course be glad to turn to him.[24]

That Clotilde's mother was inflicting psychological harm on her there is no doubt. The various physical restrictions placed on her movement by her mother also imply that there was some amount of force used and La Roche felt some action needed to be taken.

La Roche further wrote to Irene,

[Cloto's] letters plainly show that her attachment
to me is due to more than friendly affection. I
have to confess that this attachment gladdens
my heart and the prospect makes me happy . . .
[but] I am aware that I am the only young man
whom Cloto knows and that her attachment to
me is the consequence of that special situation, so
that it would constitute a sort of robbery to profit
from it.

La Roche was taken off guard; though affectionate, Clotilde had never revealed to him the depth of her feelings in person in any way. As she had written to her father since the age of eight, it was easier for her to unburden herself in a written form.

La Roche was an exceptional human being – handsome, talented, intelligent, energetic and the nicest man Clotilde had ever known. In addition, as she spent an extraordinary amount of time with him, it was somewhat inevitable that she would fall in love. It was not the romantic love between two adults but an intense worshipful infatuation of a young girl for her teacher.

La Roche unwittingly fed her adoration through letters, the following excerpt is from one he wrote to Baroness von Stockhausen in the fall of 1891,

> I received Clotilde's drawings. I liked them very much . . . All the items portray their real character. They are free of the mistakes that most architects make in that their renderings show the affectation of the architect rather than nature of the original. This mistake is understandable since the 'gentlemen architects' are usually not objective enough to immerse themselves in a task in an unprejudiced way. It is very refreshing to experience an exception to this sad rule. I am sure it is not unwarranted to draw a conclusion about the whole character of the person who possesses this rare ability. Recently, I saw architectural drawings by Rieth, an architect from Berlin that were presented with the pretension of genius. However, they were nothing but an individual style applied to dreadful ideas. How rare are the people who truly sense the beauty in things, who are free from the worship of such an illusion. Therefore, the few who find each other have to stick to together tightly![25]

H.B. finally addressed the situation. By July, it was decided that Julia, Clotilde and Christopher would move to Rome early the next year. They would stay in Florence until H.B. could find a suitable apartment large enough for all of them.

The year of 1891 ended in a blaze of fire. On the night of 26 December, in their apartment in the Palazzo Canigiani, Clotilde stayed up all night to attend to her dying grandmother, who, as Clotilde wrote to her father, was 'falling into infancy, she no longer knows what she says or what she does'.[26]

The other adults in the household – Julia, Candida the housekeeper and the Baroness's chambermaid – were all confined by illness to their own beds. At half past four in the morning, Clotilde heard a loud knock at the door. It was Santi, the concierge, who wanted to know why there was such noise coming from the Brewster apartment. It was so loud it jolted him from a sound sleep.

As they made their way through the enfilade of rooms, towards her father's sitting room, the sound of flames and the crashing of stones could be heard coming from within, but a cloud of dense smoke prevented Clotilde from entering the room. Clotilde raced down to the street, and looked up at the windows to assess the situation. They were so brightly lit she hesitated no longer and sounded the alarm. She sent Santi to the neighbors, whom she knew owned a telephone, to summon the fire department. The tenants came pouring out into the street in various states of dress. Twenty firefighters and eight policemen arrived on the scene. They broke the windows and entered by ladders where they found the ceiling was in flames. They opened the doors to the room which created a rush of air through the apartment. Firefighters began to douse the room via three water pumps working from the street.

Heedless of her own safety, Clotilde ran in to the burning room with the firemen in a desperate attempt to save the family portraits and other precious objects. She carried out as much as she could and directed the servants to remove the furniture and roll up the carpets, items that could fuel the flames. The fire quickly spread to Julia's sitting room, and Clotilde gave the orders for the Hildebrand's bust of the Baroness von Stockhausen to be removed and her mother's book cabinet filled with rare editions. 'I was only just in time because a huge quantity of masonry collapsed as the beams failed and the stone floors sagged above', she wrote. The corridor and staircase were packed with furniture.

Finally, the fire was put out. It had started in the chimney above the wall separating the two sitting rooms. The ceiling beams became overheated and self-ignited, burning from the inside out. Luckily, thanks to Santi, the fire was caught early – a third of the ceiling of H.B.'s room and much less of Julia's were burned. Both rooms were uninhabitable.

There was much damage to the furniture but the most significant loss was the oil portrait of her American grandfather, Christopher Starr Brewster, which had been close to the ceiling and thus more exposed to the flames. It was unrepairable, suffering burn holes and large areas of peeling paint.

Throughout the series of the night's events, Julia was on the verge of collapse and incapable of taking action. She remained near her mother, who was completely unaware of the drama unfolding around her though there was 'an unparalleled commotion and din'. The Baroness died a few days later; Julia was inconsolable. She had 'worshipped her mother, to whose shortcomings her eyes were lovingly blind', as H.B. wrote to Ethel Smyth just after the tragic event.[27]

In late January, Julia, Clotilde and Christopher joined H.B. in Rome. La Roche allowed the secret correspondence to continue but they were 'to only write each other about philosophy, architecture, about books, etc., but nothing else'.[28] As Clotilde wrote to Nini, he wanted to remain her friend, The letter was very nice and clear. It would really be impossible to demand more from him – so my reason tells me. I will have to control my feelings – as far as I am able. He does not want to tie himself down; rather, he wants to be totally free. He wants to me to be free as well. '*Qui vivra verra*'.[29]

The late winter and early spring of 1892 was spent in Rome, but Clotilde returned to Florence in mid-April to pack up their possessions from the apartment on via di Bardi, bidding goodbye to her friends. During her stay Clotilde assisted Hildebrand with an architectural commission for Count Giuseppe Rasponi dalle Teste. He and his wife Angelica Pasolini lived at the villa Font'all'erta, just outside of Florence and were constant visitors to San Francesco di Paola. Angelica was very close to Irene Hildebrand and Adolf had created a stunning bronze bust of her in 1887. Rasponi owned a number of estates and occupied himself with agriculture including the cultivation of tobacco in Barbialla. Clotilde was friendly as well with the Rasponis, especially with Rezia their daughter.

I have good news to give you, I did work for Count Rasponi and I think he is going to pay me. It's lovely, isn't it? This is the first money I've earned! I know how I will spend it (my letter wouldn't be complete without that word) I am going to buy a bottle of champagne and celebrate with my friends; Art, Liberty, Independence long may they live, but you can be sure that we will toast you just as loudly. Here's what it was about: Rasponi must rebuild a church and a prior's house on his property; La Roche was responsible for the design. The prior saw and accepted them, but they didn't please Rasponi in its layout and architecture. Hildebrand had another idea, and I was put in charge of doing the drawings, first plans and elevations and then a large perspective sketch of the ensemble with trees and clouds and shadows – a large pen drawing!

That is how I corrupted the good prior and made him prefer my drawings to those of La Roche, who had not done a perspective. Rasponi was very happy as well and Hildebrand told me that La Roche could not have drawn any better. I am very proud.[30]

The First World War brought an end to La Roche's architectural work as with so many architects in Europe. Though Switzerland was not involved in the war, the economy collapsed and there was a complete halt to construction activity. During these years, La Roche did not remain idle; he organized his research materials gathered in the winter of 1889–90 to produce a chef d'oeuvre on the architecture of India, *Indische Baukunst*, published in six volumes during 1921–22 and financed by his friend, Alfred Sarasin.[31]

In the summer of 1922, while vacationing in Celerina, Switzerland, La Roche went out for his usual evening walk – and vanished without a trace. His heartbroken widow suspected suicide. She would later write to Dr Emil Gratzl, an Orientalist who had been advising La Roche about his book, that her husband had lost all interest in the India photographs and went on to relate La Roche's agitated state: 'It was incredibly sad, to be witness of the deterioration of his mind. He was infested with a severe mental illness, which would most probably have led to dementia within a short time. He knew this for certain and he wanted to escape.'[32] His body was never found and he was officially declared lost on 28 September 1928.[33]

Clotilde would always have a place in her heart for La Roche. He not only honed her architectural skills but helped her transform from an immature teenager into a confident young woman. Later, ignorant of his early death, Clotilde would recommend La Roche as a teacher when her nephew Ralph expressed an interest in studying architecture.

5

ROME AND THE WORLD'S FAIR

At the beginning of 1892, Clotilde was at a crossroads in her life. Her mother's health had deteriorated to such an extent that the family left Florence to permanently to live with H.B. in Rome. Clotilde left her home, her friends and her teacher Emanuel La Roche. In addition, she yearned to become a professional architect and lead a life of independence in England (fig.13).

Profound changes were happening in Rome – a transformation of its physical appearance which had been put in motion 20 years before. In 1871, Rome had been declared the capital of the newly formed Kingdom of Italy and immigrants poured in from Northern and Southern parts of Italy at an alarming rate. As a consequence, there was an unprecedented need for new government office buildings and housing.

Those in charge of the government, as well, desired Rome to be transformed into a modern metropolis to rival other European capitals; a master plan was drawn up in 1873 and revised in the 1880s. It was an ambitious building program which included the establishment of new traffic patterns throughout the city, and the development of new residential and administrative districts near a large rail station outside the city walls.

Parts of the historic city fabric were razed to achieve these goals. For example, to create the dramatic National Monument to Victor Emmanuel II and the main traffic artery of Via Cavour, large areas of Capitoline Hill were removed along with an ancient neighborhood where Julius Caesar grew up, a labyrinth of a narrow alleys, shops and markets called the Suburra.

Clotilde advised a friend to visit soon as historic Rome was changing and being aesthetically destroyed,

> Evermore ugly straight streets are being built and more and more is excavated. The Ponte Sant'Angelo (Bridge of Angels) is spoiled. They are building large, broad quays along the Tiber and are tearing down the old picturesque houses which used to be reflected in the river. Instead, they are replacing them with squares. I know that this is nothing compared to what is left. The splendor of ancient Rome will always supersede the destruction, but the city is losing all its charm.[1]

As Clotilde alluded to, one of the most controversial projects, was the urbanization of the River Tiber which involved the wholesale demolition of structures on the north and south sides to make way for embankments – the massive retaining walls built to prevent flooding. The construction started in 1876 and lasted 50 years.

The regeneration of the waterfront indiscriminately wiped out everything in its path with total disregard for historically significant

13   Clotilde Brewster in Rome about 18 years old.
The Brewster Archives at San Francesco di Paola

structures. Already demolished were the Baroque staircase at the Porto di Ripetta (demolished 1890) and the Palazzo Altoviti (demolished 1888). Over the course of the years, the scenic wall of dwellings which seemed to rise straight out of the water and features such as courtyards, pergolas and terraces overlooking the river disappeared. These views had inspired European artists for hundreds of years, from Giovanni Battista Piranesi to Camille Corot. The final result would be a functional but flat and lifeless wall (fig.14).

Though Clotilde was homesick for her old home and friends, there was much to distract her in Rome. If Florence represented the Renaissance, Rome embodied the grandeur of the ancient world. 'You cannot imagine how wonderful Rome is and what a magnificent impression the city makes! Above all, the Roman ruins are splendid and the Colosseum is so gorgeous that one cannot even describe it.'[2] Clotilde, as one noble Italian woman would later recount, was in love with Rome as was 'every true artistic soul'.[3]

After buying a book of Piranesi prints, Clotilde wrote to Adolf Hildebrand: 'I could swear that I am myself just a few lines on an old engraving, that the columns surround me, the churches and the fountains, and the priests, and the carriages, and I am nothing but a silhouette, dreamlike and unreal.'[4]

Remnants of ancient Rome could be seen even from Clotilde's bedroom window in the Palazzo Ferrini Cini, the Brewster's first apartment in Rome, which overlooked the Temple of Hadrian in Piazza di Pietra. The Temple dates back to 145 CE and its surviving side colonnade had been incorporated into a papal palace designed by Swiss architect Carlo Fontana in the 17th century.[5]

Their landlady, Countess Cini, was part of the Italian aristocracy: 'I've visited her several times with father and have dined there. She always has a court full of counts and dukes but she is very natural and simple.'[6] Once, noted Ethel Smyth, Countess Cini arrived unexpectedly to visit with the Brewsters in their apartment, accompanied by 'two of her faithful admirers; one a Knight of Malta, de Brazza Savorgnan, brother of the explorer who is governor of the French Congo, the other a most picturesque old marchese who is chamberlain to the King'.[7]

The Countess Cini, née Adele Piacentini was an attractive widow with a dusky complexion, dark hair and eyes. Though she had two grown sons, she was still elegant and possessed a seductive charm.[8]

In February of that first year, Clotilde was invited by Countess Cini, to the *veglione* – the masked ball held at the end of Carnival, the elaborate celebrations before Lent. By tradition it was a decadent affair in which ladies were permitted to

ROME AND THE WORLD'S FAIR   45

14   Baroque staircase at Porto di Ripetta *c.*1860. The Royal Danish Library – Art Library

go alone in disguise through the crowds and could according to an American magazine, '*intriguer* and mystify to their hearts content, as long as they keep their voices at the regulation falsetto pitch, without experiencing an impertinent answer or an insolent proposition'.[9]

To conceal their identities, the Countess Cini, her sister and Clotilde put on satin masks and wore over their gowns the traditional black domino – a voluminous full-length cloak with cape, narrow pointed hood and wide sleeves – and went by carriage, without male escort, to the Teatro Costanzi. Not being forewarned (such things were not discussed with young ladies), Clotilde was surprised at the licentious nature of the event and the behavior of the two women.

The countess and her sister had to alter their voices. It was astonishing – incredibly wild – there were many gentlemen with masks but also many without. Then the two ladies attached themselves each to a man, and I did the same. Everyone was on familiar terms with one another, and said outrageous, shameless things. The gentleman, of course, wanted to know who the ladies were and tried to tear off their masks. The countess was very nice and didn't pay any attention to me – I was free to do whatever I wanted. I too said shocking things . . . Naturally, I mixed only with the nobility or officers. A few of them thought that they might know me. It was incredibly fun. We stayed until 4 o'clock this morning! The time flew-by. The countess was then recognised and to end the evening as wonderfully as it had begun, we went with our cavaliers to Donnie's and ate and drank champagne. It was very beautiful – *but can you imagine* – if I had really known someone very well – you know what I mean – how would it have ended then? Indescribable![10]

Clotilde very soon after was seized by remorse. She wrote to La Roche to describe the ball and confess her own eager participation, hoping that he would find it in his heart to forgive her. 'I told him about the ball; I wonder whether he now thinks I have sunk so low as to be unworthy of his gaze. If that were the case, I would never go again into such company. I hope though, that he will not be too severe, and will understand human weakness.'[11]

Within a week, she accompanied her Uncle Henrich von Herzogenberg to a large event at Otto von Fleischl's, a physician at the Austro-Hungarian Embassy.[12] There were 120 people in attendance, all in formal dress. Clotilde was overwhelmed by the glamour – the ladies wore 'long dresses with trains, décolleté, fans!' She was asked to dance and pretended she knew how. A bumbling archaeologist brought her over to the buffet table and she had to be on her guard in case he 'put vanilla on the fish and mayonnaise on top of the dessert'.[13] There were countless archaeologists in Rome due to the excavations; new treasures were being unearthed every day. Clotilde was to become good friends with one of them, Georg Heinrich Karo who was doing manuscript studies in Rome and would later become the director of the German Archaeological Institute at Athens.

More invitations followed, dinner at the Guerrieri-Gonzaga's, a visit to the Mengarini's, a reception at the Piacentini's among other social events those first few months.[14] Clotilde was enchanted. Escorted by her father, she entered a world of superficiality and worldliness which Julia despised, H.B. thought amusing and Clotilde found exhilarating. Julia was so reclusive in Rome that people mistook Clotilde for H.B.'s wife and invitations arrived addressed just to the two of them.

By June, the family was back in a rented house in Nyon, Switzerland, where Clotilde and Julia were again at loggerheads. Every interaction was cause for argument. Clotilde made matters worse by emphatically and persistently stating that she was leaving home as soon as she was old enough. She had been entertaining the idea of going to England for at least a year and a half, when H.B. had written to her regarding a meeting he had with interior decorator, Agnes Garrett. In 1890, H.B.'s sister, Kate de Terrouenne, hired Garrett to design and decorate her sitting room at Champhaudry, her cottage in Sandillon, Loiret, France.[15] After an introduction through Kate, H.B. consulted Garrett about Clotilde's ambitions and sought her advice.

At this point in time, relayed H.B., architectural education was primarily through one's association with an architect and his atelier:

Here is how things work in England: You don't go to a school of fine arts like in Paris. There is one but the best architects don't come from there and look down on it. You apprentice with an architect for five years; which is to say you pay a considerable sum for the privilege of working with him. You work as much or as little as you want, but if you work hard and if the master takes an interest in you, he gives you some of his work to do on your own behalf and after five years you in turn become a master. It seems to me that it is a very good system because you are immediately in practice.[16]

Agnes, together with her cousin Rhoda Garrett, trained with Daniel Cottier, a decorator, furnisher and glass-stainer in London and then with architect John MacKean Brydon.[17] They thus became the first women in Great Britain to officially apprentice to an architect. In 1874, they opened their own business, calling themselves 'architectural decorators'.[18]

Agnes Garrett was from an extraordinary family; in addition to her cousin Rhoda, there were her two sisters – Dr Elizabeth Garrett Anderson and Millicent Garrett Fawcett – and her niece, Philippa Garrett Fawcett. All the Garretts were active in the Women's Suffrage Movement and individually were pioneers in their own fields. Elizabeth was the first woman in England to qualify as a doctor; Millicent was active in the movement for higher education for women and was one of the founders of Newnham College in Cambridge; Millicent's daughter Philippa was a mathematician and educator. Their influence was widely felt – as H.B. wrote to his daughter in 1892, 'In the Fawcett-Garrett circle, one is right in a clan of active and distinguished women and their friends. This is a fairly powerful coterie that welcomes with open arms any young person who looks promising as a recruit for a good cause. You see I work behind the scenes. I am preparing an entry for you.'[19]

Agnes Garrett and Millicent Garrett Fawcett both thought Clotilde needed to wait before joining an architect's office because of her youth but Agnes suggested that she submit an original work to the Chicago World's Fair. It was, as H.B. wrote, 'a way to introduce yourself to the world and can be a good opportunity'. In fact, a year before, in July 1891, Clotilde read a newspaper report in disbelief that the next World's Fair, to be held in Chicago in two years' time, was to feature The Woman's Building, an exhibition hall specifically built to showcase the products of women's industries in fine art, crafts and literature and document their progress through the ages. Most importantly for Clotilde, as she wrote to a friend, the hall was to be designed by a female architect. A number of American women architects had competed in a design competition for the building.

Agnes Garrett spoke highly of Clotilde's aspirations, H.B. wrote to her, and had in mind two architects she could apprentice with when she was old enough: Basil Champneys, College architect for Newnham College, and Richard Norman Shaw, the most well-known and respected architect of the day.

In the summer of 1892, determined not to interrupt her architectural studies during the family stay in Nyon, Clotilde traveled to Geneva numerous times per week to the office of Jacques-Elisée Goss (1839–1921), a well-respected and prolific architect whose principal works were the Geneva Opera House, the Hôtel National and the headquarters of watchmakers Patek-Philippe. He set aside a sitting room with a drafting table for Clotilde's exclusive use.

Goss was very personable and friendly, even inviting Clotilde to his home to dine. He very much liked Clotilde's design for a house and instructed her on its construction. Clotilde told him she was considering submitting drawings of it to the World's Fair, an idea which Goss encouraged, as she told Nini Hildebrand, '[Goss] says I should send the drawings of the house to Chicago and praised it very much . . . Now that father, mother and Goss (who is the premier architect in Geneva) say that I should do it, I am telling myself that maybe the design isn't so bad and that I should go ahead'. She continued, 'But if La Roche dislikes it, then all the other opinions of the world can go to hell. I won't continue with it. In the meantime, however, I must work harder than ever before, since Goss is urging me on . . . Goss takes great pains to help me and wastes a lot of time trying to teach me something. Blast! What an idiot I am – I still have so much to learn. He tells me, though, that I don't need to rush. I have time.'[20]

La Roche, it appears, approved the design as by November and still in Goss's office, she completed six pen-and-ink drawings of a villa to submit to the Woman's Building at the World's Fair – which, by a curious coincidence, Ethel Smyth's music was to inaugurate.[21]

As the Brewsters owned property in Manhattan, and as Clotilde was legally a citizen of the United States, she would have had to submit her drawings through the New York Board of Women managers who were in charge of procuring the best items to be exhibited from their state.[22]

Only some 14 women were active in architecture in the United States in 1893;[23] five were chosen to exhibit their work in the Woman's Building: Sophia Hayden, Lois Lilley Howe, Minerva Parker Nichols, Anna Cobb – and 18-year-old Clotilde Brewster.

In America, the routes women could take to become an architect, at this time, were varied. They could attend one of the architecture programs at the rare universities that had recently begun to admit them. Or if one had an architect in the family who thought it appropriate for women to enter into the profession, he might provide some training, give encouragement and use his connections. It was also possible to enter the profession through the building trades if one had enough money to build speculative houses and an interest in studying architectural books and journals on one's own. Finally, if the woman was quite wealthy, private tutors could sometimes be found. Those university programs that admitted women provided an alternative to traditional male paths to becoming an architect such as apprenticing to a carpenter or working in an established architect's office. (These routes were generally closed to women.)

The paths followed by the other four female architects exhibiting in Chicago in 1893 illustrate some of the variations. Sophia Hayden (1868–1953), from an old Massachusetts family, was the first woman to be accepted to the four-year architecture program at the Massachusetts Institute of Technology and obtained her degree in 1890; she won the nationwide architectural competition for the Woman's Building, which was based on her thesis project. Lois Lilley Howe (1864–1964), also from a well-to-do Massachusetts family, was Hayden's MIT studio mate but enrolled in a special two-year program. She was the runner-up in the competition for the Woman's Building and went on to form an all-female architectural practice. Having a family member in the architecture profession enabled Minerva Parker Nichols (1860–1949) to pursue her design studies and follow in her grandfather's footsteps; in 1893, she was the only woman to run a solo architectural practice in America. The career of Anna Cobb (1830–1911) of Newton Highlands, Massachusetts and Pensacola, Florida, represents one of the very few ways women of her earlier generation could become architects; a hardworking real estate speculator from an impoverished but respectable family, she made the crucial transition from constructing homes based on plans from carpenter books to designing houses herself. Interestingly, of the exhibitors, only Anna Cobb and Minerva Parker Nichols were architects of actual buildings at the time of the planning of the Fair.[24]

Sophia Hayden's only known work is the Woman's Building. The enormous stress of construction led to what was called a 'brain fever' and Hayden did not see the project to completion. Discussions followed in journals of the day questioning whether women were physically capable of being architects. *The American Architect and Building News* in December 1892 stated:

> It may be that Miss Hayden's experience has been unusual, but the planning and construction of

any building with the accompanying dealing with clients is always liable to be 'especially trying' and it seems as if it was a question not yet answered how successfully a woman with her physical limitations can enter and engage in the work of a profession which is a very wearing one. If the building of which the women seem so proud, whether justly or unjustly need not be discussed here, is to mark the physical ruin of its architect, it will be a much more telling argument against the wisdom of women entering this especial profession than anything else could be.[25]

In fact, it was Hayden's lack of experience rather than her sex which contributed to her nervous breakdown. Though she had graduated with honors from MIT, she was unable to get a position in an architect's office and worked as a mechanical drawing instructor in a Boston high school. When she won the competition for the Woman's Building, she had no practical experience in construction.

At the same time that Clotilde was preparing her drawings for Chicago, she was eager for her future plans to be put into action, as she wrote to her friend Nini, 'Recently I told father I could not wait two years to go to London – it would be impossible, I want to go next winter, I cannot stand it any longer. I want to work, not for the sake of working, but for the experience of working in an atelier where I can learn the practice and move forward.'[26]

H.B. though, thought her still too young to enter into an architect's office in London, but a compromise was reached – attending a woman's college in England for a year in the interim might be possible. There she could study mathematics and acclimate to the manners and customs of the country. H.B. persuaded Julia to agree and within weeks a letter was sent from Newnham College to Julia with instructions as to how Clotilde was to apply for admission, enclosed with the regulations of the Higher Local Examination and the examination papers of a former year. No doubt, the Garrett sisters had a hand in H.B.'s choice of a school for his daughter. Clotilde was ecstatic – she would spend the spring of 1893 preparing for the exams in the Mathematical and Language Groups. Her new life, free from the troubled relationship with her mother, was about to begin.

6

NEWNHAM COLLEGE

In spring 1892, after a long and difficult period in her life, Clotilde's father, H.B., gave her some hope for the future (fig.15). Although he felt she was too young to enter directly into an architect's office in a foreign country, he agreed that she could spend a year at Newnham, a women's college in Cambridge, to study mathematics and acclimatize to the British way of life. Although she still had to wait until she was 18 to go, the prospect of leaving home lifted her spirits. For his part, H.B. would spend more time in Italy, caring for Clotilde's mother, Julia. Clotilde had a pang of regret for a beloved father who was sacrificing his freedom for hers. To a friend she wrote, 'I feel quite sorry for father . . . Now I'm free and he has to pace up and down on the carpet, stand watch and feel the weight of the chains.'[1]

Clotilde originally intended to sit her entrance exams at Cambridge University in December 1892 and, if accepted, begin school in January. Unfortunately, the school sent the necessary paperwork to Nyons, France instead of Nyon, Switzerland where Julia, Christopher and Clotilde were staying. She would have to wait another six months for the next scheduled examination – another frustrating delay. Finally, in June, she was tested on analytical geometry, algebra, trigonometry, Italian and French; on the last day she took a four-hour long exam on the German language. Passing with flying colors, she spent the next year studying

15   Photograph of Clotilde Brewster, about 20 years old. The Brewster Archives at San Francesco di Paola

Descriptive Geometry for Engineers; Static and Dynamic Mechanics; and Differential Calculus. Much later as architecture training came under the control of academics rather than practicing architects themselves, these subjects would become standard courses in Britain. For Clotilde these

51

courses would provide her with an exceptional foundation for her career in architecture, more so than the average pupil in an architect's office. She also took some general education courses such as languages and literature as befitted a young woman of her social class.

After the entry exams were over, Clotilde and her father spent some time in London before joining Julia in Zurich, Switzerland for the summer where Clotilde also planned to work. During this short visit to London, H.B. and Clotilde went to museums and the theatre, met with old friends of H.B. and visited extended relations. This would be Clotilde's first introduction to people who would later become her clients in a few years' time.

From Newnham College where she was staying during her week of entrance exams, Clotilde relayed her picturesque impressions of Cambridge to her mother:

> With their severe porticoes and their spiral staircases the old colleges must have been convents in former times – everything is delightful – the bridges and the streets and the silent river – the magnificent allays! The Gothic colleges with their walls rising from the river are reflected in the water with perfect clarity. The river runs along an endless number of Gothic and Renaissance style buildings, passes under countless bridges, flows under the shade of elm trees and loses itself in distant meadows where herds graze.

But it was London which most impressed her. In the same letter she relates,

> The day we arrived was splendid; it was much warmer than in Italy! Immediately father and I went for a walk in the city. Westminster Palace which we saw in the evening fog was quite pleasing. It's modern and in my opinion quite successful. When you need a lot of windows this is the style for you. It's pure Gothic. And St. Paul's which we saw the following day is magnificent; I'll bring you some photographs of it. All in all, I was not expecting such beautiful things – but there are a number of hideous houses as well; you couldn't call them houses really but black cardboard sheets with rectangular holes – however there are many beautiful <u>modern</u> buildings the like of which I have never seen.

Julia's response must have been negative as Clotilde then replied,

> I received your letter, many thanks – you are very harsh regarding the Gothic; I presume you are thinking of your plates pierced by ogival windows – that would be hideous I agree, but it's not that at all. It's about the 'perpendicular' which is something else entirely. There is not *Wandfläche*; the whole thing is just the arabesque in stone, the solid surface appearing only as stone tracery, dividing the voids in compartments, creating shapes pleasing to the eye. The whole is only <u>one</u> Gothic window and not a grouping of windows. But you can judge for yourself by the photograph.[2]

The Gothic and Renaissance styles of the Cambridge colleges which Clotilde described in her letter were not reflected in Newnham, which was first established in the 1870s. According to Margaret Birney Vickery in her book *Buildings for Bluestockings: The Architecture and Social History of Women's Colleges in Late Victorian England*, the founders of Newnham wanted a 'homey and domestic' atmosphere which would impart a non-threatening appearance to parents and potential benefactors. Consequently, a domestic style popular with the middle classes and dubbed the Queen Anne was the architecture of choice. It was loosely based on 'Old English' buildings from the reign of Queen Anne (1702–14), but borrowed many elements from different eras and other styles. Features from the Classical, such as pediments, lunette windows and pilasters, were used informally in original and artful compositions.[3]

Sidgwick Hall, Clotilde's residence, was built in the architectural language of a country manor. It was constructed of red brick, with white trim and sash windows. It featured whimsical Flemish gables, decorative brick aprons under the windows and Swan's neck pediments and Palladian windows in the side bays. Each girl had a small room with plain white walls, a fireplace and a bed that was made up to look like a sofa during the daytime so friends could visit. Besides its own dining hall, Sidgwick boasted a newspaper room and a music room. Astonishingly, there was no library.

Newnham little resembled what Clotilde envisioned. Unlike Girton, the other women's college at Cambridge, it did not seek to imitate the academic culture of the male schools. Rigorous study and examinations were considered too stressful for the delicate female constitution, and, as women would not be competing with men, it was ultimately deemed unnecessary. The students who came from the wealthier classes should be educated enough to run philanthropic organizations, but for the average young woman, the main purpose of her education was self-improvement. For them, Newnham functioned as a finishing school.[4]

Clotilde took French literature and mathematics at Newnham, but had to go into Cambridge to the men's colleges for her German literature and engineering courses. She was the only woman in the class for engineers and thoroughly enjoyed it. She makes no mention of what Miss Graves, her fellow mathematics student, described as the dreadful way women were treated while walking to their lectures in Cambridge: 'the men assemble to see us & laugh & criticise us'. On the contrary, Clotilde was rather amused at the students' behavior and thought their antics were harmless jokes.

When Clotilde returned in January for the Lent term, she found the atmosphere more to her liking. There was much less socializing, societies and games. She had more time to study and wasn't 'obligated to spend the evenings sitting stiff as a board in people's homes'.[5] In March, Miss Helen Gladstone, one of the vice principals, called her into her office to tell her how pleased she was with her work.

In April, the school lifted some restrictions, which suited Clotilde. After a short visit home at the break between the Lent and Easter terms, Clotilde wrote to her mother,

> I'm back in my cell which is even more isolated than that of the monk who watched the Crusaders leave for the Holy Land – as I can see nothing but a dirty courtyard and a small patch of sky – dirtier still. But it suffices; with a good fire and some books many other crusades have been made. I am very happy here and I can go up and down by a small back staircase whenever the desire strikes me – usually after dinner as we can go out in the evening now. It's more fun than in the day because we can sit on the banks of the Cam and look at the light boats pass, our hearts full of envy.[6]

By mid-May she was looking forward to the end of term. Student life at Newnham left much to be desired but in the end her year there served a useful purpose. Newnham was not what she imagined but she came to recognize its value, nonetheless. The community of Newnham was a microcosm of the wider society. Though women's roles in Victorian England were still rigidly in place there was much talk of female emancipation which would help ease the path for those wanting to enter into the professions. Clotilde's next step would be a jump from an all-female environment into the all-male sphere of an architect's office.

7

LADY PUPIL IN REGINALD BLOMFIELD'S OFFICE

We are working hard; we went to Norman Shaw's, the most celebrated architect of the day; he is charming – an old gentleman, tall, svelte, handsome, full of life; a type of court physician, friend to his illustrious patients; he would have taken me – unfortunately he is retiring from business. Let us not speak of art! – because who retires from art if at one time one has made it – but he no longer has an office. It's such a shame, but he has promised to help us. The difficulty, as he says, is that so few architects count architecture among the arts; for most it's a profession and that I do not want. So, eliminating those who do not want me and those I do not want there is not much left.[1]

(Clotilde, letter to her mother, 29 June 1894)

After leaving Newnham College, Clotilde and her father looked for an architect with whom she could apprentice. They were having some difficulty but eventually went to see renowned architect Richard Norman Shaw whose work had enormously influenced domestic architecture and was instrumental in creating and popularizing what is today known as the Queen Anne style (fig.16).

At the time a great battle was raging among architects about whether architecture was on the same footing as sculpture and painting or more affiliated with the building trades. Starting in the late 1880s there was a push by the Royal Institute of British Architects (RIBA) to transform architecture into a tightly controlled profession by introducing examinations and issuing diplomas. Richard Norman Shaw and many other leading architects, called the Memorialists, fought against this, believing artistic sensibility or talent – a fundamental qualification for designers – could not be tested. Artist-architects, attracted by the philosophy of the Arts and Crafts movement, sought to dissociate themselves from large commercial firms who mechanically produced buildings in a style they were most familiar with, or in a style that was currently in fashion. The Memorialists viewed these commercial architects as mere engineers, surveyors and commission agents.[2]

In 1894 the pupilage system, which dated back to the 18th century, was the most common route to an architecture career. If the architect was a capable master, a pupil acquired much practical knowledge, learned to draft, measure, oversee construction, run an office, etc.

Richard Norman Shaw arranged an introduction between Clotilde and a young architect named Reginald Blomfield. She was soon articled with

16   Photograph of Clotilde Brewster taken at her rented rooms at 96 Philbeach Gardens, London, SW5, the home of Letitia and Henrietta Cole. Photographer: Mary C.D. Hamilton. The Brewster Archives at San Francesco di Paola

him for three years at the cost of £135 per year, the equivalent to £23,618 in 2024.[3] The cost was high (and the work menial) but the expectation was that if you had been a pupil of a prominent architect, he would pass on work and introduce you to his wealthy clients later on. For his part, Blomfield admired Shaw enormously and would have been happy to accommodate his rather curious request to take on a female pupil.

Blomfield's future looked bright. William Morris and many Arts and Crafts leaders were counted amongst his acquaintances and friends.

Very much immersed in the current architectural scene, he contributed to the publication *Architecture, A Profession or an Art* (1892) and was an early member of the Art Workers' Guild. He had recently published a book titled, *The Formal Garden in England*, which was well received and soon would bring in clients. During Clotilde's first year in the office Blomfield was hired to apply his garden design concepts at Godinton House near Ashford in Kent. It was to be one of Blomfield's most successful designs. Additionally, during Clotilde's tenure, he developed the 'Wrenaissance' style for which he is well known. It was based on the classicism of 17th-century architect Christopher Wren, which Blomfield considered more traditionally English and 'a sounder basis' for the future of British architecture.[4] Two notable projects produced during this time in the 'Wrenaissance' style were Blomfield's entry for the St Paul's Girls' School competition and the enlargement and reordering of Heathfield Park in Sussex.

In July, just after signing her articles of pupilage, Clotilde elatedly wrote to her mother:

> Blomfield's office is in the Temple, the district of barristers. You see them busily running to and fro in their robes and wigs. This is the oldest part of London – it's enchanting! – in an old house built by Christopher Wren, spiral staircase, quiet courtyard with a lawn and trees and a fountain that sings – this is my future home . . . To return to Blomfield – he is very tall, red beard, blue eyes – makes a very nice impression. He has spirit, in short, as an individual we could not have found better. He is young and has not done much but all the architects we saw speak with great respect for him. This is not a little thing! I begin on October 1st. He will give me work to do over the summer. I need to measure and draw some buildings in Freiburg.[5]

In August, Clotilde joined her mother in Freiburg-im-Breisgau, Germany, where, as requested by Blomfield, she measured the Kaufhaus, a famous medieval merchant's hall. In the time-honored tradition of male architecture students who came before her, she experienced a baptism by cobwebs, insects and grubby filth found when crawling about in old attics. She wrote to her father, 'When I got back my dress was covered from top to bottom with tiny insects, in my collar there were 12 of them; as for the rest – they jumped, they stung, they whirled. It was enough to drive one mad.'

In spite of the infestation, Clotilde completed measured drawings of the Kaufhaus which she presented to Blomfield at the official start of her apprenticeship. He was much impressed and exclaimed that he wished his other pupils had done so well.

He put her straight to work copying drawings so she would learn how to draw in the English manner which she soon mastered. By November, Clotilde reported that Blomfield thought her drawings 'nobby' (which Clotilde assured her father was Blomfield's highest praise.) She quickly rose up the office pecking order and by the following March, in 1895, Blomfield entrusted her to draw a large sheet of elevations with a plan and section of a house that he had remodeled to submit to the Royal Academy. A fine draftsman himself, Blomfield bestowed on his new apprentice an exceptional honor. Clotilde proudly wrote to her father that Blomfield said to everyone who asked him 'how his new lady pupil was getting on' that she 'worked twice as well and as much as any other pupil he has ever had'.

Like the other pupils in Blomfield's office, Clotilde was encouraged to go to South Kensington Museum to sketch the architectural models and plaster casts that were on display. Before work each day she read books on building construction and her Saturdays were spent visiting the old buildings and churches of London. Friends of her father opened their doors to her so she could document their house decorations, woodwork and chimney-pieces.

The Blomfields would often invite Clotilde to their home. There she socialized with architects such as Richard Norman Shaw, Edward Prioleau Warren, Inigo Thomas and Frank Loughborough Pearson. Good wine, good food, good company and conversation – these visits to the Blomfields were often elegant and intimate affairs: 'Yesterday I lunched at the Blomfields' and then we went horseback riding. We were a party of four – Blomfield, his sister, Warren and me. Excellent horses – we rode as if possessed. The entire day was enchanting. We left after a lunch consisting of pheasant and other delicacies. We returned by moonlight, drunk with happiness and fresh air!'[6]

When her internship first began there were practical aspects of having a female pupil in the office that caused some concern. Blomfield fended off curious friends and colleagues who dropped by, wanting to catch a glimpse of the new lady pupil. The room she was assigned was sited away from the center of the busy office.

In addition, being a lone young woman working in a business district she was unable to lunch in the local restaurants. Finding it difficult to travel back and forth each midday to where she boarded, Clotilde managed to secure a membership in the Writer's Club, a London club for women journalists and workers in illustrative art. She described the scene to her mother:

> I have been to see the club – there are some curious creatures there! Above all correspondents of inferior newspapers, their hats pulled down over one ear and a briefcase under the arm; then there are poetesses with pendulant ear-rings over their backs wearing dressing-gowns embroidered in sunflowers. Also, old spinsters who call

themselves 'antivivisectionists', and others who are champions for the emancipation of women, etc. etc., *enfin*, a whole lot of enchantresses. Never mind, the club is two steps from my office and I can conveniently have my meals there.[7]

In the office, Clotilde exuded a tremendous enthusiasm and confidence and was by far, the most experienced pupil. She organized architectural competitions between the pupils, inveigling Blomfield to act as judge. She also helped and encouraged the others who lagged behind. She coerced Blomfield into inviting the students to the Guild expositions; there she witnessed back-biting jealousies and harsh criticisms amongst the architects exhibiting and attending.

There were four young men in the office – two employees and two pupils. Having a female in the office was such a rarity that it turned all their heads; Clotilde reported: 'The four of them strive to make themselves useful to me – light the gas for me – lend me brushes. God what a life!'[8]

There was 20-year-old Philip Bauhof, Blomfield's former pupil who had recently been promoted to his assistant. He did much of the drafting in the office; he was the son of a tailor who had immigrated from Germany and the younger brother of the multi-talented Frederick Bauhof, a Paris-trained painter and professional singer. There was also a Mr. James, Blomfield's clerk of works.

The other articled pupils when Clotilde started were Percy Feilding (fig.17) and Lionel Crane. Feilding was a new pupil along with Clotilde and was much older than the others at 27. Many years later, he was to become Clotilde's husband. He had graduated from Balliol College, Oxford in 1891 with honors in the school of jurisprudence but had been unhappy working in a law office for the previous two years. Though holding no

17 Percy Henry Feilding in his 20s.
The Brewster Archives at San Francesco di Paola

title himself, he was from the aristocracy. Percy was surrounded by wealth, but had no fortune of his own and was perpetually in debt. He had a nervous disposition, but hid it well, and made a good first impression. Upon meeting for the first time in 1901, Clotilde's father wrote to Ethel Smyth about Percy, 'Charming English manners – shy and natural, a quick and refined artistic taste, great ignorance and a kind of humourous modesty.' Somewhat superficial, he placed particular importance on appearances, from clothing down to calling cards. He always appeared impeccably

LADY PUPIL IN REGINALD BLOMFIELD'S OFFICE   57

dressed and on occasion donned spectacles to give himself an air of seriousness.[9]

He lacked the most basic drafting skills. Clotilde commented,

> Feilding, the new pupil, is 7 feet tall, has a large thin nose, lines at the corners of his mouth, neither beard nor mustache – very smart – around 25 years old. He is from the beau-monde . . . He takes up architecture as a hobby and knows nothing – to the great joy of us all. Right now he copies my drawings! He traces them I mean. I'm in clover.[10]

Seven feet tall was an exaggeration though Percy was well over six foot.

What he lacked in skill he made up for in quick wit. On a group trip to the South Kensington Museum, Clotilde laughed at a dreadful sketch Percy had drawn. He smartly responded by presenting it to her as a gift. Later she found out through Philip Bauhof that her derision so rattled Percy that he was unable to sketch at all during the next week's excursion to the museum. Alarmed at how her words affected him, Clotilde set aside time to tutor him, and encouraged his efforts. Unfortunately, his drawing skills would always remain poor and Clotilde did much of his drafting throughout his career.

Besides being quick witted, Feilding was quick tempered and on more than one occasion, got into physical altercations with the other men in the office – the first one with Lionel Crane after he ground Lionel's monocle under the heel of his shoe as an April Fool's Day prank. Fights in offices were not an uncommon event. Blomfield fondly recalled a number of rows he was involved in while training in architect Arthur Blomfield's office, his uncle. On one occasion he reported that 'the office wit, a muscular little red-headed man, became intolerable, and having warned him that I should go for him if he continued to annoy me, I went for him with a low tackle, and after a brief but vigorous struggle got him where I wanted, and spanked him soundly'. There were no hard feelings though. 'My antagonist was a sportsman, and we were excellent friends afterwards.'[11]

Blomfield's third pupil was the gentle and shy Lionel Crane with whom Clotilde shared a workroom. He was the 18-year-old son of Arts and Crafts artist and book illustrator, Walter Crane. Clotilde thought him a lamb 'who unfortunately has no more brains than a sheep'. He had begun his apprenticeship two years before, but Clotilde quickly surpassed him. Without resentment or guile, he told her: 'I know I am only a duffer. I can't do anything!' Lionel was the subject of much teasing in the office,

> He is designing a house and from time-to-time James, the residential designer or Philip (I only know his first name) the clerk, give him advice. 'I'd stick a tower in,' says he, and he does what he is told. 'I'd put some storage at the corners,' says the other, in the tone of someone who says 'Put more pepper in the curry'.[12]

He took their teasing with good humor.

Lionel fell completely under Clotilde's spell, something of which she took advantage, staging incidents where he would spring into action for her: 'Yes, Lionel is a love – he picks up my instruments when I drop them on the ground – which happens constantly. He obeys my commands; he is most definitely my page.' When Blomfield favored her over the other pupils to execute an important work, Clotilde asked him if he wasn't jealous; he replied, 'Oh no, you are so much cleverer; it's only fair!' Clotilde confessed that had their positions had been reversed, she would have clobbered him.

The only one put out by the general office behavior was a 'new boy' named Harold Falkner who arrived a year after Clotilde. Socially awkward, he was uncouth and extremely sensitive to the office banter. One example suffices. It took place in early December 1895, during the time Clotilde, Falkner and Crane were preparing for the Royal Academy entrance examinations:

> Have I told you that Falkner had influenza? The others were afraid and Bauhof came in with a large bottle of ammoniated quinine . . . James brought in cod liver oil that he made us take and Crane brought castor oil. How good those two oils tasted compared to the quinine! Falkner returned and thought he was in a pharmacy. We said to him it was to avoid catching his infection and he left. He wrote to Blomfield to complain. Our dislike for him has increased, as you can well imagine.[13]

Clotilde continued:

> Finally, after having gotten some fresh air for a week, he returned, bringing with him a beautiful drawing. Even Blomfield could not have made it (a capital). We all were suspicious, especially Bauhof, of Falkner having gotten some help. Why does he draw much worse than Crane at the office but beautifully at home? Everyone is conspiring. We are setting traps. He is surrounded by nets. He must fall!

The drawings were part of a submission package presented to the Royal Academy for entry into its school of architecture. In the first part of the admissions procedure, a candidate to the academy had to present a number of sketches as proof of ability. If the sketches showed superior talent, the candidate passed and was allowed to move onto the next level of examinations.

As the day of the examination approached, Falkner's behavior became increasingly grating. Tempers ran high. Clotilde wrote,

> Falkner is becoming more and more unbearable. He is indescribably vulgar. Every sentence, every word, every intonation is loutish. Even James is shocked by it. It is not just what he says that is annoying but the way he says it. As for the rest, we hardly see him from our side of the office and we speak to him as little as possible. When he expresses an opinion there is absolute silence and then we continue as if he hasn't spoken. We do not deign to listen to what he says. Occasionally Feilding crushes him with a pompous phrase or sharp epitaph – but it makes no more of an impression on him than water on a duck's feathers. Feilding was telling me his troubles when Falkner arrived with a tub and bottle of fixative and pretending to blow on Feilding says: 'Let me fix that smile on your face'. Feilding, seized with rage, showed him the door.[14]

Presenting oneself for entrance to the Royal Academy was complicated. Prior to submitting one's drawing samples, a form requested by a member of the Academy from the Registrar had to be filled out. Along with this, certificates from an Architect-Member of the Academy had to be submitted, testifying to the ability and morality of the candidate.

Clotilde asked Norman Shaw to write a certificate attesting to her skills and certifying that she had studied architecture. 'Blomfield must write me one as well, giving details of my moral character. For Crane he wrote 'Absolutely satisfactory' – which overjoyed him', she wrote to her father.[15]

Clotilde was more revealing to her friend Nini Hildebrand, stating that Blomfield was behaving like a monster. An articled pupil was customarily given time to prepare drawings for submission. Blomfield, rather than lightening her work load at the office, increased it. The number of people he employed was small, and some years his office quite busy. Above all, projects were his priority and not the education of his pupils. Blomfield was remembered by many as an aloof and remote master who had no time to instruct them.[16]

Drawings were not signed and the aspirants' names were not revealed to the judges until the end, in order to prevent preferential treatment or favoritism. Among the drawings Clotilde submitted was an original sketch and detail of a capital of the *Mercato Nuova* derived from her own work executed when she lived in Florence, Italy.[17] She also borrowed some drawings from Shaw in preparation. In a letter he sent along with the drawings he gave her advice on the examination, 'I am glad you think the drawings may help you a bit. They are really quite easy, please take great care with the "unders". Sir Fred Leighton who is really the most intelligent Architect on our body, is very exacting and as he thoroughly understands them he picks out the smallest defect – on the subject drawing & cast he is much more lenient.'

He also shared with her his thoughts that,

> The absolute careful drawing, the patience, skill & refinement necessary to achieve that result must tell somehow, and I am sure that the man – (or woman) who has done that, must know far more about a Corinthian cap than the draughtsman who goes scampering through his drawing in the ordinary perfunctory manner – and with the results that we all know, only too well.[18]

There were only five places at the academy they were competing for. The judges only passed four people to the next level, leaving one place vacant. Clotilde was one of the privileged few.

Not surprisingly, the pupil who started with Clotilde, Percy Feilding, did not attempt to present himself as a candidate. Both Lionel Crane's and Harold Falkner's submissions were rejected by the Academy committee. Blomfield was dumbfounded. After exploding in anger, he recovered himself sufficiently enough to shake Clotilde's hand and congratulate her. To have two male pupils fail must have reflected poorly on Blomfield's teaching abilities, but to have a female pupil pass as well, must have been a cause for some embarrassment. A woman in the profession did not quite fit into the scheme of things and an architect's office was fundamentally an old boys' club.

Another rejected applicant was Ethel Mary Charles, one of only two other women besides Clotilde training to be architects in England at this time. (The third woman was Bessie Ada Charles, Ethel's sister.) Richard Phené Spiers, Master of the Architectural School at the Royal Academy, had informed Lionel Crane that Charles was to present herself to the academy at the same time as he and Clotilde. The faithful Lionel passed on this information to her. When news of Miss Charles's failure arrived, Clotilde wrote to her father with satisfaction, 'Miss Charles, who has been at George & Peto for three years, has failed as well! Can you imagine? I didn't have a chance to show the way to that child for very long.'[19]

The next stage of the examinations was intense. The candidate, now called a probationer, had to produce the following drawings:[20]

* A sketch in perspective of some subject set by the Master of the Architectural School, and executed in one day within the walls of the Academy.
* A plan, elevation and section copied from a subject given to them in the same style as the drawings originally submitted.
* A drawing from a cast made in 12 hours in the Architectural Class Room.

Every evening Clotilde went straight from the office to the Academy to sit the exams. She slept and ate little during this time.

Today was the first day of the exam – until three o'clock my courage was astonishing – then complete collapse – they flocked around me, I was offered tea, hot water, brandy, etc. I took nothing. Crane, seeing my pitiful state, would have been happy if I did not take the exam – finally at 6:00 I was there and in a state of reaction. I didn't tremble at all. The other three young men were there as well; we were set to work, drawing from a plaster cast – it hasn't been bad at all; I'm no longer afraid. Two of the young men have nothing to fear, but the third! They will give us the order to draw from memory on Wednesday. I am glad that this was not given today. Imagination makes the unknown terrifying – and the memory plays you false – now I have no more fears – nothing to dread. Even if I fail, I will have passed 15 pleasant days.[21]

She finished the drawings early and left for Italy on an extended holiday. When the results of the examination came out on Wednesday 29 January, it was Lionel Crane who wrote to tell her she had passed. She spent the next five weeks visiting her father in Rome and in Florence working for Adolf Hildebrand, who asked her to join him in his Munich home for a year after she completed her internship as he was now getting as many architectural commissions as sculptural.

When she returned, she was taken aback that Lionel was no longer in the office, 'Crane is gone – what misery. Blomfield chased him away or to be more exact, advised him to work elsewhere, saying it was for his own good.' 'Alas, my *cavalieri serventi* is no longer here – we miss the sweet Crane. He is at George & Peto, but comes to see us at the office in the evenings.'

The office had changed. Falkner worked in the adjacent room much to her displeasure. As for Percy – 'Feilding I have not seen again. It seems that he worked for two days in a row – astonishing – and then took eight days of vacation to recover.'[22] He came and went as he pleased confirming Clotilde's first impression that architecture was just a pastime for him.

The reality of the Royal Academy was a let-down. It appeared completely disorganized to Clotilde. In March 1896 she wrote,

It seems that I have 18 months at the academy before I can enter the upper division. Waterhouse is giving the course right now. Blomfield advised me not to go. I'll wait for another one. I don't understand this institution – there is nobody to go to for information. Spiers contradicts himself with every sentence – the secretary does not want to be disturbed – the registrar is never there – still, it will be fine come what may. I'll keep you informed of what is happening.[23]

Alfred Waterhouse, born in 1830, was a colossal figure in Victorian-era architecture with 360 works to his credit, most famously the Natural History Museum in South Kensington and the Manchester Town Hall. Many of his Gothic Revival style buildings were highly colorful and patterned. Blomfield had an intense dislike of Waterhouse's work which he described as 'horrible red terra-cotta combined with red brick which he used in most of his Insurance buildings'.[24]

In March 1896 the workload was growing. Blomfield had been invited to submit a design for a limited competition for the St Paul's School for Girls in Hammersmith, a project on which Clotilde, as well as the others were involved. 'We are working like slaves in the office; sweat drips from our foreheads. Blomfield is in a state of extreme excitement. We are going so fast that he's lost his mind. He bombards James and Bauhof with insults. He even called Falkner 'a damned idiot'. I am the only one who has escaped thus far, but it will come.'[25]

Not much is discussed about the office in her letters for many months. In December 1896, she

18   Front elevation of proposed country house for Hermann Levi. Drawn by Clotilde Brewster.
Architekturmuseum der TUM, Sign. hild-208-43

traveled to Florence to work in Adolf Hildebrand's studio, first on a mausoleum and fountain, then on a villa for the composer Hermann Levi located in Partenkirchen, Bavaria, Germany. She and Hildebrand both composed the designs, and she alone drafted them. Hildebrand then sent the pencil drawings to Munich to his staff for to redraw in ink (figs 18 and 19).[26]

By March, she had begun to supervise construction of her own Arts and Crafts style cottage in Farnborough, Hampshire, she called the Rushes. She was also designing and constructing mantelpieces for her father's new apartment in the Palazzo Mattei in Rome.

Things changed for Blomfield in 1897. In late January, Clotilde reported that Norman Shaw awarded 'the prize' to Horsley for the design of St Paul's School for Girls in Hammersmith which she and the others had worked on a year before. Shaw, as the adjudicator, chose the 'Wrenaissance' style building conceived by his ex-pupil Gerald Horsley, as the winning scheme against the opinion of the other committee members.[27] Furious, Blomfield went to Shaw to demand his perspective drawing be returned to him, intending to send it to the next Royal Academy exhibition (fig.20).[28]

As the year progressed, Blomfield's commissions dropped off and he disappeared from the office

19   Rear elevation of proposed country house for Hermann Levi. Drawn by Clotilde Brewster.
Architekturmuseum der TUM, Sign. hild-208-42

OVERLEAF

20   Design competition design worked on by Clotilde Brewster and others in
Reginald Blomfield's office. RIBA Collections

for long periods of time. In early April, Clotilde arrived only to discover that Blomfield had rearranged the office, renting two inadequate rooms. He put Clotilde and James into a room with only one window. James's table was placed in front of it, and Clotilde's drafting table placed at random in the middle of the dark room. Bauhof and a boy named Squire worked in the other room, amply supplied with light from two windows. Falkner, seeing the situation, absented himself. Feilding, as usual, had not been seen in the office for some time. She informed Blomfield that she couldn't work under these conditions. Blomfield, rather than addressing the issue, asked her why

LADY PUPIL IN REGINALD BLOMFIELD'S OFFICE   63

he hadn't seen her in the office. After responding that there was nothing to do so she stayed home, Blomfield informed her that she could ink-in old drawings, something so beneath her ability at this point that she took it as an insult.

Clotilde recorded the exchange verbatim in a letter to her father: Blomfield: 'So you want to reform the system of teaching in England – it's the only way to learn – I inked-in during three years at my uncle's office.'

Clotilde would have none of it, 'I don't want to reform the system if system it is. I have no doubt but it is excellent for the masses but you must admit that there are different speeds of learning. Some take three years, others two. I have squeezed the art of inking-in dry and mean to go on to something else – anything else. As to its being the only way to learn and the only thing to be done, I don't agree with you – if it were the case, what would be the use of going to an office – borrow a roll of drawings, ink them in – according to you one would be an architect!'

Blomfield, outmaneuvered, tried to end the discussion, 'Alright Miss Brewster, when I get St. Paul's to rebuild I'll let you know – perhaps you will come then.' Clotilde got in the final word, 'I am afraid I should never come were I to wait for that, but a cottage will do.'

'Exeunt Blomfield', she continued. 'James, Bauhof and Squire were there, jaws hanging open. What do you think of this? It's not true that that is the system – otherwise – why doesn't Norman Shaw take students? He must have enough old drawings. Why doesn't Inigo Thomas take on any and why does he say that an architect with nothing to build shouldn't take on students? . . . I can write specifications, turn out working drawings etc., I know the practice of the office as well as Blomfield. But what one is missing is the touch, the lightness of hand, the grace of the pen. I devote myself now to the cultivation of this and to the development of ideas. By speaking, your opinions are formed; by designing your style!'[29]

Clotilde's internship came to an end in June 1897. She had two options at this point, accept Adolf Hildebrand's invitation to work with him or go out on her own. As H.B. spent a number of months each year in England and her brother Christopher was to attend Cambridge University, Clotilde decided to stay in England.

She was registered at the Royal Academy until 1899 but does not discuss it further in letters except once when in the spring of 1897 she submitted a watercolor of a house she designed. 'Well, the Academy sent back my amazing painting with their compliments. Again, a blunder on their part, the first one was to admit me as a student, the second to reject this immortal work! But the difference is that in the first case the judges didn't know the names of the candidates and in the second, the names were not only visible – but the principal thing!'[30] Although she never explicitly states it, her words imply she was being discriminated against due to her gender.

8

THE NEW WOMAN AND THE PROBLEM WITH DUENNAS

As women gained more freedom in the late Victorian age, a new ideal of womanhood began to emerge. Labelled the 'New Woman', she first appeared in novels and plays, as in the works of Henrik Ibsen and Henry James, and featured in newspapers and countless articles in magazines geared toward the growing female market. She was educated, independent and believed her sphere was not confined to the home.

In reality, the choices were still very limited for women who desired to escape the drudgery associated with housekeeping and motherhood. For the middle-class woman, the difficulty lay in gaining a foothold in careers while simultaneously maintaining their social status. Most of the small number of women who had the privilege of a university education did not enter public life. Those who did increasingly pursued caring roles as teachers, nurses and social workers – considered acceptable womanly occupations and regarded as natural extensions of their biological make-up.

In early 1899, the organizers of the International Congress of Women asked Clotilde to speak at their next convention to be held in London that summer. It consisted of a series of world conferences where existing women's organizations met to address questions of women's rights and suffrage. The Congress featured the many different paths women were forging. In Clotilde, they found someone who pushed boundaries – achieving what few if any woman had achieved before – the elevated status of a professional. Unlike other art workers such as painters or sculptors, architects had substantial professional and complex legal responsibilities, not only to their clients but to builders they hired and to local governments and planning boards where they built.

Not political in nature, Clotilde never saw herself in the context of a woman who happened to be an architect but as an architect who happened to be a woman (fig.21). She did, however, enjoy the special status her gender bestowed on her and began her speech, 'At the present moment women architects are, in Europe at least, but a handful—a small handful. It is by no means unpleasant to be one of the few.' She then proceeded to put forth the misconceptions of many of the profession and then debunked them:

> An architect is a cross between the human and the monkey species; it is a very agile creature that spends its time on ladders and rafters, bounding from rung to rung or joist to joist, and swarming up pipes with the assistance of all the prehensile organs that nature may have endowed it with.

21   Photograph of Clotilde Brewster aged 24.
The Brewster Archives at San Francesco di Paola

Further, it is a creature that swears at workmen—for without swearing how is it possible to exercise and influence? And it dirties its hand and its clothes. 'Let women furnish and embellish our homes; they may go as far as interior decoration: building must be left to men.'

Truth, however, forces me to declare that no extraordinary agility is necessary in my profession, that violent language is not of material assistance in it, and that it is possible to plan and design a house, to draw up the specifications, and see that the work is properly executed without rolling head over heels in mortar, or otherwise disfiguring one's self.'[1]

The speech struck a chord. In 1901 an article on Clotilde was published in *The Lady's Pictorial*, titled *Architecture as a Profession for Women* in which Clotilde was described as a pioneer.[2] One aspect of a woman architect's life, that was ignored in both her speech and the *Lady's Pictorial* article was the difficulty a woman faced obtaining employment at a firm after completing her training. This issue was fleetingly addressed in 1891 in an article by interior designer Agnes Garrett who advised potential woman decorators to open their own offices: 'Keeping the business small, and as it were personal, will always prevent large fortunes being made at it, and it will, in consequence, I think, be entrusted more and more to women.'[3]

Not expecting to be hired in a firm, Clotilde took Garrett's advice and opened her own office from her rooms where she was boarding in 1897. Though starting small, she was determined to get clients. She offered financial incentives to friends who would get her any type of design work,

> I got a letter from [Louis de] Glehn who is giving me an order for a £20 mantelpiece – I like him more and more! This is friendship! It's for one of his friends at Clifton. I am asking 10% for decorations – £3 per hour like Blomfield will come later– my motto is S.P.Q.R. – small profits quick returns . . . Half of my profits will go to Glehn; it will be £1 for him and the same for me – not much, but little things lead to big ones.[4]

Adolf Hildebrand's studio continued to be a rich source of work and she traveled down to Italy each winter season. In February 1898 she designed the base the Siegfried Fountain later placed in Worms, Germany (fig.22):

68   CLOTILDE BREWSTER

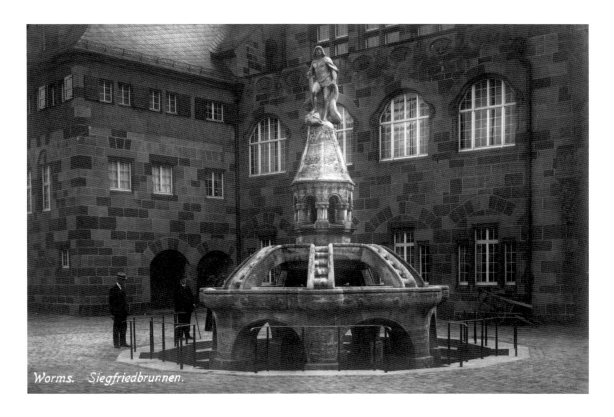

22   Siegfried Fountain in Worms, Germany. Clotilde was asked by
Adolf Hildebrand to design the base. Author's collection

The sitting room is mine, where I have a huge amount of clay that I must convert into a fountain of seven crosses in an umbrella shaped frame and crowned with Saint Siegfried in chain mail – the idea is given; it is up to me to discover the proportions and form. In the evenings I do all the drawings for the exhibition monument for Hamburg and the rest of the time I draw for myself.[5]

She worked for Hildebrand on other projects and developed a crush on the client, Count Giuseppe Rasponi, for whom Hildebrand was doing a country house remodel and a new tobacco warehouse in Barbialla.

I spent a delicious month here – work, friends, pleasure and I ended up getting '*una cotta ma una di quelle cotte*' (as Rezia Rasponi says) on her father – so that I carry away a soul that is torn. In Barbialla we had a divine day – first, two hours with him in a little two wheeled carriage. Hildebrand followed alone in an omnibus. Then the castle planted on the hill with a large courtyard and a well in the center shaded by a Holm Oak. Behind the ivy-covered church was a great view of the hills crowned with small castles. The church bells rang; the peasants left and greeted the Count. Then came the peasant women smiling as they passed. All that was missing was Figaro. It was so beautiful – it remains etched in my memory

THE NEW WOMAN AND THE PROBLEM WITH DUENNAS   69

23   Drawing illustrating Clotilde's superior skill at formal drafting. Courtesy of Amanda Feilding

24   The Alfred Williams Hearn and Ellen Joubert Hearn mausoleum in Trabuquet Cemetery, Menton, France. The Brewster Archives at San Francesco di Paola

as a romantic stage set. Rasponi's construction lower down in the plain was beautiful. We and Hildebrand stood amazed; the proportions are perfect.[6]

Back in London she continued to work on the tobacco warehouse but also recommenced projects for her English clients (fig.23):

> I am trying to correct and redo an exterior stair for Rasponi's tobacco depot. It will be very pretty. But this mirror for Cohen is giving me more trouble than a palace – it must be large and carved and majestic and artistic and in mahogany! It's not architecture he gives me but a rebus.[7]

As was typical even for male architects of that day, Clotilde received commissions from relatives, such as a mausoleum in the form of a tempietto for her cousin Ellen Joubert Hearn, library bookshelves for her father, and a villa in Rome for her cousin Anne Frankenstein (figs 24 and 25). In September 1900, Clotilde's aunt Kate asked her to visit and 'give me ideas, plans, etc. which could be executed in spring', for her newly acquired country house, *Le Temps Perdu*, in Ury, Seine-et-Marne.[8]

Much of her time was spent networking and meeting new wealthy potential clients, through friends and social events. She flattered them, attended their fashionable weekend parties, participated in hunts and games such as billiards and cards. From Lady Feodora Gleichen, Clotilde obtained a letter of introduction to Lady Margaret Brooke, Ranee of Sarawak in 1900. A number of years later when the Ranee purchased Greyfriars in Ascot, she commissioned Clotilde to reorder and decorate her new home.[9] The Ranee charmingly wrote in early 1904, 'I do so want to see you 1stly because I love you, 2ndly because I want you to help turn my house into a simple livable abode.'[10]

25   Library at the Palazzo Antici Mattei.
The Brewster Archives at San Francesco di Paola

Many projects failed to materialize: At a weekend party hosted by Sir George and Lady Elizabeth Lewis in 1902 at their home in Overstrand, Norfolk, Clotilde chatted with Lady Sophia MacNamara, lady-in-waiting to Princess Louise. They spoke of architecture and Lady MacNamara, Clotilde reported to her father, 'is coming to see me here and is going to give me her house to construct when the South African mines are on the rise'.[11] In June 1900, Madame Wolkoff dropped by to discuss the possibility of Clotilde building a school for her in Russia. The Brewsters knew the Wolkoffs in Rome.[12]

26   Likely the proposed country house for the sister-in-law of Countess Benckendorff as it in the Russian classical style. Courtesy of Amanda Feilding

As Clotilde would potentially earn about £500, she wanted her father to come to a dinner she was hosting, which Madame Wolkoff was to attend.[13] The presence of the suave and elegant H.B., she believed, would increase her chances of successfully obtaining the commission. Though Clotilde visited the Wolkoff's estate at Muromtsev, Russia in 1903, the school is not alluded to again.[14] This was and is fairly typical of the architecture profession. Even after securing commissions and producing designs, most structures are never built. She did, however, get a commission for a large country house in Russia in January 1904 for the sister-in-law of her friend Countess Sophie Benckendorff, most probably Countess Maria Sergeievna Benckendorff.[15] The project was likely built as writer William Buchan wrote in his memoirs: 'One of her projects was a splendid country house in Russia, with copper domes, for some branch of the Benckendorff family' (fig.26).[16]

Many of Clotilde's clients were women and made up of one particular type of patron, wealthy women who were advocates of women's rights and equality: Lady Mary Ponsonby; Dr Lillias Hamilton; Countess Marianna Soderini and Alessandra de Frankenstein, to name a few. Some of these patrons and their projects are explored in detail later in this narrative.

Clotilde ambitions went beyond the domestic architecture sphere. There were discussions of her

72   CLOTILDE BREWSTER

designing an Italian National Theatre to showcase Eleanora Duse, the most famous actress of her day. The theatre was to be built on Lake Albano near Rome on land donated by Henri de Frankenstein, who proposed Clotilde Brewster as architect, and Duse, 'who would like to see woman occupy positions other than those of fond dalliance . . . jumped at the suggestion'.[17] Clotilde produced designs and drawings, but the theatre was never built.

Another tantalizing project was a possible museum for Henriette Hertz. Hertz was a German-Jewish patron of the arts and hostess of a cultural salon at the Palazzo Zuccari in Rome. She had a second home in England. Clotilde wrote to her father for his help:

> Hertz has an architect whose plans she finds atrocious and I aspire to replace him. Eugenie Strong knew this and brought her to me. I showed her my drawings. She liked them and once again I live in hope.
>
> . . . Until then I ask you to tell Marianne and Madame de Frankenstein that if they see Miss Hertz to sing my praises and recommend me as architect – *che genio, non c'è che lei! Non c'è che lei!* [What a genius; there is no one like her!] They only have to say that! Tell me what Maria Cara says about the Palazzo Soderini. If she doesn't like it, prove her wrong and say that Hildebrand thinks it's perfect – her opinion could have influence on the blind.[18]

Unfortunately, Hertz's museum was never built and her art collection went elsewhere.

Though her practice was thriving, Clotilde's living arrangements were a continual source of stress. Given the era's attitude toward female sexuality, Clotilde rightly believed the smallest indiscretion might damage her reputation and adversely affect her career. She had to conduct herself in a manner that was above reproach. Women who showed any signs of licentious behavior became social outcasts.

During her internship in Blomfield's office and for some time after, Clotilde boarded with two unmarried daughters of Sir Henry Cole, founder of the Victoria and Albert Museum, Letitia 'Tishy' and Henrietta 'Henny', who took the rules of propriety very seriously. Not only was Clotilde's reputation at stake, but their own as well. They had little money and depended on supplementing their income by taking in boarders. Clotilde assured her mother that she was in safe hands as 'their world is composed of spinsters and old ladies – and here and there like a rare truffle, a small abbot, very thin. Alas, not a single wicked little prince!'[19]

Having spent a number of years with the Coles, Clotilde longed for more independence and planned to establish her own house. Appearances demanded she have an older woman live with her whom she dubbed a 'duenna' and whose role was to provide moral protection.

After much searching, a distant cousin Emily Halkett (1864–1945) was to live with Clotilde. She had converted to Roman Catholicism and had been residing in a convent of the Benedictines in Rome for some time with the intention of joining the order.[20] Plans were made to have Emily leave the convent and move to London.

Emily's father had been Aide de Camp and Equerry to King George V of Hanover (1819–78) and she and her sister Nora had been in the service of Queen Marie. Her grandfather, Sir Hugh Halkett (1783–1863), was a British soldier who had joined the Hanoverian army in 1813 and distinguished himself at Waterloo during the Napoleonic Wars.

The family had fallen on hard times until 1890, when their brother, Baron Hugh Colin Halkett married American heiress Sarah Phelps Stokes and saved the family from financial ruin. At the time of her marriage, it was reported that, 'Baroness Halkett carried $1,000,000 abroad'.[21] This is the equivalent of $34,525,000 in 2024.[22]

Through the influence of the Roman Catholic Archdeacon of Westminster, whom Emily knew well, Clotilde managed to obtain a long-term lease on the property on Barton Street, steps away from Westminster Abbey. Besides carrying out extensive renovations, Clotilde landscaped the back garden installing brick paving, planting fig trees and clipped topiaries. She constructed garden structures as well; at the far end of the yard was an arbor with classic pilasters and an arch on which flowering vines grew.[23] She had her father ship over pieces of furniture from Italy and painted the interior of the house in subdued colors, producing the effect of 'silence and shadows'.[24]

By early fall of 1898 Clotilde and Emily were fully installed in their new home. It started off promisingly. Emily got on well with Clotilde's friends and a canon whom Emily knew hired Clotilde to design an altar for a church in Exeter. 'The center section is dominated by the Last Supper of Christ, painted on a surface of tiles . . . The rest is of carved stone. On one side, a panel of roses and on the other side not lilies but pomegranates.'

Soon though, Clotilde began to regret the living arrangements. They discovered their personalities clashed – Clotilde thought Emily vacuous, infantile and offered no intellectual stimulation. Emily, as well, treated the house as if it were her own and she had equal rights to it, freely inviting friends over and infringing on Clotilde's workspace.

There was also the issue of Emily's brother, Hugh. At first, Clotilde welcomed socializing with Hugh Halkett and his social set. Networking with wealthy potential clients was part and parcel of obtaining high-end commissions – Hugh knew people in high places who could aid Clotilde's career. At the time, Clotilde and sculptor Lady Feodora Gleichen were working together on a design for the proposed monument of King Alfred, to commemorate the one thousandth anniversary of his death. The invitation-only competition had not yet been publicly announced as it was still in the planning stages. Artists campaigned early to influence those in charge. Louis de Glehn (brother of painter Wilfrid de Glehn), Clotilde wrote, 'procured a promise of an invitation for me for the King Alfred monument competition that Feo Gleichen has still not been able to get!'[25] Based on this promise, Clotilde and Lady Gleichen commenced their design work. Clotilde also extracted a promise from Ethel Smyth to talk to people she knew. Baron Halkett assured her he could get her a total of four votes.[26]

It soon became evident that those potential votes from Halkett might come at a high price as the more Clotilde got to know him, the more nauseated she became. 'All of Halkett's friends and stories emit a stench of miasmas, swampy plants and stagnant water', she wrote to H.B.[27] Unfortunately, Halkett and his friends took a great liking to Clotilde. Besides dropping too often by her house, they invited her out to dine and to the theatre, often not extending the invitations to Emily who was left home alone. Clotilde wrote her father of their numerous indiscretions in great detail.

When Ethel Smyth learned from the art critic Edmund Gosse that there wasn't going to be a King Alfred monument competition and that an architect and a sculptor would be chosen instead, Clotilde saw no reason to keep Emily in the house. Making arrangements for her brother Christopher to stay with her for a short time, Clotilde evicted Emily.

Clotilde's next 'chaperone' was Mary Sheepshanks (1872–1958), the daughter of the Reverend John Sheepshanks who had been made Bishop of Norwich about six years before. An educationalist, Mary later became involved in the suffragette movement. In 1913, she was hired as secretary to the International Suffrage Alliance at its new London headquarters, and between 1914 and 1919 edited the Alliance's monthly journal, *Jus Suffragii.*[28]

The contrast between Clotilde's and Mary's upbringings was extreme. In Mary's unpublished memoirs, she described her childhood as almost Dickensian. One of 13 children, she was born and raised in a vicarage in the bleak outskirts of Liverpool. 'One or two streets were squalid slums where from time-to-time fierce fights took place between the Orange factions and the Roman Catholics. Viragos fought with fenders and fire-irons in defence of their tenets or merely drunken brawls.'[29]

It was an austere household where religious observation was strictly followed – including fasting on Fridays and church all day Sunday. There were no books or newspapers in the house and her parents disapproved of any type of pleasure. Her brothers had the privilege of attending boarding schools, while Mary was required to traverse seedy neighborhoods every day on the other side of Liverpool because she wanted to attend secondary school.[30]

Mary went on to attend Newham College, attending for a full four years. Afterwards, she became a social worker at The Woman's University Settlement in Nelson Square and in 1897 began working at Morley College for Working Men and Women, where she was offered the position of Vice Principal at a 'semi-volunteer' salary of only £100 a year.[31]

By January 1900, Mary Sheepshanks had moved in. She occupied H.B.'s rooms until his annual summer stay in London when she willingly withdrew up into the attic rooms. Unlike Emily, she was unassuming, compliant, intelligent, a good conversationalist and perhaps most importantly, was almost never home. For a long time, the new arrangement went well.

Clotilde's friends and family belonged to an aesthetic world which unapologetically worshiped beauty and the arts and enjoyed pleasurable entertainments such as attending plays and concerts. Clotilde's international background, made an impression on Sheepshanks, 'Clotilde was thus very cosmopolitan, and her friends were of various nationalities and cultures, and different from any people I had yet met.'[32]

Clotilde's friends who came and went from Barton Street were examples of the New Woman as well – Eugénie Sellers Strong, a British archaeologist; Jane Ellen Harrison, a British classical scholar; Caroline Grosvenor, British novelist, artist and founder of the Colonial Intelligence League for Educated Women; Alice Brisbane Thursby, an American social and arts patron and daughter of socialist philosopher Albert Brisbane, and Angelina Frances Milman, the author of *Sir Christopher Wren* and a translator of Fyodor Dostoyevsky's *Poor Folk* from Russian into English.

Angelina, known as 'Lena', frequented literary circles and corresponded with numerous authors including Henry James, Irish playwright George Moore and British novelist Thomas Hardy. She was one of the ladies Hardy (when in London and between appointments) tutored in architecture at 'astonishingly low fees, to fill up the time'.[33] Clotilde most likely met Lena through Ethel Smyth, as H.B. wrote to her from Rome in April 1898, 'This afternoon, Miss Milman and a friend of hers that I do not know, are due to come and have tea. Miss Milman is the daughter of the Governor of the Tower of London. She is a friend of Ethel's and Henry James': allgemeine, culture, literature, music, art; nice manner, a little deaf; between 30 and 40 years old.'[34]

Clotilde wrote her own impressions of Lena to her brother Christopher: 'She is awfully nice – human and intelligent and very busy making a pretty mosaic (metaphorically speaking) of people – if you fit into the pattern, she loves you, if you don't she casts you aside. I happen to fit in and one notices her contemplating the result with satisfaction!'[35]

As H.B. noted, Lena had an unusual London address. Her father, General Sir George Bryan Milman, was the governor of the Tower of London, a position which came with an apartment. The family also had an apartment in the Foscarini Palace in Venice. One summer, she invited Mary Sheepshanks which Mary remembered fondly: 'The best boys took us out on the lagoon in the evenings and we had supper as the twilight came on. One night we went to a grand party at Sir Henry Layard's palace. The canal was alive with gondolas lit up with lanterns, the beautiful rooms were alive with people, and on the walls hung Sir Henry's great collection of pictures.'[36]

Mary Sheepshanks met other friends of H.B.'s and Clotilde's, including Édouard Rod whom she thought was out of touch with the lives of ordinary people:

> Édouard Rod, the French novelist, once came on a visit, and as I was generally out at my job, he asked how it was that I was so often absent. I told him that I was at work. 'Ah, que c'est beau le travail, absolument inutile, mais tout de même!' [Ah, how beautiful work is, completely useless, but all the same!]

Ethel Smyth was a constant and important presence in Clotilde's life and when H.B. was in London, she would drop in at 1 Barton Street often. Sheepshanks described her as 'the most dynamic human being I have ever met. Her vitality never flagged and could on occasion be overwhelming'.[37]

Ethel invited Clotilde to an endless number of social and family events. The Smyth sisters were so fond of Clotilde that they tried to arrange a marriage for her with their brother, Robert Napier Smyth. Clotilde immediately rejected the idea. In general, Clotilde tremendously admired Ethel but was not blind to her faults. She irritated Clotilde on numerous occasions, sometimes carrying tales to H.B., 'Clotilde has dyed her hair in front in the most palpable way (bright orange streaks). Why not? But the amazing thing is she says she has done nothing whatever to it! and really shuns the conversation. Queer – very queer.'[38]

Through her association with Ethel, Clotilde made the acquaintance not only of those in art and feminist circles but also many from the aristocracy, including Lady Ponsonby, Countess Feodora Gleichen and Empress Eugénie, the widow of Napoleon III. Clotilde first met all three women in 1897. Ponsonby became a client for two projects, a library addition to her house and a *succursale* (chapel) on her property. Gleichen was a both a client and collaborator. In 1900, Gleichen commissioned Clotilde to design a colonnade for a project in Paris for which she was paid £20.[39]

Clotilde became a friend of the Empress in her own right. When at her Farnborough cottage, Clotilde would often visit Farnborough Hill for tea or dinner. Through the years she would amuse her father with gossipy stories of the Empress and her entourage. Besides the invitations to Farnborough Hill, the Empress once invited Clotilde to spend time aboard *The Thistle*, her yacht, in 1902, during Cowes Week.[40]

It was another cosmopolite, Clotilde's debonair brother Christopher, with his good looks, perfect manners and flirtatious behavior who disrupted Clotilde's and Mary's happy living arrangements. Christopher arrived in September 1901 for an extended stay in England. Mary Sheepshanks enjoyed long conversations with him when he visited Barton Street and thought of him as a new friend.

In 1901, Clotilde invited Mary to spend Christmas with them at Abendroth, their country house overlooking Lake Constance in Heiden, Switzerland which she and Christopher had recently inherited from their late uncle, the composer Heinrich von Herzogenberg.

The setting was magnificent:

> There's a wonderful view – the lake with Bregenz in the distance and the Rhine which undulates

through the meadows. Everything is covered with snow; it is a pity that you cannot come now; it would have pleased you; everything would have pleased you and the sled races are a dream . . . Christopher has the genius of a general; he brought some furs from Basel – some tubs, eiderdowns, fish, some fruit, everything the heart could desire. The snow is deep; it is very warm in the house and we are happy.[41]

Unfortunately, the 21-year-old Christopher began to court Mary. To him, it was merely a lighthearted game, but Mary interpreted it far more seriously. She grew increasingly passionate, seeking opportunities to be alone with him. Alarmed at the situation, Clotilde abruptly cut short their stay in Heiden, taking Christopher to the Hildebrand home in Munich. Mary begged to accompany them, but Clotilde refused. Mary's feelings were further hurt when Christopher, despite promising to write to her, failed to do so.[42]

Clotilde stayed abroad that winter and spring to work with Adolf Hildebrand, first in Munich and then in Florence until early April. She then spent time in Rome. Christopher as well, stayed with the Hildebrands and in early May, Clotilde wrote to Mary Sheepshanks to tell her that Christopher was engaged to marry Lisl, Adolf and Irene Hildebrand's daughter.[43] It must have come as a great shock to Mary as she did not respond to Clotilde's letters. She returned to London in early July to find Mary was gone but had left a curt note informing her that she could not say for sure what her future plans were, leaving Clotilde in a financial bind. Mary eventually did return to Barton Street but was there only for propriety's sake – their early rapport was never to be restored.

As for Clotilde's love life, she had set her sights on Percy Feilding, who had been her fellow apprentice in Reginald Blomfield's office. Percy, in regard to Clotilde, was alternatively interested and then inexplicably indifferent and their courtship dragged on for some years.

Early in 1901, Clotilde wrote to her father on the state of their relationship; Percy seemed to be making a move, but as she explained: 'He is highly strung and at the same time easily startled – then he bolts and we are back to square one. One advances but it's slow – it seems as though this could go on forever.'[44]

Late that March, when Percy was visiting in Italy at the invitation of Clotilde, her father tried to nurture the romance as he wrote to Ethel Smyth, 'Things seem to be going well and of course I am a slave to them and their developments. I like Feilding very much, better in fact than any other young man I have come across. He also has Christopher's approval (no easy thing to obtain), the sympathy of the Frankensteins, Mrs. (Robert) Crawshay's enthusiasm and the Soderinis' praise.'

He continued that though Clotilde was obviously in love, he did not detect reciprocal emotions in Percy. Clotilde, he wrote, was 'Love in smiles and dimples. And there is nothing moonstricken in him, but a visible admiration and some traces of fondness. It may all lead to nothing, but they must have the best chance I can give them.'[45] Mrs. Robert Crawshay was Mary Leslie (1858–1936), daughter of Sir John Leslie, 1st Bt and Lady Constance Dawson-Damer. She was a close family friend and aided Clotilde in her romantic endeavors – inviting Percy to every event Clotilde was to attend. Everyone thought a proposal of marriage was imminent, but Percy refused to take the bait.

In June, after another upsetting reversal in their relationship, Clotilde rationalized her desire to marry Percy to her father:

If one makes a love match, the less one knows about the person in question, the better. One has a long way to go before the blindfold falls off. If one makes a marriage of convenience, the profession and the appearance are enough. He's an architect; he looks nice; I like him – I certainly won't find someone more satisfactory, for convenience and for love. You will tell me that if I miss this particular train, it's not very serious; this is very true from the point of view of 'sentiment' – but this is, in my opinion, false from a 'sensible' point of view. And it's always upsetting to miss the train – it's hard to be calm when one has *eisenbahnfieber* [railroad fever].[46]

It was only after his father died in early 1904, that Percy asked Clotilde to marry him. She accepted and wrote her father a long letter in which she romantically described her future bliss. Percy's letter to H.B., in contrast, was brief and somewhat awkward. In it he revealed he had admired Clotilde for many years and had recently come to love her. Regrettably, he went on, he was virtually penniless and had to repay a large debt, 'Here I must tell you what I have to offer and this I am afraid will be a matter for surprise . . .'[47]

Percy's mother, Lady Louisa soon wrote to H.B. to begin the discussions of the financial arrangements. The Feilding family required that Clotilde's estate be put into a trust. Lady Louisa would also settle on her son and his future family a considerable sum in trust which Percy could not touch. Christopher Brewster explained the particulars to his wife, Lisl, right before the wedding,

> According to English fashion a settlement under trustees has to be made, that is to say part of Clotilde's fortune 160,000 frs has to be in the hands of two people, and they must see that this capital is never touched, under no circumstances whatever. Clotilde has the interests, and may invest the capital as she likes, but she can't get at the money itself.[48]

Christopher underestimated the amount; it was substantially higher. 'They believe that I only have £6,500 and we are not going to undeceive them', Clotilde wrote to her father.[49] £6,500 is equivalent to £990,471 in 2024.[50] She also owned several properties. Clotilde never revealed the total extent of her wealth and hid her assets from the lawyers, keeping the money in foreign bank accounts.

The resemblance of the Brewster-Feilding marriage to the unions of rich Americans to poverty-stricken nobles was not lost on Clotilde. In this scenario, she was the foreign heiress. Years later she doubted her own son Basil's survival skills. Upon learning that the 18-year-old Basil had contracted chickenpox during a visit to Christopher's home in Florence, Clotilde wrote to her brother,

> If Basil shows any tendency to scratch, I <u>beg you</u> to tie his hands to the sides of the bed so that he cannot scratch in his sleep. If he were pock-marked he would lose his chance of marrying an heiress which would be dreadful as everyone knows that the house of Feildings has always risen in the world via heiresses! and in no other way – *mi raccomando* – his complexion above all else – let him swear and curse but if you tie his hands, one to the other <u>under</u> the bed he can't get them to his face.[51]

As Clotilde's May wedding day approached, Mary Sheepshanks suddenly left 1 Barton Street for a few months. She did not want to risk meeting Christopher again.[52] After her marriage, Mary settled into Clotilde's former rooms. To her great regret, Mary never found love and was never to marry. 'I kept on the Barton Street house with two friends and remained there for some years. My partners married one after the other and their places in my household were filled by others, but I continued my spinsterish existence.'[53]

9

BETWEEN SPIRITUALISTS AND PHYSICIANS

Projects for the Hamiltons

Clotilde designed a number of projects in England for first cousins Mary Christian Dundas Hamilton (1850–1943) and Dr Lillias Hamilton (1858–1925). Mary Hamilton commissioned three residential projects and one mixed use project. Dr Lillias Hamilton hired her to design a nursing home.

Mary Hamilton was a single woman of independent means who had various interests in life – real estate speculation, writing poetry and supporting the women's suffrage movement. She also wrote a novel, *The Journeys of Antonia* under the nom-de-plume of Christian Dundas published in 1905.[1] For Clotilde, always on the lookout for a liberal-minded older woman for friendship and commissions, it was a perfect fit. Hamilton also mentored and advised Clotilde on investing in the stock market, an interest that developed into a life-long passion.

Clotilde first became acquainted with the 43-year-old Mary Hamilton and her companion Alice Melvill while she was studying at Newnham College in 1893. They were part of her family's circle of friends, the connection made through H.B.'s first cousin, Colonel Charles Henry Joubert, who had married into the Melvill family.

In the 18th century, the Hamilton family made their fortune through their ownership of the Pemberton Valley Estate in Jamaica, a sugar and rum enterprise which according to an 1835 document was said to have 255 enslaved individuals.[2] In 1762, with the family's new-found wealth, John Hamilton (1739–1821) and his wife Lillias Montgomorie (d.1827) purchased Sundrum Castle in Ayrshire, Scotland. In 1798 it underwent a redesign and greatly enlarged. It was at Sundrum that Mary was raised along with her two brothers, John and Lewis.

Some parts of the original castle were intimidating. Within its massively thick walls were found a number of secret passageways and a vaulted room in its ancient Wallace Tower was haunted by The Green Lady, thought to be the ghost of a Hamilton bride.[3] Perhaps the Green Lady piqued Mary's curiosity in the supernatural as later she became a member of the Society for Psychical Research and joined the London Lodge of the Theosophical Society.

Clotilde realized early on in their friendship that both Mary and Alice were religious. For her 19th birthday, they sent her, *Rubaiyat* by Omar, a Persian astronomer poet. Shocked when they found out that Clotilde had never read or even owned a bible, in February 1894, they sent her one printed 'on paper as thin as a butterfly's wing and with characters as small as microbes.' She told her father, 'You can imagine how difficult it was to respond! But it's done – I told her [Mary] I would be very interested in reading Ecclesiastes.'[4]

Mary held successful trials in mind reading at her London home, one account of which was published in *Phantasms of the Living* in 1886 and titled 'Experiment between Miss Leila Melvill [now Mrs. Lewis Hamilton] and Mr. Lewis Hamilton, September, 1885'. In 1893, at a dinner hosted by H.B. Brewster and Clotilde for the Hamiltons and Melvills, more mind reading was attempted along with an effort to conjure spirits. Unfortunately, the mind reading experiment failed and according to Clotilde, 'the spirits resisted'.

Clotilde was often invited down to Mary's country house in Rustington, called The Marigolds, which she had built in 1889. Once a sleepy backwater, this seaside town was becoming a thriving summer community which spurred Mary's interest in real estate speculation.

It had long been a favorite spot of women's rights activists Agnes Garrett and her cousin Rhoda who lived in Fir Cottage not far from Mary's house. Adjacent to the Firs, composer Sir Hubert Parry resided in Knightscroft, a home designed by Richard Norman Shaw. It was here that he composed the famous hymn 'Jerusalem'. He would go on to set music to Mary's poem 'A Hymn for Aviators', published in 1915. Parry's wife Maud was a leading suffragette in the area and Mary supported the cause by organizing fundraising fairs for the Woman's Suffrage Movement.[5]

Mary was not new to the suffragette movement; many years earlier in 1882, representing the Somerville Club in London, she presented a petition to Parliament requesting the 'House to pass a measure enacting that the Parliamentary Suffrage shall be exercised by women'.[6] The Somerville Club, the first women's club in London, was founded in 1878 and was a place where women could discuss political and social questions of the day. It was named after Scottish polymath, scientist and writer, Mary Somerville.

COUNTRY HOUSE, OLD MILL COTTAGE AND CHURCH FARM BUNGALOW

Country House

In Clotilde's 1897 proposed country house for Mary, she strove to create something quintessentially English. Mary's reaction was encouraging. 'It's scrumptious, simply the loveliest house I have ever seen.'[7] Letters are ambiguous as to whether it was built. Still, much can be gleaned from the design drawings (fig.27).

Clotilde's design derives from the vernacular Tudor style of the Sussex Weald popular in the late medieval period. In the mid-19th century, going against the current of designing buildings in the Gothic revival style, architect George Devey was already delving into Tudor style architecture, seamlessly blending its intrinsic characteristics with contemporary design principles. This trend was further developed by successive generations of architects also interested in the 'Old England' of the 16th and 17th centuries, starting with Richard Norman Shaw and into the 20th century with the Edwardian-age designers.

The house in form resembles other contemporary houses such as C.F.A. Voysey's Moor Crag in Cumbria (1899–1900), M.H. Baillie Scott's King's Close in Bedfordshire (designed around 1909) and Edwin Lutyens' Cottages at Ashby St Ledger (1913). In contrast to these houses, Clotilde emphasized the

27 Front elevation of proposed county house for Miss Hamilton. Courtesy of Amanda Feilding

building fabric details of houses of the Tudor age. The jetty beams or joists which support the upper level are visible on the exterior, cantilevering beyond the edge of the sill. There is irregular spacing of vertical half-timbering, as well as multiple leaded glass panes hung in casement windows.

The dominant roof, cross gable and heavy chimneys give it a sense of weight and solidity. Clotilde composed an asymmetrical version of a hipped roofed Wealden house – one which originally would have been incrementally added to and renovated over time giving it a picturesque aspect. Clotilde breaks down the roof massing by stepping it down on either side of the main section. The eaves reach to the ground floor level at the loggia and the side of the entry. The main section accommodates the most important spaces such as the drawing and dining rooms. The loggia is tucked under the roof's low eave line.

Local Sussex building materials such as oak timbers and clay would have been used. As commonly seen in Rustington and Sussex in general, the ground floor has coins on the corners and the window and door surrounds. The body of the house including the infill between the half timbers most probably would have been stucco. The entrance doorway is arched.

The orientation of the rooms makes architectural sense (fig.28). The drawing room, the dining room, entry hall and loggia appropriately face south, capturing the warmth of the sun during the day. The utilitarian spaces which needed to be kept cool

BETWEEN SPIRITUALISTS AND PHYSICIANS   81

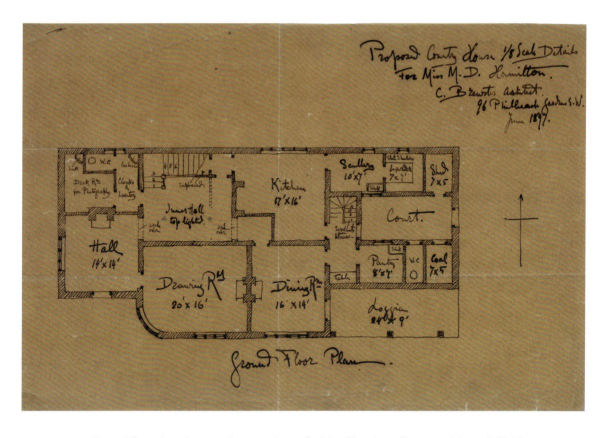

28 Ground floor plan of proposed country house for Miss Hamilton. Courtesy of Amanda Feilding

or are low on the architectural hierarchy, face north: kitchen, larder, scullery, cloak room, W.C., and interestingly, a dark room – Mary Hamilton was an amateur photographer. The kitchen was a large room, very generous in proportion and well lit; it measured 17 by 16 feet. Facing north as well was a large inner hall with stair case with a skylight above. Clotilde designed an inner courtyard off which contain utilitarian spaces and the servants' W.C. The drawing room has a simple but effective feature of a rounded corner with a round bay window. The dining room has a door to the loggia. On the upper floor there is a large artist studio north top lighted and four bedrooms. As was typical for a modestly sized house, there was only one full bath for all of the bedrooms.

Old Mill Cottage

Mary Hamilton commissioned Clotilde for two residential construction projects, a renovation of a house followed a few years later by a new-built cottage. According to Rustington poor law sheets from 1904, created by local historian Bev Taylor, among the properties owned by Mary were two houses both known collectively as 'Old Mill Cottage'. An early photograph from the 1890s shows that the smaller structure had no windows which indicates it was an outbuilding and not habitable. Later photographs show the two-story house remodeled and extended. The smaller structure was rebuilt as a cottage (figs 29 and 30).

82   CLOTILDE BREWSTER

29 Old Mill Cottage buildings in photograph of Windmill Corner, *c*.1890. The windmill was taken down in 1896. Courtesy of Graeme Taylor from the Bev and Mary Taylor Collection

30 Old Mill Cottage buildings in 1957. Courtesy of Graeme Taylor from the Bev and Mary Taylor Collection

31   Old Mill Cottage, the house. Photograph postmarked 1905. Courtesy of Graeme Taylor from the Bev and Mary Taylor Collection

32   Old Mill Cottage, the small house, *c.*1948. Courtesy of Graeme Taylor from the Bev and Mary Taylor Collection

Of the house renovation Clotilde wrote in 1899:

> I've returned from Rustington. The house is amazing. I never would have believed it would succeed so well and that it would have such a different look. The dining room is quite 'noble'. On the exterior it's no longer a shack but a house. Everyone and especially Miss Hamilton is delighted. I made £14 in profit. A beautiful spring day there, wonderful, the windmills white against the blue sky, the meadows with the river bordered by willows – a dream.[8]

An early photograph shows it as a three-bay house. Clotilde added a fourth bay. The roof was replaced and a new front entrance added. She used flint masonry for the walls of the house and for the perimeter wall separating the front garden from the street (fig.31).

Of the replacement of the smaller structure, Clotilde wrote in September 1902: 'Mary Hamilton writes that she wants me to build her a small house (rental speculation) a little confection. It's something at least – it shouldn't be difficult architecture-wise' (fig.32).[9] Clotilde recreated the side-gabled configuration of the original structure and built chimneys at either end.

Church Farm Bungalow

Late in 1902, Mary hired Clotilde to design a bungalow with shops and apartments. In June 1903, a plan was submitted and building permission was issued. This property was located on Ash Lane and known as Church Farm Bungalow. It was later renamed 'Whitecroft'. In November 1902, Clotilde wrote to her father.

> I've just returned from Rustington, where I did the plans for Mary Hamilton's bungalow. It is splendid. It is comprised of two apartment suites, a butcher's and a grocer's. There is something 'respectably rich Dutch' about it – I would even say Transvaalois; it's very good – you'll see. Miss Hamilton, very nice, gave me honey and apples and a novel in which everyone is charming and everything ends up for the better.[10]

As demonstrated by the Country House for Mary, Clotilde embraced the Arts and Crafts movement, which celebrated a variety of traditional historical styles. With Church Farm Bungalow, she was influenced by the Jacobean Revival style. Unlike the half-timbered architecture of the preceding Tudor period, the Jacobean Revival is modelled after brick and stone manors popular in the early 17th century during the reign of James I. These homes featured motifs what were brought to England through German and Flemish carvers and craftsmen. Its most distinguishing feature was the 'Dutch' or 'Flemish' gable with stone coping. Architect Basil Champneys adopted this style in his design of Newnham College. Especially familiar to Clotilde were the ornate gables of Newnham's Clough Hall (1886). While this influence is undeniable, Church Farm Bungalow may also reflect a nod to Mary's flat in the Albert Hall Mansions, Kensington Gore, London – a magnificent apartment complex with a gabled roofline designed by Richard Norman Shaw. Clotilde's use of the word 'Transvaalois' refers to similar structures built by Dutch settlers in South Africa.

As built, the exterior cladding of the building was brick.[11] A later owner covered it with pebble-dash, added an unattractive entryway and replaced the original slate roof but its elaborately shaped gables and scalloped parapet topped by stone ball finials can still be seen. Almost all the original casement windows remain except for two double hung sash windows mulled together to the right of the entryway. A number of years later, architect Edwin Lutyens rented the house for August to September 1907 (figs 33 and 34).[12]

33   Church Farm Bungalow, 1920, with corner tower. Courtesy of Graeme Taylor
from the Bev and Mary Taylor Collection

34   Church Farm Bungalow, 1920. It was later renamed Whitecroft. The entryway was a much later addition and
not designed by Clotilde Brewster. Courtesy of Graeme Taylor from the Bev and Mary Taylor Collection

Fittingly for a home built by Mary Hamilton, Church Farm Bungalow has a connection with the supernatural. During the Second World War it was requisitioned by Canadian troops and afterwards the 'Council took the property over and converted into self-contained flats. It was at this time that it was discovered to be haunted by the ghost of a lady in long flowing white robes'.[13]

PROJECT FOR LILLIAS HAMILTON, M.D.: NURSING HOME

Late in 1899, Mary Hamilton's first cousin, Dr Lillias Hamilton hired Clotilde to convert a town house into a nursing home at 29 Queen Anne Street, a terraced town house built in the 1760s in Cavendish Square, London. In April 1898, the property was described in a real estate advertisement as a 'First class Professional or Private residence with magnificent reception rooms, good bedrooms and full set of offices'.[14]

Though no drawings of this project have been found, it is worth discussing as it outside of Clotilde's usual domestic architectural work and commissioned by a well-known woman, Lillias Hamilton. Unfortunately, her high hopes for this project were dashed due to the nervous temperament and unpredictable behavior of the client.

Dr Hamilton was born in Sydney, Australia but raised in Cheltenham, England. She was a pioneer physician and author who had an adventuresome but formidable personality. Her varied career included physician in charge of the Dufferin Hospital in Calcutta; physician to the Court of the Amir of Afghanistan; farmer in South Africa and finally, warden of Studley Horticultural and Agricultural College for Women in Warwickshire. One of Hamilton's major achievements was the introduction of mass vaccination against smallpox in Afghanistan.[15]

Though amazingly accomplished, the eccentric Hamilton was a source of gossip among Clotilde and her friends as the exotic subject of hypnotism comes up in a letter to H.B.[16] Hamilton had learned hypnotism in India and intended to use it for medical ends in her London practice.

Lillias Hamilton's challenging personality led to difficulties dealing with Clotilde and the builder of the nursing home, George F. Wright of Westminster.[17] Impatient and eager to start, she had Clotilde and the builder begin the work in late January before the lease was signed, before the surveyor had completed his work and before drawings were approved by the city of London.[18] Hamilton had no understanding of the process of construction or the time involved. The surveyor demanded more and more changes resulting in a constant revision of the drawings. Heedless of the consequences, Hamilton was making continuous design changes well after construction was underway – which led to cost overruns and time delays.

In June 1900, Clotilde thought Dr Hamilton was on the brink of a mental breakdown. 'Miss Hamilton quarrels with Wright (the builder) then cries in his arms. She's hysterical and will need her hospital more than she knows'.[19] By October, tensions escalated as Hamilton refused payment to Wright due to rising costs and unfinished work.

Almost nothing more is mentioned in Clotilde's letters until the following summer. Dr Hamilton had decided to take Wright to court and in July 1901, Clotilde was required to attend as a witness. When Hamilton's case against Wright started to unravel, she began to widen her suit to implicate Clotilde.

> The opposing party changed tactics and now accuses me of complicity, fraud and collusion. It's a sign of weakness. Miss Hamilton is ready to accuse me of anything and has arranged her affairs in such a way that she is declaring bankruptcy and won't be paying anything she owes . . . Her lawyer

understands nothing, which does not surprise me. He hasn't seen the plans and doesn't know what's been done. Mr. Pollack, the judge, seems charming and stops him each time he insinuates that I swindled Hamilton with Wright. It's extremely interesting and I'm not afraid at all. I think this trial has been conducted in an idiotic way. If they had accused Wright and me of negligence, they might have a case – it's a matter of opinion but in accusing us of fraud, the game is lost. Wright's lawyer is a big wig, a friend of Sir G. Lewis. I should have liked to have been a lawyer; I missed my calling.[20]

The nursing home failed financially due in part to Hamilton's strained relationships with colleagues. It ceased operations by late 1906, though Hamilton retained ownership until her death.

In 1908, Hamilton took on the role of warden at Studley Horticultural and Agricultural College for Women in Warwickshire. Despite leading the college to success, rumors circulated about her harsh treatment of staff, some involving her use of hypnotism.[21] The British occultist, Dion Fortune worked for Hamilton at the college when she was just twenty. In the preface to her book, *Psychic Self-Defense* (1930), Fortune describes Hamilton's 'psychic attacks' on her which eventually led to her own mental breakdown.

Hamilton's long service to Studley College came to an end in 1924 interrupted only for a short period of time during the First World War when she headed the Wounded Allies' Relief Committee's hospital in Podgorica, Montenegro. She died in January 1925 of unspecified causes.

10

SOCIALITES AND SUFFRAGETTES

Projects for the Smyths

A couple of months after her mother's death on 15 September 1895, Clotilde became close to her father's mistress, composer and suffragette Ethel Smyth. Ethel took Clotilde under her wing and introduced her to her circle of friends and family, who became a valuable source of work for the young architect. She designed a number of projects in England for Ethel and her sisters, the wealthy Mary Hunter, a society hostess and patron of the arts, and the less well-known Violet Hippisley, who was friends with such cosmopolites as writer Vernon Lee, Princess Eugène Murat and Princess Edmond de Polignac.

MARY HUNTER

In his memoirs, *Portraits of a Lifetime*, Mary is remembered by her friend, the French artist Jacques-Émile Blanche.

> There is nothing to suggest that Mary Hunter, the sister of Dame Ethel Smyth, when she moved in military circles at Aldershot in her youth, was anything of a wit. As a wife and the mother of three daughters, she did not emerge from the half-light till she had become mature, when Sir William Eden, the celebrated shot and a neighbor of Charles Hunter, a mine-owner in Durham, introduced her to London Society. George Moore had initiated her into the arts and literature; Ethel, the composer of The Wreckers, a pupil of Brahms and a traveller, added certain elements of great value to the accomplishments of her sisters. The family might have remained home-biding like the Jane Austen's heroines, talking scandal and peeping out from behind curtains in their small town to take stock of the passing gentry, but fate made them cosmopolitans.[1]

Mary was born in 1856 in India, where her father, Major-General John Hall Smyth of the Bengal Artillery, was stationed. Shortly after, the family moved back to England where Ethel was born two years later. The two were very close growing up but as adults fought frequently and were often estranged. The beauty of the family, Ethel described Mary as always exquisitely dressed, 'splendidly erect' and 'radiating that sense of enjoying life to the utmost which was one of her greatest charms'.[2]

Mary, at 19, married Charles Hunter, a mine owner's son from Northumbria. They had little money when starting their life together but, in a decade or so, as the coal mines prospered, Charles would make a fortune.[3] They eventually moved into grander accommodation, leasing Selaby Hall in Gainford, Darlington from Lord Barnard in about 1890. Charles Hunter from the start of their lease made improvements to the estate while Mary zealously embraced her role as wealthy châtelaine.

At some point, Mary began to squander Hunter's fortune by lavish entertaining and by her patronage of the arts on such a scale that it eventually ruined her. In doing so, Mary became one of the most celebrated and envied hostesses of her time. She created luxurious settings where she hosted the greatest artistic, musical and literary figures of the day. Many became her close friends, like writer Henry James and American painter John Singer Sargent. Sargent's favorite sitter, he depicted her in many of his works, including the oil painting *Mrs. Charles Hunter*. He also produced a painting of Mary's three daughters titled *The Misses Hunter*.

Her wider social circle included artists such as impressionist painters Claude Monet, Walter Sickert and Antonio Mancini, all from whom she acquired a number of paintings. Furthermore, she commissioned portraits of herself by sculptors Prince Paul Troubetzkoy and Auguste Rodin.

A music enthusiast, Mary financially supported Ethel's musical career and held private concerts of other musician's works in her homes. Composers Percy Grainger, Roger Quilter and singer Elsie Swinton were frequent visitors.

Clotilde socialized often with Mary who in general, despised her own sex. She wrote to her father, 'I dined with Mrs. Hunter. She told me that among women she loves only me and Feo Gleichen. I am delighted.'[4] They saw each other much less frequently after Clotilde's marriage in 1904, but one occasion stands out. In 1910, two years after the Hunters acquired the lease of Hill Hall in Epping, sixteen miles from London, there were signs that Mary was in financial trouble. In February that year, she telegraphed Clotilde asking to have lunch with her and Percy at their house in Farnborough. Upon arriving, Mary got right to the point and asked Percy for financial assistance. Clotilde wrote to her brother in disbelief, 'Mary Hunter hardly knows Percy – she has lots of friends who are rich – without mentioning Sargent – why should she hit upon us? And why should she want money? She must either have borrowed so much that no one will lend her anymore or she must be on the verge of bankruptcy . . . It makes me laugh when I think of it. Mary in her sables and pearls comes from London to ask us in our rough and ready-made tweeds for money! I feel like the frog who said "What next?" when his tail dropped off!'[5]

There is no further mention of Mary's finances and her life continued at the same hectic pace, continuing to host large house parties. The following year, Clotilde wrote her brother that she and Percy were staying with the Hunters along with Henry James, and the painters Wilfred de Glehn and Annie Swynnerton.[6]

In 1914, at the start of the First World War, Mary and Charlie prepared Hill Hall to receive wounded officers and soldiers.[7] Incredibly though, Mary continued to entertain on a large scale throughout the war.[8] In early 1918 rumors circulated in the district about the amount of food going into Hill Hall which was very soon raided by the police, under authority conferred by the Food Hoarding Order.

That February at a Parish Council meeting, Mary addressed her neighbors, revealing how far removed she was from the difficulties faced by everyday folk. In her defense she claimed the food was being consumed and thus not technically hoarded. She said that, 'On Christmas Day 67 people partook of hospitality at the Hall, and on various shooting days during the month at least 22 beaters and six or more loaders were fed from the Hall larder'.[9]

The money eventually ran out. Charlie died in 1917 and by 1920, Mary was compelled to sell her London residence at 31 Portland Place, parting with 54 of her artworks. Five years later, she relinquished the lease on Hill Hall, auctioning all its paintings and furniture. The final blow occurred in 1931 when she sold off the rest of her possessions from her last home in Gloucester Square. Mary died less than two years later on 18 January 1933.

SELABY HALL

The earliest mention of Clotilde's commissions at Selaby is by Ethel Smyth in her memoir *What Happened Next*. In the summer of 1898, 'I knew too that he (H.B.) had been invited to Killarney, and my sister Mary had booked him and Clotilde for Selaby, where Clotilde was to build a gamekeeper's cottage; and I was to follow in his wake to both places, if possible.'[10]

No drawings of the gamekeeper's cottage have been found nor references to it in Clotilde's letters to her father. As he lived in England with Clotilde during the summer months, there would not have been any need for correspondence between them and thus no written documentation remains.

Her next commission was for a new East Entrance addition, drawings for which were found in the Durham County Records office. They are undated and unsigned but these drawings can be attributed to Clotilde through a comparison of the handwriting and the drafting style especially

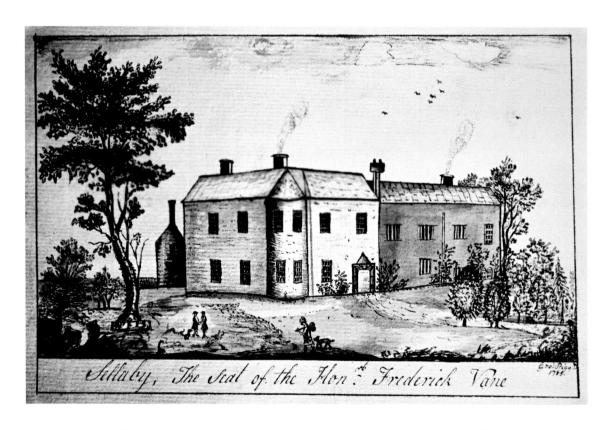

35   Selaby Hall, 1785, ink wash drawing, 18cm × 25 cm. Raby Estate Archives. Courtesy of Lord Barnard

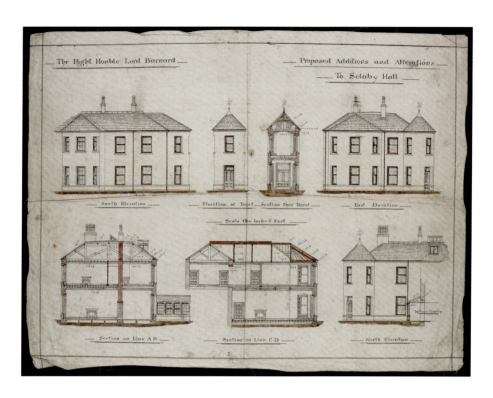

36   Selaby Hall, sections and elevations. The Story, Durham

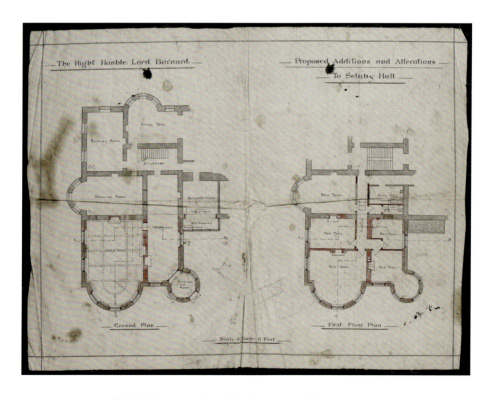

37   Selaby Hall, ground and first floor plans. The Story, Durham

to Clotilde's drawings of another project for the Hunters, Proposed Racket Court, Bothy and Stables also held in the Durham County Records Office. Though undated, the new addition is estimated to have been built about 1898.

Imbedded in what is now Selaby Hall are the remnants of a 13th-century manor house which was 'most likely U-shaped in plan'.[11] Centuries of multiple additions have completely obscured the original structure.

In a 1785 ink wash drawing, Selaby Hall is depicted as a two-story building (fig.35). It consists of a main block built in the late 18th century and, to the right, a lower structure dating back to the 16th century or earlier.[12] The main block was constructed during the Georgian era but aside from its tall proportions and multi-paned, sash windows it lacks a symmetrical composition and formal, classical details typical of the Georgian style. The most interesting and whimsical feature is a circular corner turret with a conical roof. Over the next century, several alterations were made to this block, including the addition of bow windows and the removal of the turret. The 16th-century section, as seen in this ink wash, has survived relatively intact.

The new East Entrance was built abutting the late eighteenth-century addition (figs 36 and 37). Clotilde matched the roof and eave lines and doubled its size, adding new entry in the form of a turreted tower. In doing so, Clotilde recreated the most intriguing historical element of the house while unifying it into a cohesive whole. The new design not only honors the house's history but also reflects Clotilde's love of French medieval architecture. It is roofed in ornamental shingles and topped by a copper weathervane. On the

38   Photograph of Selaby Hall showing the new turret entryway. The Bowes Museum, Barnard Castle, County Durham. To the right of the turret is the 16th-century structure

SOCIALITES AND SUFFRAGETTES   93

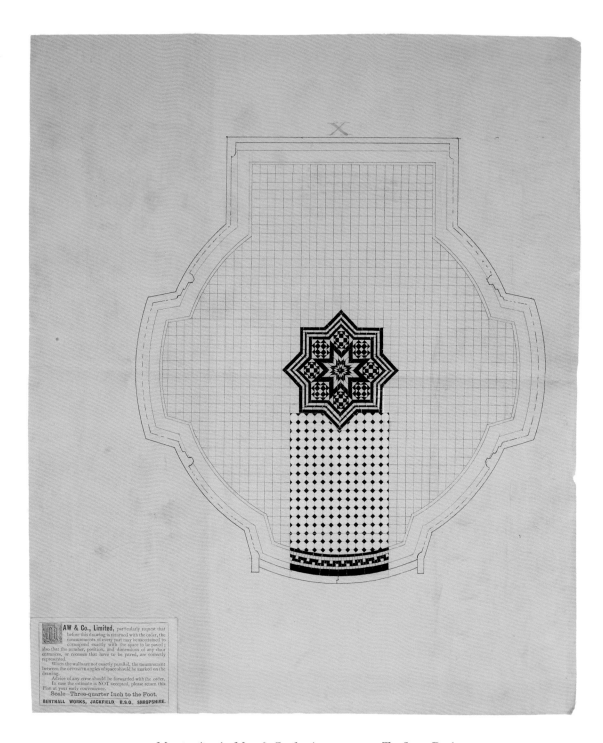

39   Mosaic tiling by Maw & Co. for the turret entry. The Story, Durham

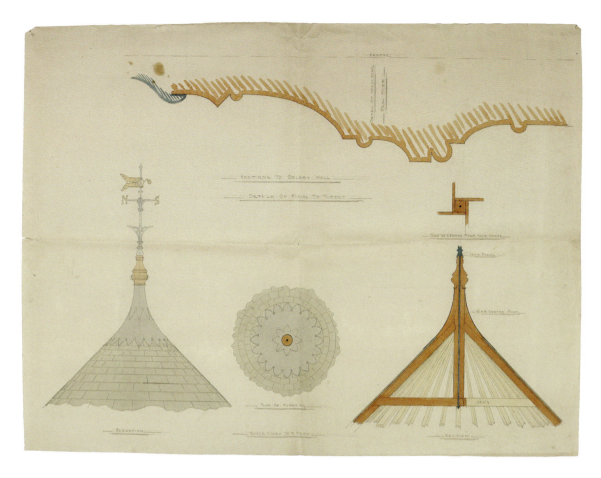

40   Details of the roof and finial to turret. The Story, Durham

turret entry floor, Clotilde designed an exuberant starburst pattern in Maw & Co. mosaic tiles (figs 38, 39 and 40).

Very grand in proportions, the new addition's Large Hall was designed to accommodate Mary's grand-scale entertaining. It measured 25 feet, 6 inches by 37 feet and featured high ceilings, two fireplaces, a high dado all around and exposed beams. In proportion to the new room, the windows are wider than in the Georgian era block. The windows, though not slavishly copied from the 18th-century originals are sympathetic to them. Most importantly, the extension transformed an undersized corridor into long wide gallery. This space was used to display Mary's extensive art collection.

On the upper floor, the curved walls make placing furniture a challenge but created much more interesting rooms – something that appealed to Mary's decorating skills. The house still exists today but the interiors are much altered.

SELABY LODGE

Much pleased with the project, the Hunters soon required of Clotilde designs for other buildings on

SOCIALITES AND SUFFRAGETTES   95

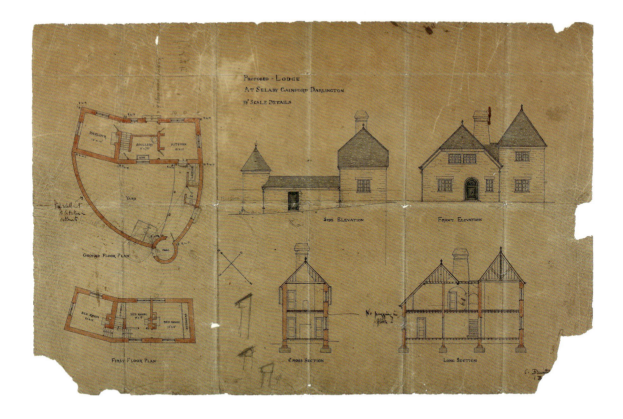

41   This is one of a number of drawings Clotilde produced for Selaby Lodge. The Story, Durham

the estate. In early January 1900 she wrote to her father from Selaby,

> I'm still here and I am staying just until Miss Hamilton has signed her contract. I changed the farm building (racket court) and I am doing something much better with a tower and arch under which automobiles pass. Hunter is very nice and has very good taste. He thinks everything I do is nice. In addition, he has asked me to build a new lodge at the entrance to the park – square tower, main building, courtyard and small round tower. Everything has a triangular layout created by three intersecting roads.[13]

The design was something very French and playful in style; Clotilde called it her 'château-fort' (fig.41).[14] In January, Clotilde wrote from her house in Westminster, London,

> Hunter is the ideal client; he has perfect taste and also lets me do whatever I want. If only he were Duke of Westminster I would have work till the end of my days. He came to see me here a few days ago and admired everything. I am sending you a trace of the Lodge. Tell me what you think of it. Do you find that the roofs are steep enough and the proportions satisfactory? It seems to me that by putting the small tower at the end and joining it with the walls gives it a grander look. Hunter said

96   CLOTILDE BREWSTER

that Lord Barnard will fear competition for Raby Castle.

As the approach to the lodge was important to get right, she asked for her father's critique,

> I want your advice for the curve of the walls – would you make the curve constant or first gentle then tight or vice versa beginning with the main building – which of these curves produces the greatest effect at a distance?[15]

Clotilde was there in December 1900 supervising the construction for the lodge as she feared the builder might not understand the complicated massing of the roof. She was still there in January 1901 as Charles Hunter wanted her to design yet another project. 'Finally – I just returned from Selaby where I was detained every day by my hospitable hosts. On the evening before my departure, Hunter said he wanted to build stables and here I am, held back.' Clotilde was anxious to return to London. 'Hunter is an ideal client but as soon as an estimate is finished, he wants another one and doesn't give you a break. Finally, it's done – God be praised.'[16] This would be a second version of the stables, commissioned 11 months after the first.

WEMMERGILL HALL

There was soon talk of moving and in 1903 Clotilde requested that H.B. campaign on her behalf, 'It seems that the Hunters are going to abandon Selaby

42   Photograph of the front of Wemmergill Hall after the Hunters' renovation. Courtesy of Mick Collinson

(their lease ends in 3 years) and establish themselves at Wemmergill in a small house which they will enlarge. I covet this work; if the opportunity presents itself, please put a word in to Mary Hunter.'[17]

Later letters indicate she was successful in obtaining the commission and though no drawings have been found, a newspaper article outlined the scope of work on the house, outbuildings and grounds (fig.42).[18] Besides extensive landscaping, major work was done on the interior and some cosmetic work on the exterior and a new porch was created:

> Gun-rooms and game-houses are alike now screened by rustic trellis-work, adorned with ivy, and the whole has a very pleasing effect. An old-style porch has been faithfully reproduced, leading into the entrance hall from the north. It projects eight feet from the main wall of the building, and is about twenty-five feet long. The ceiling of the corridor, under antique treatment, has now an old-fashioned appearance.
>
> By the insertion of an iron girder, a partition has been removed and an apartment added to the drawing-room, which is now el-shaped, and very large and commodious, the dimensions being thirty-six feet long by twenty-five feet wide. The dining-room has been paneled in representative old dark oak. The old time fire-places are commanding and very artistic. The arches at the east end, considered with the contemplated mirror effect – a growing and commendable feature in fine art and high-class furnishing – will be simply marvellous. The mirrors must be eight feet by six and herein the landscape will be deftly reflected in curious and subtle deception.

The article goes on to describe the rest of the improvements which imbued the residence with a 'subdued luxuriance'. In addition to the house, a rustic bungalow was built on the grounds for Charles Hunter's private secretary.

After the renovation, Wemmergill Hall became a magnet for the shooting parties of the aristocracy. In 1907 *The Gentlewoman and Modern Life* reported: 'At Wemmergill, which, with the last two years' successes, has become one of the very cheeriest centres for autumn hospitality, and quite famous for its sporting bags, Mr. and Mrs. Charles Hunter mean to be busy with relays of guests throughout the season.'[19] The more illustrious among them were Prince Arthur of Connaught (grandson of Queen Victoria), Jacobo Fitz-James Stuart (The 17th Duke of Alba and direct descendant of Mary, Queen of Scots), Lord Farquhar (a Lord-in-waiting to the King) and the Russian Ambassador and Countess Benckendorff.

VIOLET HIPPISLEY – BOER WAR MEMORIAL FOUNTAIN

In 1902 Clotilde designed a Boer War Memorial Fountain in Farnborough, Hampshire for (Honoria) Violet Hippisley (1864–1923).

Violet lived a more modest and quieter life than sisters Mary or Ethel. In 1885, she married Richard Lionel Hippisley (1853–1936) of the Royal Engineers who served as Director of Telegraphs in South Africa during the Second Boer War (1899–1902). Ethel, not as close to her as she was to Mary, wrote briefly of her, 'I apologise for adding that this sister, too, was very pretty, but only last week a contemporary of mine remarked: "You certainly were a very good-looking family", and if so, why not say so? Violet was altogether a charmer, very kind, exceedingly amusing, and according to her great admirer H.B., the best brain of us all.'[20] 'She was more emphatically *feminine*, I think, than any of my sisters.'[21] Among Violet's many friends was a rich American named Mary Dodge who along with the Empress Eugenie and Mary Hunter supported and financed Ethel's musical career. Dodge also provided the funds for Ethel to purchase a plot of land in Woking, where she built a cottage in 1910.[22]

At the end of 1895, Ethel invited Clotilde for Christmas week to her house at One Oak in Frimley, Surrey, near Farnborough, where Clotilde 'spent a delightful Christmas, five days in which physical, intellectual and artistic pleasures came together, were separated only to be united again even more harmoniously'. During the stay, they visited the homes of two of Ethel's sisters who lived nearby, Nina Hollings and Violet Hippisley. It was Violet who would later become a good friend, but it was Richard Hippisley to whom Clotilde felt an immediate attraction. At their second meeting, Violet was ill, and Clotilde spent time alone with him.

> The day after Christmas everything was under snow; we went on bicycles to the Hippisley's, through the Empress' woods. It was enough to make you fall in love with the countryside. Her sister was doing much better. She [Ethel] stayed with her for more than an hour while Mr. and I talked. He is <u>charming</u>. I underline because there is charming and there is charming.[23]

After Colonel Hippisley left for South Africa in 1899, Violet and Clotilde socialized frequently and formed a friendship quite independent of Ethel. It was mostly dinners and lunches with close friends in London or Farnborough, going to the theatre or musical performances. When Richard returned in 1902, there was talk about building a house. In December, she spent the day with Violet looking for a plot of land.

> Hippisley will only have me as his architect. He is a man of great intelligence. A cold to freeze boiling water – nothing very pleasing found. I'm afraid that once the search is left off that they will buy a mundane but comfortable house within their price range. In any event, I shall know before I leave and if they decide to build, I'll do the drawings in Rome.[24]

The Hippisleys in the end continued to rent accommodation in Farnborough which was inadequate for their needs; in 1904 Clotilde wrote to her father,

> Violet has a horrible little house – and lots of guests. She says to each one, 'Do stay, I hope the other one who bores me will leave' and to the other one she says the same thing. This creates a lot of complications. Vernon Lee arrived at the end in all her beauty – we had to leave. She wore a big cravat with a cameo brooch [. . .] and a sprig of flowers on her lapel – she made quite an impression! The Princess Murat had to leave. Violet is expecting Madame de Chimay, the Princess Polignac, Lena Milman, Alfred Lambert, Captain Blunt and there are only two miserable rooms for everyone. She is playing some kind of shell game, changing everyone's bed. Maybe everything will go smoothly and no one will notice a thing![25]

Though she did not get a house to design, Clotilde was delighted when Violet commissioned her for a Boer War Memorial Fountain to be located near the military town of Aldershot. The design phase started in the summer of 1902 but the budget was low and kept getting smaller. There was also an issue of water even before the fountain was built. Wanting to see this project realized, Clotilde negotiated for a free water supply.

> I went to Vawdrey's to ask him to furnish water for the fountain for free. He said I should put my trust in him; he would see to it. What a delightful man. But if I don't get the official consent from

43   Boer War Memorial Fountain in Farnborough, Hampshire. Author's collection

the authorities, I won't have any money left. First Violet wanted to donate £1000 then £700 and now it's only £500 – in a month's time the fountain will have fallen through.'[26]

Dr Vawdrey was the Chairman of the Council in Farnborough at the time and when the fountain was discussed it was agreed that the Council would supply the water.

By October 1902 the design was complete. Clotilde sent a photo of her drawing to H.B. 'Behind the memorial plaque is a small basin with a tap where passersby can drink. To the left is a little fellow to indicate the size of the monument and behind him is a semi-circular bench that invites repose. I hope that you approve of the design.'[27] In the next letter she revealed she had got an estimate but the high cost of construction might jeopardize the entire project, 'I am delighted that you like the fountain. Alas – the cost is £900 and I only have £500! But I sent the plans to other contractors and I live in hope!'[28] After much searching, she found a contractor at the right price, a Mr. Hammond of Farnborough.

Clotilde designed the details of 'Violet's fountain' at Adolf Hildebrand's studio in Florence where Hildebrand was on hand to consult and advise (fig.43).[29] Stylistically the Boer Memorial Fountain was influenced by Hildebrand's marketplace fountains and was quite different to other British war monuments of the time. It made an impression on author Maria Theresa Earle whose son, Captain Sydney Earle of the Coldstream Guards, was killed in the Boer War in 1899. In a 1906 letter to her niece Lady Constance Lytton she wrote,

> There is a memorial monument at Aldershot which touches me supremely. It stands at the cross roads just as you leave the pretty fir and heather Farnborough country to enter the ugly, neat, inartistic North Camp. It was erected after

100   CLOTILDE BREWSTER

the Boer war, no one knows by whom, and the dedication is equally anonymous. It is a large and handsome piece of stonework with steps on either side leading up to a platform, at the back of which is a large stone seat. Here the weary may rest and the sad may think. Behind this are a few old and somewhat weather-beaten trees, birches and Scotch firs. The steps and front of the platform are enclosed by a rather severe but handsome balustrading. Below this is a basin which in any other country but England would be filled by a copious fountain of water. Here the water flows from only one spout, and that only at times, into a large basin for horses to drink out of, and at either side are low saucers for smaller animals. Above the balustrade which forms the background to this fountain, and in front of the seat, is a high monumental stone. On the side facing the water and the road is written in plain letters: 'In Memory of one who died for his Country'. The execution of the design and the stone-work leaves a good deal to be desired artistically, but the idea, to my mind, is simple and admirable, and in perfect taste. Although dedicated to one in particular, it may be appropriated as a memorial to all those who lay down their young lives in war, and it is a most suitable ornament to the entrance of a great camp.[30]

COIGN

In the spring of 1910, Clotilde quite unexpectedly designed a version of Ethel's newly built house called Coign in Woking, Surrey. She wrote to her brother that out of the blue, 'Ethel turned up and spent two days here making me draw plans for her new house as she does not like her architect's plans! – the fifth set – poor man.'[31] Permission to build was granted soon after. Ethel Smyth's unpublished memoirs leave out any mention of Clotilde but outlines her contentious relationship with her architect-builder.

> To go back to my cottage. Connected with it is a tragedy which I am certain would not have happened had my architect been a woman! But the day of female architects had not yet dawned, and my choice fell on a Woking man I knew and liked – Arthur Messer by name – who had built a lot of houses in the neighbourhood.

Ethel at the start of construction was in Vienna where her work was to be performed. When she returned, she was shocked to find that much of the house was built but her requested design changes had not been carried out.

> Mr. Messer was so pressing in assuring me I need not come till the walls were up (like the conductors who always try to keep me away from rehearsals till is too late to correct the tempi they prefer to yours) . . . Seldom have I been so furious. The walls of the upper storey were rent down (some by my own hands) and a curt note sent to Mr. Messer . . . Had I been rich the foundations would have been relaid![32]

It is uncertain how much of what was actually constructed was influenced by Clotilde's design as original drawings of the house have not survived.

Ethel's move to Coign marks the start of her time as a leading suffragette. For two years, from 1910 through 1911, she left off her musical pursuits to commit herself entirely to the movement. It is here she composed the suffragette anthem, *The March of the Women*. In 1911 when the census taker came to her door, she refused to give him any information. Instead, she wrote in bold letters on the census form itself, NO VOTE NO CENSUS.[33]

II

ROMAN HIGH SOCIETY MEETS THE LADY ARCHITECT

Projects for the Frankensteins

Clotilde was asked to do four projects in Rome by various members of the Frankenstein family, Alessandra (1846–1921) and her two children, Marianna (1868–abt 1951) and Henri (1866–1934): The Palazzo Soderini, the Palazzo Frankenstein, the facade for the workshop *Laboratorio Santa Caterina* and the Villino Frankenstein.

After her mother's death in 1895, Clotilde's father began a new phase in his life, one in which he played an active part in the social life of Rome. Margaret Chanler, an American living in Rome, wrote of her friend H.B. in her memoir, *Roman Spring*.

> He had a handsome apartment in the beautiful old Palazzo Antici Mattei, where he gave excellent dinners and knew how to bring together the most interesting people. The Pasolinis and the Abbé Duchesne were among his favorites; Count Pasolini use to call him *il bel sauro* (the handsome sorrel), and complained that the ladies, his '*Maria cara*' among them, were all too partial to him. Brewster was indeed unusually attractive – tall, blond, distinguished-looking, he was at once friendly and remote. He had a romantic past that was never mentioned by those who knew about it, and naturally never by him.[1]

Abbé Duchesne was the director of the French School of Archaeology in Rome. Count Pier Desiderio Pasolini dall'Onda was an Italian historian and politician. His '*Maria cara*' was the preservationist and photographer Countess Maria Pasolini Ponti.

H.B. Brewster's hospitality extended beyond Rome's residents. Margaret Chanler introduced him to her friends Edith Wharton and her husband Teddy during Wharton's research for her book, *Italian Villas and Their Gardens*. Wharton was favorably impressed, both with H.B. and Clotilde,

> We have lunched with them twice, & little Miss Brewster, who has completely captivated Teddy, has been most kind about getting *permessi* for inaccessible villas, even to forcing the doors of the villa Albani when everyone else had tried & failed. Mr. Brewster I like greatly & should like to see often & the whole milieu is so sympathetic & charming that I leave with great regret.[2]

H.B.'s social connections, particularly the influential women of Rome, greatly contributed to Clotilde's professional success in Italy. The Frankensteins, in particular, sought her services. The family matriarch, Aleksandra 'Alessandra' Kronenberg, originally from Warsaw, Poland, hailed from a prestigious lineage. Her father, Henryk Andrzej Kronenberg, was a prominent physician and philanthropist who converted to Roman Catholicism and was ennobled by the Russian Empire in 1875.[3] Dr Kronenberg was an exception in the family in that most of the Kronenbergs were Polish bankers and industrialists. The founder of the family was Alessandra's grandfather, Samuel Eleazer Kronenberg, a merchant who established the S.L. Kronenberg bank. Somewhat unconventional, in 1808, he 'broke with Jewish tradition, shaved his beard, and began to wear European-style clothes'.[4] When he moved outside the Jewish district, he attended the progressive German synagogue in Warsaw and was an active member of the francophone Bouclier du Nord Freemason lodge. Alessandra Frankenstein's uncle was Leopold Kronenberg, an industrialist who was considered the richest man in Poland. He hired Napoleon III's architect, Hector Lefuel to design his impressive Kronenberg Palace in Warsaw.[5] Lefuel had previously designed the addition to the Palais de Louvre in Paris.

Alessandra's late husband, Edward Frankenstein was born into a family of Jewish origin from Kutno.[6] He was a well-known violinist in Poland before entering into government service in 1856.[7] He eventually became an attaché at the Russian legation in Brussels and it is there that he raised his family.[8] It appears they had a second home in France as on his death certificate it states that in May 1888, aged 60, he died 'at home' at no.52 Boulevard Malesherbes, Paris.[9] His widow was 40 years old; his son Henri was 21 and daughter Emilia 'Marianna' was 20. With Edward's death, the family moved back to Poland.

Within a year an old Italian count passed through Warsaw. Marianna's family induced her to marry him and she reluctantly obeyed.[10] This was a second marriage for Count Edoardo Soderini (1853–1934) who had been widowed in 1885. Following family tradition, Edoardo held a high position at the Vatican and belonged to the Black Aristocracy – the Roman noble families who had remained faithful to the Pope after the Papal states were annexed by the Kingdom of Italy.

Edoardo had only his noble name to offer her as he possessed no personal wealth of his own. His marriage to Marianna improved his fortunes and he purchased a country villa immediately after the wedding. They also established a residence in Rome and were soon joined there by her mother and her brother.

Trouble appeared very soon after their wedding. Though on the surface both appeared religious, they had very different definitions of what that meant. Edoardo was faithful to the conventions of the Black Aristocracy, and never challenged the beliefs of the Catholic Church. Marianna, on the other hand, was on a life-long quest of spiritual enlightenment. At the time of meeting him, Marianna had had aspirations of becoming a nun, but according to her granddaughter, the writer Brianna Carafa in her book *Gli angeli personali* [Personal Angels], her early religious inclinations were highly unorthodox. Marianna spoke of having wanted to become a missionary and visiting unexplored continents, of meeting fakirs and having spiritual mysteries revealed. She was greatly disappointed with the high prelates of the Vatican that her new husband invited home to dine. She thought they lacked any real or interesting ideas.

Her unusual beliefs upset Edoardo greatly, as Carafa states in an astonishing passage.

> He watched his beautiful, young foreign wife with a vague though constant fear, sometimes coaxing

her tenderly, sometimes curbing her impulses with ill-mannered and desperate reasonableness. In fact, she must have appeared to him very soon as the most mysterious, unpredictable and unknowable of creatures, full of danger and turbulence masked by her very grace, like an animal crouching among the flowers.[11]

Her embrace of new ideas extended into the realm of politics which displeased her conservative husband still further as Carafa wrote 'he violently forbade her to receive into her house a liberal who had struck my grandmother's political imagination'.[12] She became a vegetarian and practiced yoga, in that day and age considered radical acts.

Marianna regarded her husband with a certain contempt but submitted to his authority. Though never giving up her own views, Marianna channeled her energy into first making a difference in the lives of the poor of Rome through Catholic agencies. Later she would become involved in more activist organizations that fought for women's rights, welfare and education.

In 1896, she became the first president in Rome of the *Compagnia delle Dame di Carità* (The Ladies of St Vincent de Paul) and in that capacity began weekly meetings for the poor of the parish.[13]

Another early mention of her work in raising funds to renovate a church is from an 1895 *New York Times* story. No doubt to her husband's embarrassment, she had asked the Pope for a personal favor.

THE POPE YIELDS TO THE MARQUISE

Cherchez la femme! The Marquise Soderini has succeeded where all the grandees of the Vatican have failed and failed again. It may be remembered that among the presents sent to Leo XIII, on the occasion of his pontifical jubilee, was a magnificent phonograph, the gift of a wealthy American. The Pope has spent many a leisure afternoon hour toying with the instrument, and has often gratified a visitor by causing him or her to listen to some pontifical or episcopal discourse, registered and faithfully reproduced by the 'talking machine'. One thing, however, the Pope would not do. He would not let the phonograph go outside the Vatican, though a request might come from the most august personages. But when the Marchioness Soderini and other distinguished ladies of the

44   View of the Piazza del Popolo. The Palazzo Soderini can be seen to the right of the Flaminio Obelisk. United States Library of Congress

Roman aristocracy were organizing a charity sale the other day, they asked again for the loan of the phonograph, and, to everybody's surprise, the Pope agreed to lend it. And thus the phonograph has been prattling away in the voice of the head of the Church, and for a considerable consideration, to all and sundry who visit the grand bazaar at Rome for the restoration of the Church of St. Philip of Neri.[14]

Marianna found her true calling in 1906 when she authored a paper advocating for the enfranchisement of Italian women. Her work was published in the journal of the Catholic Society for Social Studies in Italy, known as *Cattolica Per Gli Studi Sociale* in Italia.[15] She was also one of the signers of the *Petizione Al Parlamento Presentata Dal Comitato Nazionale Pro Suffragio Femminile Nel Marzo 1906* (Petition to Italian Parliament Presented by The National Women's Suffrage Committee in March 1906). On this document she is listed as School Inspector.[16]

In 1909, she penned a 14-page article titled *Pauperismo: Caratteri e Rimedi* (Pauperism: Characteristics and Solutions), which was published in *Nuova Antologia*.[17] This was a subject which would develop into a passionate interest.

The First World War put a temporary halt to her work on poverty but Marianna volunteered to assist the families of soldiers called up to fight for a second time on the *comitati per l'assistenza alle famiglie dei richiamati* and served as a nurse with the Italian Red Cross. In 1916 she was awarded a diploma of merit by the Italian government.[18]

After her husband's death, she attempted to put some of her more radical ideas into action. To address the problem of affordable housing after the Second World War, she partitioned the five spacious rental apartments of the Palazzo Soderini into twenty small ones for the poor while retaining

ROMAN HIGH SOCIETY MEETS THE LADY ARCHITECT   105

her own residence intact. Many years later and still concerned with low-income housing, Marianna unsuccessfully tried to build a housing estate made up of individual villas, to be built on her own land. It was well thought out, with architectural drawings and a financial plan. She approached first the Pope and then the leader of the Communist party, both of whom paid her scant attention. Undeterred, she continued to work on this project right up to her death in the early 1950s.

Marianna became acquainted with the Brewsters when her brother Henri began to court Clotilde's second cousin, Anne Seabury Brewster, who was visiting from New York in January 1894.[19] Clotilde instantly was taken with the beautiful and intellectual Marianna.

The Brewsters and the Soderini-Frankensteins became quite close and when H.B. asked for a private tour at the Vatican to show John Singer Sargent the Borgia apartments in February 1897, Edoardo arranged it. Afterwards H.B. wrote to Clotilde,

> This visit to the Vatican very much interested me. Firstly, because the ceilings decorated by Pinturicchio are beautiful, even to my irreligious eyes; secondly, because I saw that Sargent admired a host of things whose beauty escaped me . . . In any event, it is very pleasant to accompany Sargent through the [Vatican] museums because he has a quick appreciation; he needs only a glance; 'Cristi, how beautiful it is!' and he passes by.

The visit was a success and in gratitude, H.B. hosted a dinner. 'Acting as Clotilde, Madame Frankenstein sat at the head of the table. On her right was Sargent, the guest of honor; to her left, Theodoli . . .' Clotilde responded from London, 'Your descriptions of the parties in Rome are mouthwatering. Alas, why aren't I in the place of Madame de Frankenstein surrounded by charming people – succulent dishes – I feel like Master Bridaines after his disgrace!'[20]

Bridaines is a drunken parish priest in Alfred de Musset's play, *No Trifling with Love*.

That December, H.B. wrote to Ethel Smyth of Marianna's initial interest in procuring Clotilde's services though she looked elsewhere as well. 'There is a certain vagueness in her [Clotilde's] plans on account of her having no home yet in London and also because Mme. Soderini has expressed the wish to build a house in Rome with Clotilde as architect – if she can buy the right spot at the right price' (fig.44).[21]

PALAZZO SODERINI

Address: 7 via Principessa Clotilde, Rome

It took some time to find the perfect location to build but by March 1901, everything was in place. H.B. wrote to Ethel,

> Clotilde has got the order for the Soderini's palazzo on the piazza del Popolo and they have approved her designs. It has got to be passed by the Board of Works and there are some difficulties ahead but we hope to surmount them. It is a joint affair; she gives to Clotilde the designs, and [Gaetano] Koch, a Roman architect, is to oversee the works. They share the spoils. The stranger thing is that Koch has consented. He was applied to first and failed to please with his designs.[22]

In the end, another engineer was chosen to supervise the construction, Gustavo Giovannoni. It was his first project.

Curiously, when the building lot for the palazzo was laid out, a new road was established and given the name Principessa Clotilde. It is likely that this name choice was influenced by Marianna, suggesting her satisfaction with the design. In

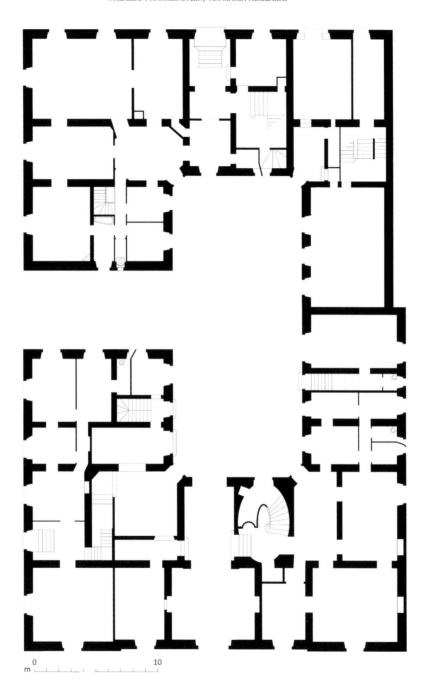

45   Plan of the abutting Soderini and Frankensten palaces was recreated by the author and based on drawings located in the Centro di Studi per la Storia dell'Architettura

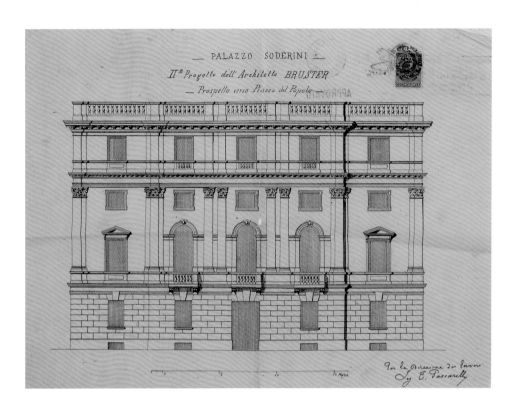

46   Permit set elevation of the Palazzo Soderini. Courtesy of the Carena-Ricotti family

47   View of the Palazzo Soderini upon completion. Centro di Studi per la Storia dell'Architettura

48   One of the elaborate ceilings at the Palazzo Soderini. A recent redecoration
uncovered an original frieze. Courtesy of the Carena-Ricotti family

addition to Marianna's personal residence with a separate grand staircase, the building also featured apartments available to rent to affluent families. When first completed, it also housed the consulate of Denmark (fig.45).[23]

Mariana wanted Clotilde to design the palace in Rome and wrote persuasively,

> We will have time to submit [designs for] the finishing touches just until we start to construct the foundations – the beginning of winter, I believe. Perhaps it is better if you do it in Rome. You will be here around Christmas I think. Perhaps it is an effect of my imagination, but it seems to me that your drawings have more grace and are more natural when you do them here in Italy than in England.[24]

Clotilde returned as planned for the winter season and permit drawings were submitted to the city of Rome in November 1901. She went through at least two versions of the palazzo before a slight variation on the second design was built (fig.46).

In February 1902, Clotilde was working on designing the Palazzo's interior and at the same time socializing and networking. 'I have enjoyed myself, made great friends with (Henri) Frankenstein, done a lot of work and I am presently employed in decorating the inside of the palace Soderini' (fig.47).[25] The interior design worked continued well into the following year as Clotilde wrote to H.B. in May 1903 from Adolf Hildebrand's home in Florence, 'I worked hard – I finished Marianna's drawings, her theatre, her woodwork' (figs 48 and 49).

ROMAN HIGH SOCIETY MEETS THE LADY ARCHITECT   109

49   Clotilde designed all the interior millwork including this mantelpiece for the Palazzo Soderini. Author's collection

Upon entering, there is a passage to the internal courtyard off of which is an oval staircase leading to the rental apartments. It cleverly echoes the plan of the piazza itself and the church of Maria di Montesanto (fig.50).

On the exterior the ground floor is heavily rusticated with angled grooves between the blocks; window and doors openings are topped by flat arches of oversized masonry and dropped keystones. The massive door is composed of deeply carved wooden panels. There is a weighty horizontal feel to this level in contrast to the verticality of the lofty piano nobile above. Separating the attic from the body of the building is a heavy cornice supported by modillions (ornate brackets) (fig.51).

Piazza del Popolo is an oval shaped square which features many architectural gems, such as the Flaminio Obelisk, the Valadier Fountains and the twin churches of Santa Maria di Montesanto and Santa Maria Dei Miracoli. Looking west, the Palazzo Soderini forms a visual edge enclosing the plaza. Though the palace's height, massing and materials had to conform to the urban context of the neighborhood, Brewster used elements to add depth and shadow to the skin of the building animating the facade – creating a very sculptural composition. On the piano nobile, paired pilasters repeat along the front and side elevations. The composite order of the pilasters was a perfect choice for a palace designed for a woman; with its leafy capital and curved volutes, this order was considered feminine and used in many Renaissance churches dedicated to the Virgin Mary and female saints.

50   Elliptical stairs at the Palazzo Soderini. Courtesy of the Carena-Ricotti family

51   The front entry of the Palazzo Soderini. The colors have recently been brought back to their originals. These were also the original colors of the Palazzo Frankenstein. Courtesy of the Carena-Ricotti family

52 View of the Palazzo Frankenstein upon completion.
Centro di Studi per la Storia dell'Architettura

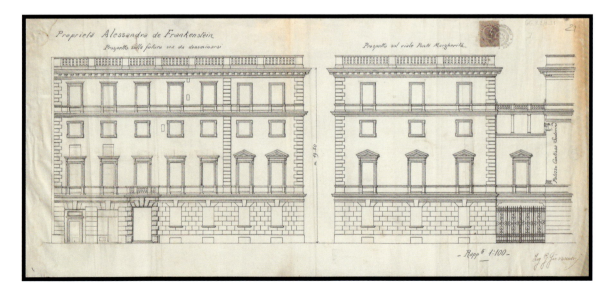

53 Front and side elevations of the Palazzo Frankenstein.
Centro di Studi per la Storia dell'Architettura

PALAZZO FRANKENSTEIN FOR COUNTESS ALESSANDRA DE FRANKENSTEIN

Address: 8 via Maria-Adelaide, Rome

Even before it was certain that Marianna's palazzo was to be built, Clotilde was paid for her design of the Palazzo Frankenstein from Alessandra de Frankenstein as H.B. wrote to Ethel Smyth in June 1901, 'It seems probable that the difficulties with the municipality will be overcome and that she will get Mme. Soderini's order. Any how she has already pocketed payment for Mme. de Frankenstein's (madre).'[26] In September 1901, a permit set of drawings was approved by the city of Rome.

Both palaces were designed together. For the Palazzo Frankenstein, Clotilde continued the lines of the Palazzo Soderini into the design, binding the buildings together into a coherent whole (figs 52 and 53). The simpler Palazzo Frankenstein was designed to support the Palazzo Soderini, rather than to compete with it, revealing its grandeur by quiet comparison. Instead of columns, there are quoins at the corners and accenting a central bay. The grooves of the rusticated masonry on the ground floor are shallower and the blocks are smaller in scale; on this level as well, there is only one simple keystone over each window opening. On the main level the windows are plain rectangles surmounted by pointed pediments. The unassuming entry, narrower than its Soderini sister, is highlighted by a small balcony above.

There is an elegant connector piece between the buildings belonging to the Palazzo Frankenstein. Its function is to connect the two but visually maintain each as a separate structure. The height is lower by one story; there is a void at ground level which is a carriage entry to the interior courtyard. The opening featured ornate wrought iron gates. There was a columned loggia, now enclosed, on the uppermost level which was topped by a classical balustrade.

LABORATORIO SANTA CATERINA FOR ALESSANDRA FRANKENSTEIN

Address: 55 via Ezio, Rome

Madame de Frankenstein assisted her daughter in her charitable endeavors but was involved in her own projects as well. She was founder and administrator of *Laboratorio Santa Caterina* in Rome – a communal house and cooperative for impoverished female workers and their families (fig.54). Madame de Frankenstein purchased the

54   Laboratorio Santa Caterina after a 1914 addition. Archivio Storico Capitolino di Roma Capitale

ROMAN HIGH SOCIETY MEETS THE LADY ARCHITECT

land on which it was to be built. Marchese Carlo Lepri was the official architect but Madame Frankenstein asked Clotilde to design the facade. Clotilde consulted her father about the fee she was going to charge Madame Frankenstein 'Madame Frankenstein asked me for a façade for her workshop. The price is still 375 francs. That's what I asked for. Do you think that's a fair price?'[27]

Henri Frankenstein

Alessandra's son, Henri, first studied law at the University of Dorpat located in Tartu, Estonia and then, like his father, entered into a diplomatic career. As an attaché at the Russian Embassy in Paris, he was put in charge of the diplomatic mail service. He kept that position until 1890 when he left for a year-long trip of big game hunting and exploration in southern Africa accompanied by two friends.

He gave a lecture on his trip at an anti-slavery conference in Rome in March 1891 at the Palazzo Altemps.[28] The lecture titled *Notes et Impressions sur l'Afrique Australe* was published that same year in *La Revue Générale*.[29] The first part extols the beauty of Africa and its people; the second part discusses the horrors of African slavery and suggestions for remedies. The adventure had a profound effect on Henri which would manifest itself many years later. In the intervening years he married Anne Seabury Brewster and had a daughter, Henrietta (later Princess Barberini).

Anne and Henri enjoyed the vibrant social life of Rome, complete with musical performances, theatrical spectacles and intellectual salons. Henrietta would later write of their life together:

> Season followed season, as they say, and the days passed by indolently, to the distance sound of the countless fountains. Life smiled on young couples, happy to live on the banks of the Tiber River whose current, mysteriously, had civilized the whole world; time seemed motionless and they tasted, as privileged people, the refined pleasures of a world that would soon crumble to dust . . . Constant meetings between friends, the luxurious palaces opened up for receptions, splendid or intimate. The tableau vivant, much appreciated at the time, of which only photographs remain, followed balls adorned with the young beauties of the day, adorned with their heavy historic jewelry.

From all appearances, Henri enjoyed the lifestyle of the idle rich. Besides being patron of the theatre, he was as noted Henrietta 'a passionate rider, owner of a racing stable, took part in horse shows and hunted in the vast plain, a poetic setting, which he was so madly in love with, that he bought the lake of Castel Gandolfo with a friend'. Then 1908, at the age of 42, Henri's life suddenly changed course. Eighteen years after his grand tour of Africa, he left Rome for Italian Somalia where he had been offered a concession – land on which to establish a plantation. It involved a great deal of hardship, both physical and personal, and would keep him separated from his family for long periods of time.

In 1911, he became director of the *Società romana di colonizzazione*. He invested his own money and brought the latest farm machinery and technology to the plantation, successively cultivating between 250 to 350 hectares of cotton and maize in a cooperative partnership with the natives.[30]

The partnership was described by his daughter, 'He delivered the seed in the hands of Somalis and, at harvest time they brought the cotton back to my father, receiving in exchange small sacks of silver rupees. They returned home dancing their characteristic 'fantasia', happy to have been able to work around their villages, rather than in distant fields!'

The local women were employed as well but given light work as some were pregnant and others old. They collected, separated and discarded the dry stems, with attached leaves, in the banana fields.[31] This was used as packaging in crates.

In a time of crisis Henri responded admirably. During a tragic famine, he brought in from Kenya wheat to distribute to his workers in lieu of money, saving the lives of thousands of families.[32]

Henri unfortunately had been in poor health since contracting an illness in Africa and died in Rome in June 1934 at the age of 64. After his death, Anne took over the concession. After two and half years she too fell ill, returned to Rome and died in September 1937.

VILLINO FOR HENRI AND ANNE FRANKENSTEIN

Address: 8 via Abruzzi, DEMOLISHED. Rome

In February 1905, Clotilde was commissioned by Henri Frankenstein to design a house for himself and his wife Anne on land he had purchased on Via Abruzzi. The budget was unusually small, between 50,000 and 60,000 francs and was being paid for by a trust set up by Anne's late father, William Cullen Brewster.

Even with a low budget, the proposed design results were successful. Her father wrote to her in March that, 'I think the design is delightful. And they [Henri and Anne] are incredibly pleased with it, as are Marianne and Madame de F . . . Of course, you will get an "*ingegnere*" here to supervise the work. That will amount to two or three hundred francs. We will choose one who is honest and hungry.'[33]

The journey was not without obstacles. There were problems with the city of Rome. The intention was to build that same year but the building commission of the city of Rome took a political stance against foreign architects and rejected Clotilde's plans. Henri Frankenstein then hired a Roman architect and engineer, Carlo Busiri Vici to attach his name to the project along with Clotilde's, but this was unsuccessful. Another set of plans was presented, a variation on the first design. These also were rejected.

Her brother Christopher wrote,

The plans were refused again of course by the *commissione edilizia*, they are exasperated it appears at a foreigner making drawings for a house in an Italian style. They would have accepted the ugliest art nouveau so they candidly confess, but that a foreigner should come and propose something Italian, 'Questo poi no'. They are afraid of foreign architects and their competition, and so here they are trying to make a monopoly. The Frankensteins are in a fix, your drawings refused, the workmen waiting to get on, and he refusing to employ a Roman architect par pique. They are thinking of copying something already existing I think and may decide on the casino of Caprarola which is a good choice![34]

This is indeed what happened. The final version which was accepted by the commission was a replica of the Casino del Piacere nel Giardino Grande di Palazzo Farnese, Caprarola. It is hard to know if Clotilde was involved at this stage as any mention of it is absent in her letters. Clotilde must have been greatly disappointed that her original project was unrealized as she considered it an almost perfect design (figs 55–58).

Given the tight budget, Clotilde had to be selective in her design choices. The exterior is characterized by a simple yet elegant classicism. There is no articulation of the walls; the grouping of three openings on the upper and lower story defines the center bay on the elevation facing the street. These are mirrored on the garden facade. The primary source of decoration are the windows and doors with their ornate surrounds. The front door is especially celebrated. It features a double leaf glazed

55   Front elevation of the Villino Frankenstein.
Courtesy of Amanda Feilding

56   Rear elevation of the Villino Frankenstein.
Courtesy of Amanda Feilding

door topped by a round pediment with a cartouche at its apex – a shield which would have contained an inscription or date with an elaborate scroll frame, bordered with ornament. French windows run along the main story. The molding of all the openings features small projecting ears at the top corners. These are then topped by alternating round and pointed pediments creating a rhythm. These undergo a transformation on the upper story windows where the pediments are 'broken'. The attic level is pierced by small, horizontal windows. On the hipped roof are terracotta pantiles.

It was to be built in what was then a suburban context and the property was planned with a garden. Walls surrounding the property were integral to the design. There are grand pillars with iron railings at the front. On the sides and rear, solid walls enclose the garden and become part of the outbuildings – the stables, and a garden pavilion. Here, atop the window surrounds, are reliefs of vases with floral displays.

After these projects in Rome, Clotilde could have easily established herself in Italy as a premier architect to a large expatriate community. Her father wrote:

> It's a shame that you have not been here these past days. You could have gotten a new commission: the Grosnowskis are going to build and they liked your drawings of the villa Frankenstein and wanted to ask you for a design. But the work must begin as soon as possible so that it is roofed in October. Otherwise, they lose a year. A certain Viviani has come up with a very banal design for them but which they will accept because he is here at hand. It's annoying. It will be a *villino* of 150,000 francs.[35]

Her brother Christopher also thought so.

> Carlo Sattler who was here the other day told me in Naples lots of things were built by an English Architect who came quite a short time ago and is making a fortune.[36]

Carlo Sattler was an architect who had worked for Adolf Hildebrand and had married Hildebrand's daughter, Eva. At this point, newly married, Clotilde preferred to concentrate on pursuing projects in England. As for the Villino Frankenstein as built, it did not last very long. In the 1950s it was demolished to make way for an apartment complex.

57   Side elevation of the Villino Frankenstein. Courtesy of Amanda Feilding

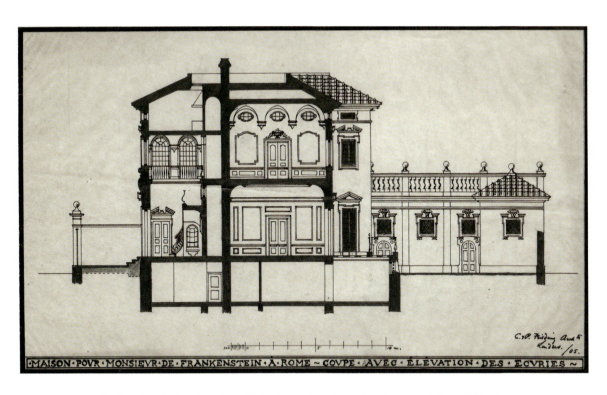

58   Longitudinal section through the Villino Frankenstein. Courtesy of Amanda Feilding

12

THE HEIRESS AND THE CASTLE

Project for Contessa Ada Telfener

In 1903, the American Contessa Ada Telfener (1857–1910) asked Clotilde to design a faux medieval castle on the ruins of a fortress in Cenerente, five kilometers from the city of Perugia, Italy.

When Ada first left America for Paris, France, she wasn't much different from other heiresses described by Lady Harriet Jephson in her book *Notes of a Nomad*. The women, wrote Jephson, were 'handsome, restless, brilliant, exquisitely dressed'. They went to 'Rome principally for social pleasures, and their interests don't lie much in archaeology or serious art. Many of them have improved their "shining hours" by a gradual evolution from an American "Miss" into an Italian princess.'[1] Ada's background story, though, is much more dramatic than most and filled with larger-than-life characters.

Ada Hungerford was born into poverty to Colonel Daniel Elihu Hungerford and his wife Eveline (Visera) in a rough-and-ready mining town in California. Originally a New York barber, Daniel preferred the excitement of a soldier's life to the mundane responsibilities of a job and family and as a consequence absented himself for long periods of time, leaving Eveline and their first child Louise to struggle on their own. In 1851, in between military tours, he opened a drugstore in Downieville, California and did some prospecting on the side in the hopes of striking it rich. In 1853, he sent for his wife and Louise to join him; Ada was born four years later. The family's lives changed dramatically when Louise married John William Mackay, a successful miner in 1867. Mackay and his partners owned the Consolidated Virginia Mining Company in Virginia City, Nevada, and in 1873 discovered a rich silver ore deposit, part of the famous Comstock Lode. This discovery became the greatest bonanza in the American West, making the men among the wealthiest in the world.

A few years later, after a failed attempt at establishing themselves in New York, the Mackays moved to Paris, France, followed by the Hungerfords. As befitting their new status, John and Louise purchased an impressive mansion at 9 rue Tilsitt, with a garden facing the Arc de Triomphe. Louise entertained lavishly in their new home, using silverware from a 1500-piece silver service from Tiffany & Co. made out of

Comstock silver, some of which John Mackay had mined himself.[2] John Mackay did not often attend these events, preferring to spend most his time in America.

Louise and Ada became so well known in Paris that French writer Ludovic Halevy portrayed them as the rich American sisters, Suzie Scott and Bettina Percival, main characters in his novel *L'Abbé Constantin*.[3] Giulia Ajmone Marsan, in her biography of *Giuseppe Telfener: Precursor of Global Entrepreneurs*, reveals that among the wealthy American colony in Paris, Louise and Ada outshone them all. Quoting an article *in Le Figaro*, Marsan reports that the Mackays arrived in Paris 'laden with gold like a galleon. Desperate for acceptance, they tried to enter high society by using outrageous and uncouth means, such as writing the menu of their dinners on small gold bars and encouraging their guests to pocket them – which they did without batting an eye – being of the nabob race.'[4]

Louise was a self-professed social climber and had hopes of marrying off her sister Ada, and her daughter from her first marriage, Eva, to titled men. Both women married into the Italian aristocracy. It was said that on the marriage market, 'princes were a little cheaper in Italy than in most countries'[5] but Eva's prince, Ferdinando Colonna di Stigliano wound up costing the Mackays much more than they bargained for. He was a gambler, violent, and a flagrant philanderer and had only married Eva for the money. The marriage was a disaster and the separation came at high price for the Mackays. Ada's marriage to a count from Rome was more successful perhaps because he had only recently acquired his title with the purchase of the royal palace of Macao from King Victor Emmanuel.

Count Joseph (Guiseppe) di Carlo Telfener, was among other things, a financier of railroads, an engineer, entrepreneur and owner of a significant number of racehorses. It was rumored that he was one of the richest men in Italy. He was university educated and had a wide variety of interests. At his death, an inventory of his personal effects showed antique weaponry, photographic equipment, and a library consisting of one thousand books, including ones on philosophy, scientific treatises and a book on the Roman architect Vitruvius.[6]

But being intelligent, successful in business and newly ennobled did not guarantee social success. In fact, among the Italian aristocracy earning one's own money was seen as base and dishonorable. If an aristocrat lowered himself by going into business, he would lose status, and any marriage with him would be a *mésalliance* – just as if he were, God forbid, 'the son of a wealthy ambitious shoemaker or a dry-goods merchant' as wrote Marchesa Lily Theodoli, an American writer and good friend of H.B.'s who had wed an Italian aristocrat.[7]

In April 1878, the newspaper *La Stampa* reported that Telfener, from a poor family, had left Italy ten years before to seek his fortune in Rio della Plata in South America. After seizing opportunity by the hair and never letting go, he returned to Italy a millionaire, bought a villa in Piazza Colonna and donated 50,000 lire to the Italian Geographic Society. After being knighted by the King, Telfener wished to establish himself in Roman society and applied to join the exclusive *Club delle caccia*, a hunting club. The old aristocratic members 'wrinkled their noses' at the very idea of having this neo-noble among their ranks. There was much gossip about the opposition but the reporter seemed confident that Telfener would be admitted.[8] In the end, he was not.

By June 1878, Telfener was in Paris where he met Ada Hungerford at a ball given by the flamboyant Henri Cernuschi, a French-Italian banker and collector of Asian art, in his townhouse facing Parc Monceau in Paris.[9] Telfener was 39 years old

THE HEIRESS AND THE CASTLE

and Ada was 19. A newspaper article would later describe him: 'He is of fine, manly presence. The beautifully shaped oval head, the long eagle nose, the intensely dark bushy beard, the thick glossy, downy hair, carefully parted and always redolent of lovely perfume, and, most attractive of all, the eyes, soft and innocent as those of a gazelle, must create havoc in feminine hearts.'[10]

Count Telfener was in Paris to attend the Paris Exposition of 1878 where he presented three of his racehorses at the live animal competition.[11] He had also been appointed Italian commissioner for the exhibition.[12] Perhaps he personally knew Cernuschi or frequented the same Italian social circles. In any case, Cernuschi's ball was one of the spectacular events given at the time. One reporter wrote:

> I have never looked upon a more beautiful scene than that I saw in the great ball-room…it was brilliantly illuminated by the new Jablochkoff electric light, and every corner available was filled with the rarest and loveliest flowers . . . And the ferns! and the palms! Where did they all come from, I wonder! It was a very dream of flowers and light . . . M. Cernuschi's ball-room . . . is quite an architectural marvel. The walls are literally hidden by thousands of Japanese antiquities, ranged up on shelves, vases of all shapes and sizes, grotesque figures of bonzes and heathen deities, quaint and beautiful jars, bronzes, generally extraordinary monsters, dogs with phenomenal jaws and dragons with impossible tails. At one end of the room stands the crowning wonder of this priceless collection: a gigantic bronze idol, FULLY FORTY FEET HIGH, hideous beyond all measure! [13]

After a courtship of nine months, Ada and Joseph married in March 1879 at the Villa Telfener in Rome. As it was held during the Lenten season, the ceremony was kept simple but was important enough that the Pope sent Monsignor Cataldi as his representative. In the afternoon, celebrations were held at the Villa Ada, another former royal residence in Rome owned by Telfener, just outside the Porta Salaria. He had renamed the villa in honor of his new bride. In the extensive park surrounding the villa, guests attended horse races specially organized in honor of the event. It was reported that the King of Italy made an appearance.[14] Telfener's extensive family was present at the wedding celebrations but Colonel Hungerford did not attend. John Mackay also could not make the wedding though he gave Ada a very handsome dowry.

For the newly wedded Ada, settling into Roman society was not a smooth transition. Seven months after her marriage one newspaper reported that, 'I am sorry to hear that one of our richest families is emigrating from Rome. Count Telfener, I understand, intends to spend the winter in Paris. His young wife, it seems, has taken quite a dislike to Rome.'[15] They spent time each year in the Villa Ada in Rome, but Paris would be their main residence through the first half of the 1880s.

In the spring of 1880, Ada and Joseph Telfener and her father Colonel Hungerford left for a visit to the United States. For Ada, it was a trip to reconnect with old friends in California, but for Telfener, the trip was a business one. Hungerford had convinced him to invest in a grand scheme to build a railway connecting New York City to Mexico City – Telfener had some previous experience as a railroad contractor in Argentina.[16] The 'New York, Texas and Mexican Railway Company' charter was signed in Paris, France in the autumn of 1880. Because of liberal land grants, Texas was chosen as the starting point and Telfener was contracted to build 350 miles of track there. In addition to investing heavily in the project, he bought large amounts of land on speculation – railroads would encourage settlement and economic growth in the area and create a demand for land. Telfener brought over 1,200 Italian laborers for the heavy construction work and thus the railway was dubbed 'The Macaroni Line' after the pasta which made up the diet of the workers.

The 'New York, Texas and Mexican Railway' enterprise caused Telfener long term financial difficulties. In 1884, he sold all the furniture in the Villa Ada and borrowed 675,000 lire (2.65 million euros) from Ada. In July 1886, the Villa Telfener was sold to settle debts to a number of Italian financial institutions. In 1887 the Villa Ada was sold to his mother-in-law with the proviso that he was entitled to live there until his death as long he remained married to Ada.[17]

In the following few years Telfener was able to partially recoup some of his loses. Early in the 1890s with government help, he successfully designed and built a summer resort in Vallombrosa, south of Florence, Italy, complete with a funicular railway which connected it to the low-lying plains of Saltino.[18]

At the time of his death on 1 January 1898, he was comfortably well-off but not in possession of his former wealth. He estate as well, was tied up in legal disputes. Eveline soon sold the Villa Ada to the Banco Romano and Ada moved into rented accommodation at the Palazzo Taverna.[19]

Lady Jephson in *Notes of a Nomad* describes her friend Ada around this period of her life, 'Contessa Telfener was one of the most singularly delightful women in Roman society. Without ever having possessed the beauty of her sister, Mrs. Mackay, she had all her charm and the liveliest intelligence. Her spirits and fun and repartee made her society an unfailing pleasure.'[20]

Ada purchased the Cenerente property in July 1901 from Alessandro Bianchi, a Perugian lawyer.[21] Besides the ruins of the old fortress, the estate included the castle's extensive 633 acres and a small villa which Ada had renovated (dubbed the Villa Ada).[22] The ruins consisted of the undercroft of the former fortress which had an unusual curvilinear wall exposed by the sloping site. Exterior doors here gave access to cellars with vaulted ceilings as it still does today. Windows punctuated its thick walls. Also remaining was an ancient round tower. In 1903, Ada hired Clotilde to design a new castle on top of the undercroft.[23] Clotilde incorporated a portico built in 1898 thus creating its L-shaped plan, the old tower at the corner. Now called Castello dell'Oscano, it sits on the edge of the hill overlooking a valley.

In the fall of 1903, when she was working on the design for the Castle Telfener, her friend, Countess Sophie Benckendorff, showed great interest in the project as she wrote to her father. 'I have so much to do I don't know where to start. Madame Benckendorff is amazing – with her taste and judgment in architecture she helped me with the Telfener castle which is going to be very costly to build – there's no doubt about it!'[24]

The connection between Ada and Clotilde could have come from any mutual acquaintance in Rome as the American colony all knew each other. In letters it is clear that Henri Frankenstein and his mother, Alessandra, were close friends with Ada. At one point, Clotilde wanted Henri to inform her of Contessa Telfener's reaction to the design drawings.[25] In February 1904 after not hearing from the Contessa for period of time, Clotilde asked her father to find out what was happening. After not finding Contessa Telfener at home, H.B. inquired at the Frankenstein's and wrote to Clotilde, 'According to what Madame Frankenstein (the mother) says, it is funds which are lacking at the moment, so that after having been in such a hurry her dream now is to do nothing.'[26]

It is assumed that Louise Mackay gave her the funds for this new enterprise and Ada, with the additional help of a mortgage, moved forward with the project. Not many original documents survive

59   A view of the Castello dell'Oscano upon completion. Courtesy of Pierfrancesco and Lory de Martino

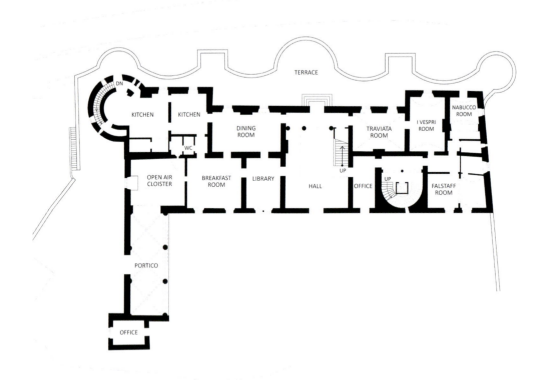

60   Ground floor plan of the Castello dell'Oscano in present day. Drawn by the author

but Clotilde was involved at least until February 1905. Ada hired Roman engineer Carlo Giuliani to oversee construction.

Ada Telfener's financial situation continued to present problems. After many attempts to get paid for her work, Clotilde asked her father to hire a lawyer in Rome. 'Tomorrow I am going to write one more time to Madame Telfener and then if I don't hear back from her, let the law take its course!'[27] She was successful. In March 1905, Clotilde wrote: 'Madame Telfener has paid 975 francs; one gets results when one is determined to be paid. Keep the address of the lawyer. It may be useful another time!'[28]

The majority of construction work was completed around 1905, although the payment of the balance to the construction company was made only in 1910. The total cost of the project, including Clotilde Brewster's fees, cost about 190,000 lire.[29]

THE CASTLE

Rather than purchase and restoring an ancient castle, Ada Telfener decided to build a new one in the Italian Gothic style (figs 59 and 60). There were a few new-built castles in Perugia which could have inspired Ada, especially the Guglielmi Castle on the Isola Maggiore. Clotilde would have taken her design cues from a castle built on the ruins of the Vincigliata outside of Florence. Sir John Temple-Leader, a wealthy Englishman had purchased and reconstructed Vincigliata Castle in the feudal style over a 15-year period. It was a place Clotilde knew well and admired.

Castello dell'Oscano is characterized by massive battlemented walls and small windows. It has four towers, three of which have corbelled parapets.

The entry doors are topped with arched hood moldings above which is a window of three trefoil-headed openings. The window is comprised of a double plane – the actual glazing sits behind it. Interestingly, in Clotilde's final house, a restoration of Beckley Park, a Tudor hunting lodge, also used this technique on a circa 1600 casement window as noted by architectural historian Christopher Hussey in a 1929 *Country Life* article, 'The Italian custom, developed in early times, was to set glass in wooden frames fixed behind the marble or stone colonettes that appear externally on quattrocento palaces. A cleaner joint was obtained thus than by fixing the glazing to the stonework.'[30]

A shallow entry foyer opens up into a grand double height hall. The space spans the entire width of the castle and features a wooden ceiling with exposed beams. The space is lit from above by a stained-glass skylight depicting the Telfener coat of arms, created by the famous Studio Moretti Caselli in Perugia.

Around three sides of the hall run a handsome staircase and a balcony supported by scrolled brackets. On the fourth side is a musicians' gallery which opens into the hall by a large span of five arched windows and wood paneling. All the wood is of a rich European walnut.

Opposite the entryway are found ornate doors leading out to a terrace, its parapet following the lines of the undercroft's curvilinear wall (figs 61 and 62).

The library's ornate bookcases and door trim date back to the Renaissance and refitted to the room's dimensions. The room's ceiling, windows and other decoration were made to match the bookcases' liberal use of gilding (fig.63).

During its time as a hotel a century later, many rooms were named after the operas of Giuseppe Verdi, a fitting tribute to Ada, who was an opera enthusiast. The salon known as the 'Traviata Room' features two elaborate portals decorated in real gold, gifts from the Savoy family of Rome to Ada. The rest of the decoration was created to match their magnificence: a stunning coved ceiling is ornately

61   The Hall, view towards the doors to the terrace. Courtesy of Fabrizio Temperini

62   The Hall, view towards the entry door. Courtesy of Fabrizio Temperini

63   The Library. Courtesy of Fabrizio Temperini

64   The Traviata Room. Courtesy of Fabrizio Temperini

65   The Traviata Room during Ada Telfener's lifetime. The doorway location was later changed. Courtesy of Umberta Telfener

painted; and the mantelpiece features carved medallions and intricate floral gilt work (figs 64 and 65).

Ada Telfener died at the early age of 53 on 30 April 1910. She had suffered for many years from a tic douloureux – an acute, shooting pain on one side of the face.[31] The pain causes sufferers to wince involuntarily, similar to a facial tic – and lasts from a few seconds to a few minutes. In August 1905, she underwent an experimental surgery in London performed by Sir Victor Horsley, a specialist in trigeminal neuralgia. It was reported that during Ada's procedure, 'part of the whole brain was taken out and the nerve which caused all of the pain was literally taken away. It was a fearful task and it was with terrible difficulty that the nerve was disentangled from the brain, but Sir Victor's hand never shook the whole time, and with as much calmness as though bandaging a finger he replaced the brain, filled up the cavity, and sewed up the open scalp wound'.[32] The operation was considered a success, but Ada continued to be in poor health for her remaining years. In 1939, Ada's daughter-in-law Pia Telfener, passed on the ownership of the castle to another American-born countess Natalie Mai Coe and her husband Count Leonardo Vitetti.

13

EDWARDIAN PROSPERITY AND PEKES MANOR AND ESTATE

When Percy Feilding finally asked Clotilde to marry him in 1904, she wrote a long letter to her father expressing her joy:

> I would like to know how to write you a pretty letter which would charm your heart, sway your spirit, put you in a good humor and please you. It has to do with Percy Feilding who has done me the honor of asking for my hand. It was yesterday, February 29th – it was he who asked – and not me who should be the one to speak according to the ancient custom. He was very kind. He said that he had no right to hope, being poor and modest, whereas I was a young lady and beautiful – or rather brilliant and loved by the world . . . . I told him that I had to think about it and having done this, today I will give him *'a little hope'* . . . I love him and I believe that between the two of us, we shall know how to build the most beautiful buildings in the world.[1]

Percy's hesitancy regarding marriage was a subject of much speculation and amusement in the Brewster family. Curious as to what prompted this new development, Christopher asked him how it came about, asking for details. Percy responded with humor but with little emotion:

> Unfortunately, however there is so little to tell. The spring may have had something to do with it – who can say? There were other signs of spring about at the time. Do you remember the two Japanese trays I bought in Rome? I hardly suppose you do, but Clotilde has an ugly theory connected with these. I had given her one of them but it was undergoing repairs for something like 3 years so that it was only ready for presentation two or three months ago. She will have it that I found life impossible without that tray and that matrimony was the sole way of recovering it. However, since she seems quite satisfied, I won't worry. There is another theory yet which seems to please her less. You can guess it from the fact that it was all arranged on the 29th of February – the only day in four years in which ladies have the privilege to make proposals.[2]

So, whether it was Percy who proposed to Clotilde or Clotilde to Percy, they happily began their married life together.

Of the two, Clotilde was the more successful architect, a fact which did not bother Percy in the least. The February after their marriage he wrote of his inferior position in a letter to Christopher:

> Have you heard from Rome, I wonder, that Cloto is to build a *palazzetto* [little palace] for the Frankensteins at the end of the *Via Abruzzi*? This is the most important order we have had since our return to business. The least important is one for a sundial at two guineas which Clotilde insisted that I should refuse for the honour of the family and of the profession: so I did and got it raised to £3- 3/-.[3]

In the same letter, Percy described their first dinner party which took place in Clotilde's London townhouse, 40 Grosvenor Road, which she had renovated the year before.

> We flatter ourselves that it was 'très réussis'. Sargent was there, so also were Maurice Baring, Lady Ottoline Morrell & others: making eight in all including selves. The cooking was good, the champagne first rate taking into consideration the fact that we are but commoners the menus bright & the company brilliant.[4]

Luckily it ran smoothly with the help of their new Italian major domo assisted by Lady Louisa Feilding's footman, loaned for the occasion.

From the date of their marriage until the First World War, the Feildings successfully juggled their architectural practice and their growing family with the help of numerous servants in both the Feilding's residences – Clotilde's London townhouse and her country cottage, called The Rushes, in Farnborough, Hampshire. According to the 1911 census for Farnborough, the Feildings employed three maids, one gardener, one manservant and a cook, which allowed Clotilde the freedom to pursue her profession.

Hiring good servants was challenging especially after her children were born – Susan in 1906 and Basil, in 1907. There were a series of inadequate nannies who ranged from variously incompetent to outright abusive. By August 1907, the Feildings had gone through quite a number of them. 'We are on our 12th (!) nanny . . . all quite impossible – they take Basil to bed with them, and lift him out of the bath by a hand and a foot!'[5] Clotilde often had to fill in until another nanny could be found.

The building trades tend to be very dependent on the economy, leading to broad shifts in activity. From 1900 to 1914, Britain saw a building boom from which architects and builders benefited. This was a time of feast for Clotilde and Percy and they received numerous commissions for work on newly built country houses and cottages, and renovations.

The more unusual commissions included a small chapel in Moscow for a Russian friend of Clotilde's cousin Ellen Hearn in 1905 and a funerary monument of a crucifix for Christine

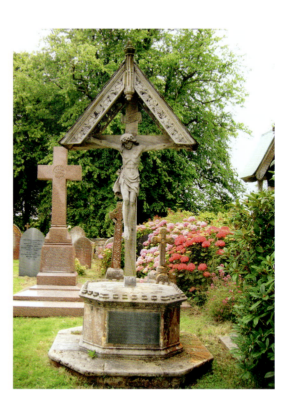

66   Funerary monument of Frederick Hamlyn. Courtesy of Janice Dennis

128   CLOTILDE BREWSTER

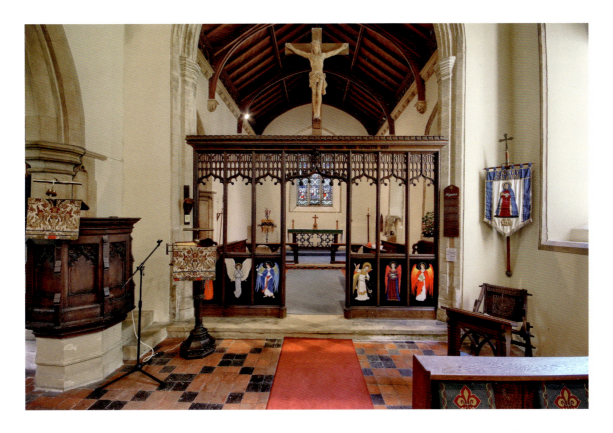

67   Rood Screen for St Mary's Church in Colkirk, Norfolk. The painted panels of angels are of a later date. Courtesy of Paul Brittain

Hamlyn Fane's husband Frederick Hamlyn at All Saints Churchyard, Clovelly, Devon. In 1912, a Feilding project was installed for St Mary's Church in Colkirk, Norfolk of a rood screen in oak. The intricate woodwork echoes the medieval stone tracery of the church's windows and is 'wholly 15th century East Anglian in feeling'.[6] (figs 66 and 67).

With their increased incomes, they extended Clotilde's house in Farnborough and created a six-acre park on its grounds – constructing terraces, planting hedgerows, transplanting trees and laying out paths and avenues.

As for the distribution of work in England, Percy would visit the project sites and Clotilde would stay at the drafting board. As she was the more skilled at drafting, and as their studio had been created from the Rushes' former stables, this suited her. This arrangement is not unusual in an architectural practice even today. One architect visits the site, records existing conditions and in the case of renovations, takes precise measurements and field notes. All this documentation is then turned into measured drawings from which designs can accurately be developed.

The drawings below illustrate the difference in drafting ability between Percy and Clotilde. They date within a few years of each other. The first drawing is by Percy for a cottage addition onto

EDWARDIAN PROSPERITY AND PEKES MANOR AND ESTATE   129

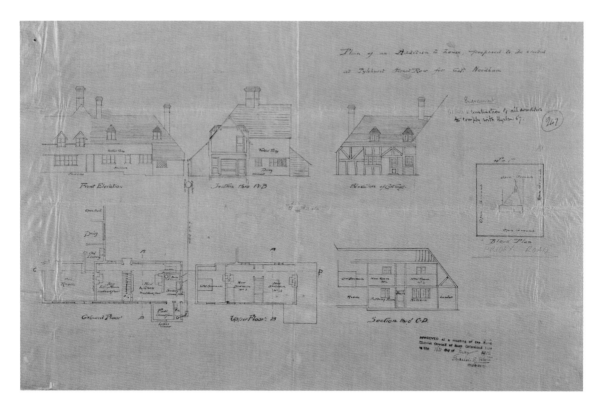

68   Tylehurst cottage addition by Percy Feilding for Colonel Needham, collection of
The Keep, East Sussex. Courtesy of Amanda Feilding

Tylehurst, the home of Colonel Needham in Forest Row, East Sussex in 1912. Though the design seems charming, it is so poorly drafted it creates the impression of a child's drawing of a house (fig.68).

The next two ink drawings dated 1908 were found in a collection of Clotilde's drawings at her last home in Beckley Park. They are proposed designs for a Bath Tower and New Porch at Lees Court in Sheldwich, near Faversham in Kent. It was originally designed by Inigo Jones and built in 1652. Percy had been hired to renovate the main house for Mrs. Reginald Halsey Laye.

Though the drawings are signed 'Percy Feilding', they are by Clotilde and very much resemble the formal inking in her other projects such as the house for Henri Frankenstein. Beautifully executed, her drawings would always bear a resemblance to those produced in Adolf Hildebrand's studio (figs 69 and 70).

In January 1908, Clotilde wrote to her father that she and Percy had received a large commission from his friend, the Hon. Terence Bourke (1865–1923), son of Richard Bourke, the 6th Earl of Mayo, and that she was working very hard on it.[7]

Terence's upbringing had been unusual. His father had served as Viceroy of India between 1869 and 1892. Too young to be sent away to school in England, Terence lived with his parents in a neo-classical palace called The Government House in Calcutta, the seat of the British government in India.

130   CLOTILDE BREWSTER

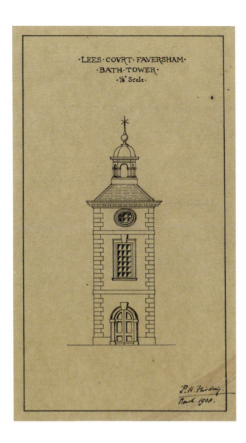

69   Proposed Bath Tower for Lees Court. Courtesy of Amanda Feilding

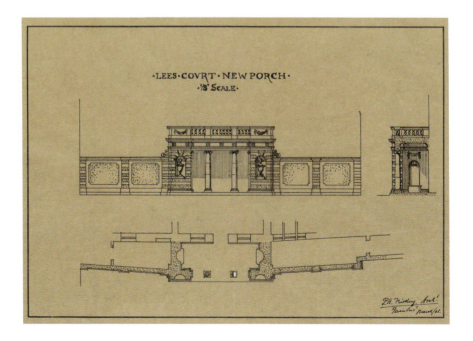

70   Proposed New Porch for Lees Court. Courtesy of Amanda Feilding

At The Government House, Terence's mother, Lady Blanche Mayo, possessed a menagerie of exotic pets including tropical birds and tame monkeys. When a British officer presented her with a newborn Bengal tiger cub, she 'was rather pleased to add such a rare jewel to the list of her favorites and shared the ownership with her son, the Honorable Terence Bourke who was about five years old'.[8] Ned, as he was soon named, slept in a basket on the colonnaded veranda at night and followed Terence and Lady Mayo around the magnificent galleries and gardens during the day. Ned behaved with Terence like an affectionate kitten, chasing after balls and playing tug of war. An American visitor, Olive Risley Seward, described the tiger cub in a book of her travels, *Around the World Stories*.

> It was pretty to see this wild creature of the forest wilderness subdued to the demurest ways of civilised life, walking with his young master, under the palms and banana trees, and among the brilliant flower-beds of the Eden gardens which adjoin the palace, followed by tall, lithe Hindu attendants. These men, in the glitter of their vice-regal livery, all white and gold and scarlet, which is purposely designed to harmonise the British colors with oriental ideas of show and splendor, escorted the viceroy's son, with watchful but deferential tread. The boy, all unconscious of the state which surrounded him, enjoyed the gay companionship of his favorite playfellow; while Ned in a gold collar and chain followed his sturdy little master in a quiet promenade, or better still, all glee and brightness, capered and leaped, in many a mad race and frolic, at his side. The dogs and cats in the neighborhood, for reasons of their own, got out of the way of the gay côrtège, and provided a wide berth for its passage through the park.

Having grown as big as a St Bernard dog, Ned's ferocious nature suddenly emerged during a rough game with Terence. When the tiger scratched him deeply on the hand an immediate change came over him.

> Never before had he smelt or known the taste of blood, and to his savage senses it was irresistibly intoxicating. They who saw him knew that he would never forget it. Instantly his whole expression changed from a frank, fearless, contented creature to that of a cunning, stealthy and cruel one . . . His tail quivered and his eyes flashed. He crouched, clutching the carpet and prepared to spring at the friend whose confiding affection made him the easy victim of treachery. But strong hands and arms were near to seize the tiger and defy his ferocity.

Terence's beloved pet was sent away never to return.

In February 1872 the Viceroy was assassinated. He was inspecting a convict settlement at Port Blair in the Andaman Islands when he was attacked and stabbed by Sher Ali Afridi, a Pashtun who had been placed in prison for murder. Feeling his imprisonment was unjust, the Pashtun swore to kill a high-ranking colonial official as an act of revenge. A heavy burden then fell upon Terence as described by Percy Feilding many years later in an obituary for Bourke: '[H]e was not seven years old at the time of his father's assassination, and in the absence of his three elder brothers in England it fell to his lot to follow behind the coffin in the State procession as chief mourner.' Their life in India came to an abrupt end. Lady Mayo and Terence returned to Ireland and Terence was sent off to boarding school at Eton.

This strange and enchanting childhood had a lasting effect on Terence; it was to influence the places he chose to live and in the houses he built. He displayed a passion for the exotic and the unusual – for bright colors – richly layered decoration and wild animals.

According to Percy Feilding, Terence as a young man intended to study languages so as to enter into the Diplomatic Service. This was derailed as

71   Château Ben Negro's Arab Room. Courtesy of Kildare Bourke-Borrowes

'during a holiday trip to Tunis the call of the East made itself felt, and there it was he went and spent the larger part of his life'.[9] He was only 18 years old when Lady Mayo purchased a property for him near Biserta.[10] There he would later develop an estate called Château Ben Negro and served, without pay, as British Vice Consul (fig.71). Seemingly without effort, he took on the traits of the local inhabitants, adopting their language, dress and way of life as described by his cousin, the diarist Wilfrid Blunt,

> Like . . . all the Bourkes [Terence] was gifted with extreme natural ability for dealing with men and generally for affairs. Terence, by this special quality, had made for himself an exceptional position in the regency of Tunis. He had learnt to talk Tunisian Arabic perfectly, and had acquired an influence with the native Tunisians of all classes, unrivalled by any other European. Of all the men I have known who have had dealings with the East, and whom I have seen engaged with them in conversation, I place him first in his power of making friends with them, for he has what Englishmen so seldom possess, an inexhaustible patience equal to the Oriental's own, which enables him to sit as they do, hour after hour, conversing with them, and show no weariness however dull their talk. This is a great power, and through it he has always been successful in acquiring their attentive sympathy, and in obtaining from them their confidence and help.[11]

This charismatic figure lived an almost fictional lifestyle, as writer Logan Pearsall Smith wrote to his sister, Mary Berenson, 'Sir Harry Johnston told me that Terence once took him on a trip into the interior, and that they mounted their horses and rode straight off into the Arabian Nights.'[12] In addition, on his estate Ben Negro, Terence bred the wild Barbary stag, known for its ferocity.[13]

While visiting the British Consul General at La Marsa just outside of Tunis, Terence met his future wife Evelyn Haines (1872–1917); they married in August 1896. The marriage produced two daughters named Jasmine and Myrtle. The family wintered at Ben Negro and summered with relatives and friends in Ireland and England, but when Evelyn fell ill with tuberculosis, Terence began looking for a property of their own in England, eventually purchasing a small country estate in East Sussex called Pekes in September 1908. Here Terence would bring some of his eastern exoticism with him but in a tamer form. Château Ben Negro would continue to be Terence's main residence though his family would spend increasing amounts of time at Pekes.

The project included entry walls and gate, entry lodge, extensive restoration of the main house and conversion of a cowshed into the 'Edwardian Wing' and creation of its columned garden. Other work included the conversion of the Oast House into summer guest accommodation, conversion of an outbuilding into a schoolhouse and new landscaping such as the creation of the front drive across the parkland and construction of a walled garden.

THE ENTRY GATE AND LODGE

At the entrance of Pekes are towering pillars capped by stone balls and flanked by brick walls into which circular windows or oculi have been inserted. These are reminiscent of a number of villa entryways in Italy, for instance at the Villa Roncioni in Pugnano. The Feildings used another oculus in a garden wall at Pekes as well. The lodge was a simple, side-gabled house with chimneys built at either end.

THE MAIN HOUSE

Pekes, a Wealden hall house, was originally built in the middle of the 15th century. Architectural historian Philip Mainwaring Johnston noted that Pekes consisted 'like so many others of its class, of a central open hall, flanked at either end by two-storied wings, in which were contained the buttery, parlour and sleeping apartments'.[14] Hidden within the current structure is its original skeleton framework of timber. The central open hall was one volume open from the ground floor to the roof and featured an open hearth. The upper floor rooms were inserted into the hall about a hundred years later.

Chimneys did not become common in English houses until the 16th and 17th centuries, and smoke from the fire thus ascended from the center of the hall and escaped through the gaps in the roof or through gablets or louvers.

In the early 16th century the house underwent a series of major alterations. Handsome stone fireplaces with Tudor arched heads were constructed on both floors. At some point the parlor was converted to an entry hall which it remains to this day.

In renovating a structure, an architect designs in response to what is existing in combination with the aesthetic goals of the client. An interesting aspect of this project is the reuse of old house parts which were incorporated into the house and other buildings on the estate where appropriate (fig.72). One was an elaborate window built in 1875 which was reused in the small new schoolhouse.

But the most striking example is the design of the entry stone porch of the main house. It features architectural pilasters in the form of caryatids (anthropomorphized columns) each with a claw foot (fig.73). They support a barrel frieze above. The choice of caryatids is not random or accidental. It provides advanced notice to an imminent architectural event. Upon entering the hall, there can be seen an ancient chimney-piece. On it is found the porch's counterpart – another pair of caryatid pilasters. The mantel depicts bearded men who are perhaps ancient gods of the harvest as they are balancing baskets on their heads filled with leafy vegetation. They are holding what appears to be scrolls of geometric floral decoration. The formal entry porch connects to a more informal and intimate space. The imagery is the same but the scale changes from large to small, public to private (fig.74).

In this hall and opposite the front door, the Feildings inserted a main staircase leading up to

72 Main entry to Pekes. Originally published in *Some of the Smaller Manor Houses of Sussex*, by Frances Garnet Wolseley, 1925, Hove Library, special collections. Brighton and Hove City Council

73   Porch caryatid, Pekes, Chiddingly. Photographer: Candida Lacey, The Brewster Archives at San Francesco di Paola

74   Chimney piece with caryatids, *c.*1910. Author's collection

75   The Front, Pekes, Chiddingly, c.1910. Courtesy of Kildare Bourke-Borrowes

a new upstairs corridor. The style of construction and materials used is sympathetic to the Tudor era architectural vocabulary of the house. The stair tower projects out onto a garden facade which is a jumble of random geometries, created over centuries of additions and extensions. The tower housing the stair features a carved stone plaque depicting the Bourke family armorial, with perhaps appropriately their wild cat crest on top.

THE EDWARDIAN WING

An L-shaped 'Edwardian Wing' was created out of an old dairy and cowshed, connected to the main house by a small passageway. The lower courses of brick are very old and laid in a pattern seen in ancient Sussex buildings. For the conversion, some courses of brick were taken down to accommodate the new design. New courses were laid on top and sections were built entirely of Edwardian brick such as the battlemented bays, the west window and the two chimney stacks (fig.75).

For the interior the Feildings used neo-classical moldings painted white; the walls were painted a bright blue. Classical barrel-vaulted ceilings lend a sense of elegance and loftiness to the rooms (fig.76). Found in the first room entered from the passageway is a plaster frieze decoration which evokes Lady Mayo's menagerie in Calcutta. Viscountess Wolseley in her book *Some of the Smaller Manor Houses of Sussex* noted that 'A modern craftsman, coming from the East and bringing with him fairy-like designs of strange, fantastic birds with gaudy plumage and

76 An interior view of Edwardian wing *c*.1910. Author's collection

sweeping tails and monkeys with quaint human visages, has transmitted them in frieze of plaster round a portion of this room.'[15]

COLONNADE GARDEN OF THE EDWARDIAN WING

The L-shaped Edwardian wing forms two of the edges of what was known as the Colonnade Garden (fig.77). At one story high and one room deep, the Edwardian Wing reads as walls enclosing the garden rather than an addition to the house. It is further enclosed by a row of brick pillars and garden walls. An exedra, the curved architectural element frequently used in Italian landscape design, is set in the rear wall and shaded by overhanging boughs of trees. It terminates an axis created by a broad path cutting through the garden from the door of the wing.

THE OAST HOUSE

Starting in the first few years of the 20th century, a new building type emerged, the repurposed oast house (fig.78). These agricultural buildings normally consisted of two circular oasts or kilns with an attached barn where the dried hops were processed and packaged. The earliest mention of this new building type was in 1903 when the *Gardener's Chronicle* listed a Mr. A.D. Hall, Esquire living at the Oast House in Harpenden, Hertfordshire.[16] By 1906 they had become popular enough in Kent that a newspaper in Nottinghamshire made note of these new 'Curious Dwellings'.

> Cottages of a novel type are making their appearance in the agricultural districts near Tunbridge Wells. They are really the oast houses, converted into dwellings, which have been lying

138   CLOTILDE BREWSTER

77   Colonnade Garden, Pekes, Chiddingly, *c*.1910. Author's collection

78   The Oast House *c*.1910. Author's collection

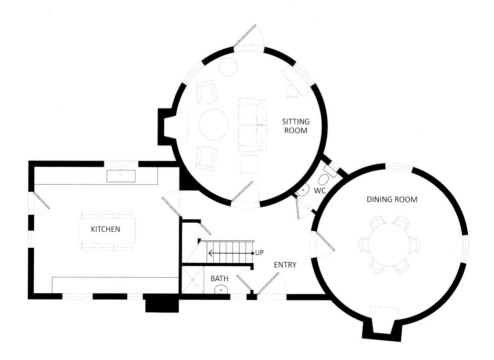

79   Ground floor plan of the Oast House in present day. Drawn by the author

idle, owing to the continually decreasing amount of produce grown nowadays in the face of foreign competition. The circular structures, when relieved with dainty little old-fashioned windows, look extremely picturesque; and in some cases they have attracted the attention of wealthy people leaning towards 'the simple life.'[17]

The following year, Mr. Ashley Dodd asked Reginald Blomfield to convert a double oast house into a potting shed, fruitrooms and a bothy for the estate gardeners at Godinton Park, in Ashford, Kent. Blomfield had designed the gardens in which the oast house stood in 1896 when Clotilde was serving her articles in his office. She likely contributed to the garden design in some capacity and undoubtedly had a keen interest in the oast house project when it was featured in *Country Life* in 1907.[18]

Not long after, Clotilde and Percy converted the Oast House at Pekes into a summer residence for Lady Mayo, Terence Bourke's mother. Work progressed steadily, and by August 1909, Lady Mayo was documented as residing there.[19]

The architecture firm of Niven, Wigglesworth & Falkner also adapted an old oast house into a home called Dial House, in Farnham, Surrey. Curiously, one of the architects, Harold Falkner, had previously studied with Clotilde and Percy in Blomfield's office. The Dial House oast was square and incorporated into a rectangular block with rooms either side. A wall was removed between the oast and the store creating a large dining room and a second story was added. Unlike Pekes and the Godinton Park oast houses, any interior or exterior trace of the original oast structure was lost.[20]

On the ground floor, a living room and dining room were created from the two circular oasts (fig.79). Large casement windows and a door to the garden were inserted with shallow-arched brick lintels above. The ground floor of the barn was converted into an entry hall and kitchen. Above are found bedrooms and a large, shared bathroom.

On the exterior, two Italian Renaissance-style medallions from the Della Robbia workshop were fitted onto the brick surface (the current clay tiles applied over the brick are a later addition). Over the entry door is one of a Madonna and Child surrounded by putti and the second medallion is a lovely tondo portrait of a lady (fig.80). The building explains its own identity. It announces in effect, that this structure was the domain of an estimable mother and noblewoman.

At the start of the First World War in 1914, Terence returned to Biserta to serve as British Consul and Representative of the Ministry of Shipping. During the war, he was completely cut off from his wife and family in England except for one extended visit between June and October 1915. Sadly, this trip would be the last time he would see his wife and mother. Evelyn died in 1917 and Lady Blanche Mayo in 1918.

When Terence returned to England in 1919, he was in poor health and barely able to walk. Percy remembered that, 'Indeed, it was due to his untiring exertions, almost unaided, and the strain of the work at Biserta, which had suddenly grown to be far heavier than any one man could cope with, that his health, never robust, finally broke down . . . During the war,

80   Tondo portrait of a lady above an Oast House window. Courtesy of Pamela Berry

> Biserta, from being a quiet and inconspicuous neighbour of the White City, Tunis, had, owing to her splendid harbour, suddenly become one of the busy and important place of the Mediterranean, and, with its mix of population of Arabs, French, Italians, and Maltese, a hotbed of race-jealousy and contesting interests. No one knew how to steer a safe course among these shallows better than Bourke, with his tact, his cosmopolitan training, and his *savoir faire*; and all alike, officials, colleagues, equals, and subordinates, had for him an unbounded respect, if not real affection.[21]

Thereafter he spent most of his time at Pekes with his daughters but managed with the help of friends to travel to Ben Negro once a year. He died in Biserta on the 13 May 1923, and his body transported back to Chiddingly Church for burial.

14

HOME SWEET HOME: STONEHILL, CHIDDINGLY, EAST SUSSEX

We are so tied here by building and farming that we cannot get away even for a day. We came here last November and are picnicking in this old house with only a rather inefficient married couple to look after us altogether and we find it very amusing, even absorbing but it is also monopolising. We are running a sort of a milk walk and are farming some 70 acres of land – half arable and the next few weeks are critical ones for seed sowing etc. The house is very small but when we have enlarged it as we hope to do this summer you will have to pay us a visit. It is charming country and wonderful air and views. We have about 70 acres of woods which are full of primroses, violets, hyacinths.

(Letter from Clotilde to
Lady Ottoline Morrell. n.d.)[1]

During their many visits to Terence Bourke's property, the Feildings had become enamored by this part of East Sussex. In 1911, Clotilde purchased Stonehill Farm, featuring a silvery oak timbered house built in the 15th century (figs 81 and 82).

The project included restoration and small additions to the house: among these changes were the extensive landscaping of the property, the creation of walled gardens, the conversion of a barn into play areas for the children and an architecture studio plus the construction of new farm buildings and cottages. Originally, the Feildings had had much more ambitious plans for adding onto the house but due to the First World War and the subsequent labor shortage this was not realized, though some modest additions were built.

It can be hard to separate Clotilde's and Percy's individual contributions to their architectural projects. Fortunately, in the case of Stonehill, deeds and real estate sale particulars still exist along with family letters. It is clear that Clotilde was the sole owner of Stonehill, paid for all building works, and was the leading force behind the architectural design. Writing to her brother in 1913, she asked him to contact the man who handled the Brewster financial affairs, which makes it clear who was funding the project.

> Will you please settle with Bates which of my securities to sell about £600 or 700 worth. I need it for buildings done here – Cottages £300, garden wall £300, farm buildings £400, barn reroofed with tiles £60, odds and ends repairs, doing up the house etc. £40. Total £1,100. I have paid all but farm buildings and I am very short of money indeed!![2]

81   Stonehill Farm from *Old Cottages and Farmhouses in Kent and Sussex* by Edward Guy Dawber, 1900. Author's collection

82   Front of Stonehill Farm after renovation. Photographer: Christopher Brewster, The Brewster Archives at San Francesco di Paola

Like Pekes, Stonehill was a Wealden Hall house. It featured jettied end bays with the center roof eaves supported by large curved oak braces oversailing the center section of the facade. The vertical timber members are unusually close together. Before purchase, Clotilde sketched the front of the house and sent to Christopher; she already envisioned the restoration of the massive arched doorway and the projected bay window on the ground floor.

Though they did not sell their house in Farnborough, the Feildings proceeded to move into Stonehill in the autumn of 1911. They lived there while the building works were taking place even though the house was in a poor state, as revealed in a letter from Percy's friend Logan Pearsall Smith to his sister Mary Berenson: 'Percy Feilding and Clotilde are going in for farming, and are now living in great squalor in a little 14th Century rickety old farm-house about 30 miles from here and near to Terence Bourke. They have cattle and chickens and quarrels and mud and manure – but Percy makes it all very amusing, and I hardly suppose that it will last very long.'[3]

In a letter to Christopher in early 1913, Percy goes into detail about their living arrangements during construction. They lived entirely in one room for over a year and were plagued by bad weather.

> If it interests you to hear of our life as farmers there is plenty to tell you. It is not at present all beer and skittles, let me assure you. There are moments when my head swims. It is all so simple on paper but when you come to deal with flesh and blood whether it be the flesh and blood of cows, heifers, pigs or natives it all becomes so frightfully complicated.[4]

Early on there was trouble with the 'natives'. They started off with a full staff of servants but very quickly the number dwindled. The cook left after the third day, due to conditions being too primitive. Their cowman regularly turned up drunk; he lasted six weeks. The nursery maids were caught stealing; they were sent away. Then next to go was the man in charge of the farm named John Hammond. Percy's temper had at last got the better of him.

> Finally, John H. fell foul of me and I of him. I hardly knew which – my patience had been wearing out and in one of my stormy moods I spoke the words that were in my heart; they were not altogether so unreasonable as you might suppose. J.H. became abusive: abusive of me and even more so of the place which he described as bloody (he might well and better have said muddy) and many other disgusting and hastily chosen epithets.

They would have to make do with a much reduced staff in the years to come.

After about six months of living in the house, Clotilde designed a new layout that included additions for Stonehill during a stay in Florence with the Hildebrands. She then sent the plans to Percy for his review. The drawings unfortunately have not survived but what can be gleaned from Percy's letters is how at this late date Clotilde continued to solicit Adolf Hildebrand's opinion.

Percy sent her his thoughts:

> I have been studying the plan of Stonehill. I think the change between the Dining room and Schoolroom <u>excellent</u> for a great many reasons but I do not at all agree with Hildebrand about [the] position of [the] front door. I do not like to walk up against a wall and often a vista through a house is charming. I like your servants plan very much; my only fear is that you exaggerate the natural fall of the ground and that to carry out your plan one should have to move a great quantity of earth which could be an expense. I am giving thought to the lay out of the garden but I find it difficult

to plan anything in my mind without some idea of the levels and that is all hazy in my mind now. I rather wish the ground fell away a bit quicker both for the house's sake and the garden's too.[5]

The ensuing years after the purchase showed significant progress. In a 1916 letter to her brother, Clotilde revealed,

> We have brought the carved cassone into the entrance and hung Arthur's red brocatelle over it. It looks stunning with the gilt looking glass you gave me hanging over it. You would not recognise the house. It looks elegant and theatrical, no longer humble and sordid. On the whole I am glad we are not going to build a large house. It is dreadful to be over housed.

That spring the gardens came into magnificent bloom with 500 anemones, 36 delphiniums, 18 roses, masses of phlox and peonies besides innumerable seeds all of which Countess Sophie Benckendorff had sent Clotilde as a gift.[6] Countess Benckendorff also sent a large number of fruit trees to Stonehill.

The restoration entailed major work. Much of the house had to be underbuilt in brick. Extensive restoration of the windows was carried out. Almost none of the windows were original to the house and the Feildings replaced them with style-appropriate lead lattice glazing, preserving the existing molded oak frames and mullions, replicating them where necessary. Window openings which had been bricked up were also restored. The kitchen was remodeled and new plumbing installed. The original arched doorway which had been partially walled up was brought back to its original configuration and a massive new nail-studded oak door was created.

A key focal point of the facade is the generous bay window, which was created by the Feildings, as noted in a *Country Life* article of 1923, 'To his

83   The new bay window in present day.
Author's collection

immediate predecessor [the Feildings] is due the roomy bay window which looks out at the grassy forecourt on the entrance side of the house, for the fashioning of which window the molded mullions of the original window above served as a precise model.' In designing the bay, the Feildings very carefully preserved the historic concave sided lozenge bracing between the ground and upper floors (figs 83–85).

During their years at Stonehill, Clotilde bought more and more land in the surrounding

84 Stonehill study with view of new bay window. Originally published in *Country Life*, 5 May 1923, Future Publishing Ltd

85 One of the bedrooms located above the study at Stonehill. Originally published in *Country Life*, 5 May 1923, Future Publishing Ltd

neighborhood. £900 was spent on Beards Farm, a nearby property at risk of development which would obstruct their views of the South Downs.[7] During the First World War, Clotilde would go on to purchase the adjacent Charity Farm, Gatehouse Farm, Carter's Farm, Beeney's Farm, Strood Farm and a small holding on Gun Hill. Percy purchased three small tenement cottages in nearby Muddles Green.[8]

The Feildings eventually did find a builder and in 1919 some modest additions were made. Desirous that Christopher should come to visit, Percy wrote,

> I do hope that there will be no more wars in our time! Surely, we in our generation have had enough of them and when things get completely settled and all these passport difficulties are rounded off you must return the visit and tell us what you think of Stone Hill with its extensions. We think it quite out of the common run of things.[9]

A two-story replacement of the single-story lean-to kitchen was built with a remodeled kitchen, new chimney stack and a water closet. The story above featured a covered 'open-air' balcony. The extension imitated the half timbering of the original house. A new arched doorway gave access directly onto the rear garden. New windows with lead lattice glazing brought the morning light into the space.

The framing of the covered balcony tells a different story. It is not a balustrade on the upper level but a framing out of walls and windows. The Feildings most likely intended to enclose the space but the construction was not complete at the time the photo was taken (figs 86–88).

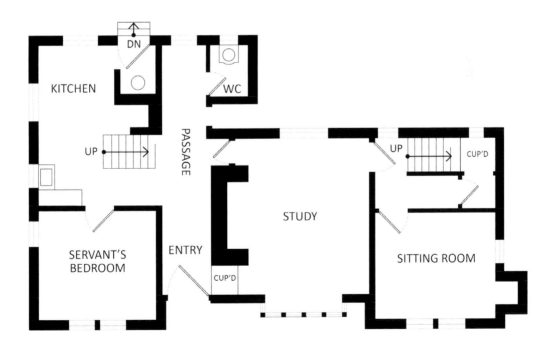

86 'Sketch Plan of Ground Floor' redrawn by the author from *Country Life* illustration published 5 May 1923

87   Garden side of house featuring the Feilding's addition with roofed balcony and new chimney stack. The lower half of the addition is obscured by the chicken coop. The barn can be seen to the right of the house. Originally published in *Country Life*, 5 May 1923. Future Publishing Ltd

88   Rear-garden side of house in present day. The roofed balcony was, at some point, enclosed. Author's collection

89 View of the barn garden walls under construction. Photographer: Christopher Brewster.
The Brewster Archives at San Francesco di Paola

LANDSCAPING

We have built the kitchen garden wall and are going to build the terrace wall of the entrance drive the total difference of height is 15'-6', 4.60m. Not so bad – what do you think? The terrace wall will continue all-round the S.E. and S. side of the house. It is quite extraordinary how easily one can make differences in levels and there is nothing that makes more [of an] effect, I think. Look at Italy, nearly every house on different levels. In England all is flat – the ground is the same. The only difference being that in England the lump is thrown into the hole whereas in Italy the hole is thrown onto the lump. Exactly the same amount of earth is mound and in the first case you have dullness in the second fun![10]

Influenced by Italian architectural concepts, Clotilde tended to plan houses that closely related to the surrounding terrain, often incorporating terraces into her designs. When purchased, Stonehill, except for the facade facing the street, was surrounded by sloping fields of grass.[11]

The major exterior work encompassed the creation of terraces and walled gardens. Clotilde thought Stonehill was too close to the road. With the construction of the forecourt walls and garden, the Feildings created more separation from the street and a formal setting for the house.

Another, higher wall separated the future barn garden from the forecourt and ran from the barn to the house (fig.89). Inserted in the wall is an archway connecting the two spaces. Viscountess Wolseley in 1937 recounted that against this wall flourished climbing plants, '. . . a wisteria and a magnolia. We see also the red foliage of a sumach, planted near the wall in another part of the garden by a previous owner and its red leaves seen above the wall cast a glove of warmth in autumn'. Red brick paths were laid out. In a nod to Clotilde's Italian childhood and love of Italy, a cypress tree was planted to the right

HOME SWEET HOME: STONEHILL, CHIDDINGLY, EAST SUSSEX   149

90   View into the Kitchen Garden with its stepped brick wall. Author's collection

of the bay window. Adjacent to the barn garden, a very large walled kitchen garden was created with a unique stepped wall traveling down the slope. In April 1913, the kitchen garden was nearly finished, all '650 feet of it'.[12] Where each section steps down it curves (fig.90).

OUTBUILDINGS

In April 1913, Clotilde wrote to her brother of her plans to turn the barn into a 'playroom, studio, etc'.[13] In addition to the studio, the Feildings created a garage within its volume. There is a brief mention of it in the 1923 *Country Life* article, 'Of the rest, there is no occasion to note more than the barn—half as large again as the house, and, therefore, so big that the garage provided at one end of it is almost unnoticed.'[14]

Though its function had changed, it still looked like a barn in its historical setting. The Feildings preserved its original form and features on the exterior and judging from what can been seen today, treated the interior in a similar fashion.

Like other farm buildings of its age and place, the barn at Stonehill features a half-hipped design and a catslide roof. The building is constructed with a timber frame and plaster infill, with three sides clad in weatherboard. It is roofed with clay tiles. On the street side (north-west), the barn doors were preserved, including two sets with pointed arches dating back to the time of construction. The pair of doors furthest left provided access to the garage which was tucked under the catslide roof. The south facing side originally featured a barn door, which has been replaced with a large wooden window with views into the barn garden.

The interior is completely open from floor to ceiling, creating a voluminous hall-like space and exposing the entirety of its oak timber framing. A wall separates what was once the one-story garage from the main space. Above it, in the loft, a room was created which is open to the main living area. Access to it is via a rustic staircase.

The first known barn conversion of this type was by Margaret Asquith on her property in Sutton Courtney in 1912 and first published in *Small Country Houses: Their Repair and Enlargement* in 1914. The barn was remade as an annex behind her newly constructed house. Asquith's architect Walter Cave retained the building's original characteristics while creating a sitting room below and a bedroom on the upper level.[15]

Dr Timothy Brittain-Catlin in his book *Edwardians and Their Houses* published in 2020, states that Margaret Asquith's remodel was a 'revolutionary thing to do', as before this, the gentry who wanted to live in an old building would have altered it to look like a conventional house. It is unclear whether the Feildings were aware of Asquith's project when they remodeled their own barn, but they were undoubtedly at the forefront of the movement in sensitively adapting agricultural buildings into residences.

The old cow shed which is attached to one end of the barn was also converted into habitable space, perhaps for the schoolroom, workrooms and guest accommodation. The horse stable which stood opposite the cowshed was demolished to build the wall separating the new barn garden from the house forecourt. A new barn, stables and cow shed were built elsewhere on the property at a good distance from the house (fig.91).

91   View of farm building, granary and attached laborer's cottage. Photographer: Christopher Brewster.
The Brewster Archives at San Francesco di Paola

HOME SWEET HOME: STONEHILL, CHIDDINGLY, EAST SUSSEX   151

92   One of the new cottages at Stonehill. Photographer: Christopher Brewster.
The Brewster Archives at San Francesco di Paola

COTTAGES

Clotilde built at least two modest sized houses on the property (fig.92), perhaps with the intention of renting them as she wrote to her brother:

> The cottages are nearly finished and so nice that I feel inclined to keep one <u>entirely</u> for you – three bedrooms, two sitting rooms. If you preferred a house entirely for yourself you can have it. Meals here with us of course, I am sure you will like the cottages – £150 apiece. I am delighted with them.[16]
>
> (Letter to Christopher Brewster from Clotilde)

Though isolated, the Feildings received many visitors including the merely curious. In 1915, Oscar Wilde's former lover stopped by, surprising Clotilde, 'Lord Alfred Douglas has been here several times. He does not look in the least like his portrait or sound a bit like his poems. In fact, I doubt it being he.'[17]

In 1918, aristocratic friends from Italy, Marchesa Etta de Viti de Marco and her daughter Etta paid a visit to the Feildings. As there were food shortages during the war, running a farm had its advantages.

> Etta had the large room with the fireplace. Etta II, the room you were in and the bathroom was for both – we had a brick path laid to the post office (E.C) – a great improvement and Countess Benckendorff sent us a <u>wonderful</u> Dutch cheese which saved the situation. Etta eats no bread, rice, spaghetti, milk or butter which makes it uncommonly difficult to feed her but there were eggs (3 a day!), fish, vegetables, fruit, ham and beef. Percy surpassed himself with sweets and we all worked hard. Susan was so tired that she went to bed and stayed there for 3 days. I fear influenza and gave her quinine and brandy and I have only just

recovered! Two people make a lot of extra work – hot water, hot water bottles, fires, cooking, serving, etc., etc.[18]

After the war, Britain and Europe were in a state of social turmoil. In February 1919, Clotilde wrote that her brother-in-law, Major General Sir Geoffrey Feilding's car had been vandalized, 'Things are serious here – Geoffrey had his motor car smashed up by dissatisfied soldiers (he was not inside luckily) he never says anything but now he says the situation is very grave. Percy is upset about it.'[19]

Soon the trouble came to Chiddingly right to the Feildings' doorstep. In May, their foreman fomented trouble by getting other farm laborers to suddenly quit. In addition, he caused damage to the farm equipment and the animals,

> Well since last I wrote we found out that our foreman – is a political agitator, a trade unionist, a Bolshevik! He broke the cultivator – said it would have to go to Lewes – we mended it in an hour – injured the horse's shoulder – so that we had to run and get a friend to lend us one – in fact was always putting spokes in our wheels. I was miserable because he was so rude to Percy that he [Percy] got heart palpitations and he did not like to put the man in his place lest he should work less well. But the cowman told Percy that he [the foreman] was going to leave us even if it was in the middle of haymaking.

Clotilde had to put off a planned trip to Italy to stay with Percy, who though he was only 53 years old had developed heart trouble.

There was a violent interaction between Percy and some workers which would signal the end of their time at Stonehill. In mid-October 1919, the Feildings suspected their carter of stealing oats from the granary. Percy put it under lock and key, taking two sacks out a day to give to the carter to feed the horses. The horses though, were getting thinner and thinner and Percy accused the carter of neglect. The carter became furious and demanded that Percy give him the key to the granary, insisting he needed it to properly care for the animals. Percy refused. Clotilde wrote to her brother that the carter 'shook his fist in Percy's face and said: "You call yourself a gentleman!" "No, I don't", said Percy, "but I am one for all that". Percy thought he was going to hit him but he kept his eyes glued on him and eventually he went away after he had received notice to quit.'

The following night, Percy caught two men and two women loading wagons with wood. Percy demanded of one man his name which he refused to give. When he lit a match to see the name on the wagon, the man struck Percy in the face. 'Percy lit another match and recognised the men, one worked for the timber merchant who bought our pit props.'[20] The other man was the son of the fired carter. Furthermore, Clotilde was told, down at The May Garland, the local pub where the Bolsheviks met, the feelings against local farmers were very great and there was talk of shooting the Feildings.

The carter's wife was Clotilde's only servant and she left when her husband was fired. The work was overwhelming now. On Christmas Eve 1919, Clotilde again wrote to her brother.

> You must think me a brute not to have answered your letter at once . . . I must tell you that I am writing by lamplight [at] 7am and that my head feels empty – but I have so much to do that I thought if I don't get up at an unearthly hour I shall never get my letter off to you. I have all the washing up to do as well as cooking – we have no woman at all now – the coal to fetch, the fires to light and wood to carry – the hot water bottles to get – the oil stoves and lamps to fill and the house to clean – besides feeding chickens, ducks, dog, cats, guinea pig – by the time I have done I can't write letters.[21]

HOME SWEET HOME: STONEHILL, CHIDDINGLY, EAST SUSSEX

To escape the unpleasantness, Percy had been spending time at Garsington Manor near Oxford, the home of his friend Philip Morrell and his wife Ottoline. Clotilde wrote to her brother that during a visit Percy saw a house that he coveted and that 'Stonehill is in disgrace at present'.[22]

By February and without consulting Clotilde, Percy impulsively made an offer on a property seven miles north-east of Oxford. Though heartbroken, Clotilde tried to put a positive spin on it in a letter to her brother. In it, although she says 'Percy has bought' it was actually Clotilde who was the purchaser and legal owner.

> I have great news for you, Percy has bought 350 acres in Oxfordshire with a very fine Henry VIII house! He came back and told me that we must sell Stonehill to pay for it and I was awfully upset – but I have been to see it and it is very beautiful and I have accepted the inevitable so we are selling this place . . . it has more ground and arable than we have here, only a small wood with a heronry in it. The house has two moats around it and three towers. I will send you drawings – a solid cork screw staircase and all the rooms are over 12ft high. It is elegant, it has style and it is in the centre of the property – all the same I am very sad at leaving here.[23]

In April, Clotilde wrote to Christopher that J.M. Barrie the playwright of *Peter Pan*, had purchased Stonehill. He had intended it as a gift for his twenty-year-old ward Michael Llewelyn Davies, who along with his four brothers was the inspiration for the characters in Barrie's *Peter Pan*.[24] Perhaps Michael, who suffered from depression, wasn't interested as it was soon passed back to the Feildings. A tragic fated awaited Michael; he drowned a year later in May 1921.

Sometime during 1921 or 1922 the house was on the market again, and finally sold to a Captain H.P. Dick. It was featured in *Country Life* in May 1923.

15

MOATED GRANDEUR AND SHABBY CHIC: BECKLEY PARK

Most of the workmen have left. We now have a bath with plated taps Hot and Cold and two lavatory basins and a sink in the kitchen and three W.C.s. The first time the W.C. was used Basil was the elect. The moment the plug was pulled we all ran round to the cesspool, helter skelter to watch the arrival of – the paper let us say – but nothing arrived and we are still waiting for it! Basil had to tear himself away and go back to school a week ago. However, the water runs through very satisfactorily so we ask no questions and only admire one more of nature's mysteries.[1]

(Beckley Park, May 1921,
Clotilde to Christopher Brewster)

Beckley Park was built in 1540 by Lord Williams of Thame as a modestly sized hunting lodge surrounded by three moats located on an ancient Roman road from Dorchester to Bicester. It was passed down through his descendants until purchased by Clotilde Feilding in 1920.[2] The house, so remote, so old and so long in the same family became an object of curiosity when it was put on the market. From Stonehill, her house which was for sale in Chiddingly, she wrote to her brother in April 1920 of Beckley, 'Two people who came to see Stonehill spoke of it as the famous house near Oxford . . . "The moat" is a very good setting – the house is famous. Sir Alfred Mond wanted to buy it. Asquith went there the day after we had bought it' (figs 93 and 94).

The style of the house was Elizabethan, modern for its time and characterized by height, narrowness and symmetry. The interior harkened back to an antiquated medieval floor plan – a hall, parlor, buttery and kitchen. The house at time of sale to Clotilde was falsely described as in 'excellent condition' but featured fine paneling and a staircase of solid oak. The ceilings were high.

On an eight-foot high rubble plinth rests Beckley's plum-colored brick walls, laid in a repeating diamond pattern with stone mullioned windows of leaded glass. Beckley's windows were placed high on walls, windows then being designed only for the admission of light and not for the framing of picturesque views. The approach to the front door is over a cobblestone bridge built the same year as the house.

The three tall gabled towers or projected wings on the garden facade form Beckley's E-shaped plan. The center tower houses a corkscrew staircase, and the two flanking it were originally built as privies or garderobes which discharged the sewage directly into a moat; the section at the base of

93 Front view of Beckley Park before the First World War. Photographer: Norman Taylor. Author's collection

94 Garden view of Beckley Park before the First World War. Photographer: Norman Taylor. Author's collection

the towers was at some point filled in to create a terrace. This configuration of the toilets positioned high up and articulated on the exterior was often built in medieval castles and signifies the original owner was wealthy.

In July 1920, when Clotilde was 46 and Percy was 53, they moved into Beckley. It was their last design project and would entail a sensitive restoration of the house and moat, the creation of Italian-inspired interiors and the design of ornamental topiary gardens (figs 95 and 96). At this time, Clotilde also purchased two properties in Beckley village: a picturesque, thatched cottage called Cripps, and its neighboring wheelwright's house which was the setting for the novel *Cripps, the Carrier: A Woodland Tale* by Richard Doddridge Blackmore. Beckley Park's literary claim to fame is that it was the model for the manor house in Aldous Huxley's 1921 novel *Crome Yellow*.[3] In 1925 Clotilde would purchase an adjacent property called Middle Park which she would later refer to as 'The Farm'.

The garden side was dramatic in comparison to the austere simplicity of the front facade. In 1929, *Country Life* wrote that it was 'the gables at the back that constitute the architectural beauty of the house'. Aldous Huxley in *Crome Yellow* thought otherwise and called this view 'severe, imposing, almost menacing' (fig.97).

The Feildings still moved in aesthetic and intellectual circles perhaps more so after their move to Beckley Park. Lady Ottoline Morrell and her husband Philip were close friends and frequent visitors. Percy had maintained a close friendship with Philip over the years, visiting the Morrells at their homes in the Bloomsbury district of London and at Garsington Manor, their country estate in Oxford. Clotilde's more recent connection to Lady Ottoline was through Maria Nys, whom Huxley married in 1919. Maria was a Belgian wartime refugee who lived with the Morrells. Clotilde knew Maria's uncle, painter Georges-Marie Baltus (1874–1967), who was also a friend to Lady Ottoline. Baltus' wife, Silvie 'Vivi' Hildebrand, was Christopher Brewster's sister-in-law and one of Clotilde's childhood playmates. Vivi and Georges had moved to Britain when he accepted a position at the Glasgow School of Art in 1905 as a lecturer of the history and techniques of art.[4]

95 View of topiaries in present day. Author's collection

96　Front of Beckley Park after renovation. Originally published in *Country Life*, 23 March 1929, Future Publishing Ltd

97　The garden side of Beckley Park in present day. Author's collection

Aldous Huxley, after a 1921 visit to Beckley Park with the Morrells, parodied the architecture and occupants – both guests and owners – in his novel. Following its publication, an outraged Lady Ottoline Morrell accused Huxley of using her friend's conversations verbatim. She also suspected that Maria Nys greatly assisted him with the book. If Huxley did reuse conversations verbatim, it suggests that the topics of conversation at Crome were similar to those at Beckley Park. Interestingly, in one chapter, the character Mr. Scogan, inspired by the philosopher Bertrand Russell, debates the appropriateness of certain architectural styles:[5]

'The great thing about Crome,' said Mr. Scogan, seizing the opportunity to speak, 'is the fact that it's so unmistakably and aggressively a work of art. It makes no compromise with nature, but affronts it and rebels against it. It has no likeness to Shelley's tower, in the "Epipsychidion," which, if I remember rightly –

"Seems not now a work of human art,
But as it were titanic, in the heart
Of earth having assumed its form and grown
Out of the mountain, from the living stone,
Lifting itself in caverns light and high."

No, no; there isn't any nonsense of that sort about Crome. That the hovels of the peasantry should look as though they had grown out of the earth, to which their inmates are attached, is right, no doubt, and suitable. But the house of an intelligent, civilised, and sophisticated man should never seem to have sprouted from the clods. It should rather be an expression of his grand unnatural remoteness from the cloddish life. Since the days of William Morris that's a fact which we in England have been unable to comprehend. Civilised and sophisticated men have solemnly played at being peasants. Hence quaintness, arts and crafts, cottage architecture, and all the rest of it. In the suburbs of our cities you may see, reduplicated in endless rows, studiedly quaint imitations and adaptations of the village hovel. Poverty, ignorance, and a limited range of materials produced the hovel, which possesses undoubtedly, in suitable surroundings, its own "as it were titanic" charm. We now employ our wealth, our technical knowledge, our rich variety of materials for the purpose of building millions of imitation hovels in totally unsuitable surroundings. Could Imbecility go further?'

The popularity of architectural styles that evoked 'Old England' mentioned by Scogan (Russell) emerged during the Edwardian age due to a profound resonance with the social, artistic and philosophical movements of the time. As explored in the book *Edwardians and Their Houses* by Dr Timothy Brittain-Catlin, it was also the architecture of choice for Liberal politicians in England, and reflected their ideological stance on social reform and land ownership. Liberal politicians favored architectural styles that symbolized their progressive views and aspirations for a more equitable society. Often distancing themselves from the grandeur associated with Georgian and Palladian designs linked to the aristocracy and enclosure movements, Liberals preferred architecture that felt organic and rooted in English history. This influenced the style of domestic architecture during the building boom which was fostered by cheaper land that became available after the establishment of The Small Holdings and Allotments Act of 1908.

Crome's owner, Henry Wimbush, responds to Scogan explaining that for Sir Fernando, the original builder of Crome, sanitation was of paramount importance and was the overriding force in its design. In fact, Wimbush proudly states that in 1573 Sir Fernando, published a book on sanitation titled *Certaine Priuy Counsels by One of the Maiestie's Most Honourable Priuy Counsels, F. L. Knight*, which addresses the matter with 'great learning and elegance.' Placing the toilets up high was not driven solely by practical sanitary concerns; Sir Fernando also had spiritual reasons. In the third chapter of his *Privy Counsels*, Wimbush tells Scogan, Sir Fernando argues that the necessities of nature are so base and brutish that they can make us forget our nobility as the universe's noblest creatures. To counteract this, he advised placing the privy in every house nearest to heaven, in rooms with windows offering extensive and noble views. The walls should be lined with bookshelves containing the finest products of human wisdom, such as the Proverbs of Solomon, Boethius's 'Consolations of Philosophy', the apophthegms of Epictetus and Marcus Aurelius, Erasmus's 'Enchiridion', and other works that testify to the nobility of the human soul.

In an uncanny echo of *Crome Yellow*, *Country Life* in its 1929 article on Beckley Park states that, 'Among the books that await writing is the *Chronicon Cloacinum*, a history of sanitation' and goes on to discuss at great length the toilets. Cloacinum derives from the name Cloacina, the Roman goddess of the sewer.

RESTORATION OF BECKLEY PARK

Restoring the ancient house was an enormous undertaking. It took deep pockets and tremendous energy. Beckley at the time of purchase, did not have electricity or heat. Windows were broken or missing. The garden was overgrown and the moat was dried up and in great disrepair. As money was tight, much of the restoration had to be done by the Feildings' own hands.

By November many of the windows were still not glazed. The Feildings often waited till they could source the appropriate glass but even then, Clotilde had to do the work herself. 'There are nine panes of glass broken in the hall window and it is freezing. I must set to and mend them. I have become a

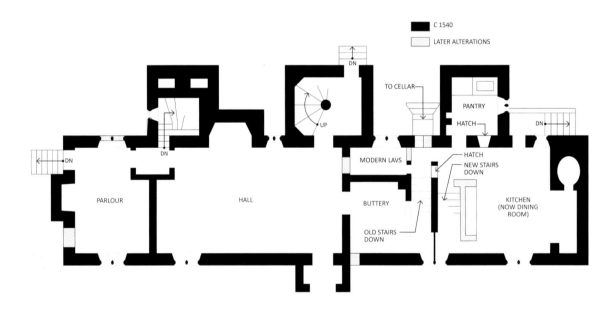

98   'Ground Floor' of Beckley Park after the Feilding restoration, redrawn by the author from a *Country Life* illustration

99   The hall at Beckley Park with hand forged chandelier. Originally published in *Country Life*, 23 March 1929. Future Publishing Ltd

glazier.'[6] She also stripped the paint off the paneling in the parlor, all the doors in the house and the beams in the dining room.

The stripping of the Jacobean oak paneling in the parlor was never completed and was later presented as a design feature when the house was profiled in magazines. In a *House and Garden* (New York) article, a description reads, 'At one period the paneling was evidently painted. The upper part has been scraped and cleaned and the lower left as a dado.' *Country Life* wrote, 'The parlour has Jacobean wainscot to just above eye level, above which the plain studding has been hung over with bluey grey damask. The wainscot has been only partially cleaned of its paint, gaining thereby a pleasant mottled surface more interesting than the plain wood.' Clotilde made the valance and all draperies herself from new and vintage fabrics her brother sent her from Italy (figs 98–100).

Clotilde enthusiastically embraced Beckley Park and its restoration but for Percy, older and in ill health, it was overwhelming. He began to regret having acquired Beckley so impulsively.

That first December after purchase a deflated Percy wrote to Christopher:

If I seem a little depressed it is partly the weight of obligation unfulfilled and partly the cold of this cursed country. No room in the house can by any and all means be raised above a temperature of 47 Far [Fahrenheit] except the kitchen where we have all of us taken refuge. C[lotilde] is cooking

MOATED GRANDEUR AND SHABBY CHIC: BECKLEY PARK   161

100   View of the parlor with Jacobean wainscot and curtained upper wall. Originally published in *Country Life*, 23 March 1929. Future Publishing Ltd

the supper and S[usan] is engaged in a work of art. I am sitting writing on my knees, clad in a fur coat bought at Munich and with my feet in the oven: the hot plate is my table; the odour of pork sausages frying within a yard of me.'[7]

During a family trip to Italy to visit Christopher in the summer of 1921, Percy saw a villa and farm he wanted both families to purchase. To do so would entail the sale of Beckley Park – an idea which Percy seriously considered. The Feildings had already made expensive improvements including installing electricity, plumbing and rebuilding the moat walls – everything, in fact, which had turned Beckley from a 'very dilapidated farm into a gentleman's place'. All this, Percy was 'prepared to forfeit'.[8]

When Clotilde strenuously objected, he seemed to relent, but had not given up on the idea. He spent the month of September calculating what the property cost to run including rates and taxes, insurance, upkeep and outside labor. He wrote to Christopher, 'In showing my figures to Cloto, I was amazed to find her quite agreeable to the idea of selling only she is anxious that we should not talk of doing so at present outside the family circle. Either the idea is growing less obnoxious to her or else the horrible influence of Basil is unmoored.'[9] Their son Basil, then 14 years old, had taken to Beckley as much as Clotilde had but now it was Clotilde who seemed to relent as the following April, she wrote to Christopher that they were unable to travel to Italy that summer as she had to get Beckley in shape, in order sell or rent should they want. In the end, Clotilde's desire to stay at Beckley held sway over Percy's wish to leave. Their thoughts then shifted towards turning Beckley into a profitable enterprise.

As their architecture practice ended, due to the First World War, the Feildings found themselves in want of money. The economy was in turmoil and many estate owners were selling off their large homes to buy smaller ones which were less expensive to maintain. Very few people had the means to hire architects. Clotilde made her views on the profession of architecture as a source of income known when Christopher's son Ralph gave up on the idea of studying architecture and decided to pursue another career. 'I am quite delighted, because I feel that he will be happy and get on with his work and succeed. I did not believe architecture would suit him – it is delightful to be an architect if one is a *mecenas* but if one wants to earn money it is awful!'[10] A *mecenas* is a patron of the arts and thus if one had a calling to be an architect, it would be better to be independently wealthy.

Their relations were also looking for ways to respectably earn money, including Percy's older brother the celebrated Major General Sir Geoffrey Feilding, KCB of the Coldstream Guards. The fact that the aristocratic Feildings were descended from the Habsburgs made their loss of status all the more shocking, as Clotilde noted:

> What do you say to our buying tapestries and sharing profits? After all, everybody is making money as best they can – why should not we. Geoffrey has bought a washing machine – you put the dirty linen in on one side and the electric light plug and it comes out all ironed on the other. He is taking in all his friends' washing to make money. When a KCB, D.S.O C G M H P Q R S T Hapsburg becomes a washer woman it seems to me that one can kick over the traces and sell furniture at a profit. Tell me what you think of my idea.[11]

Percy, many years ago, had previous experience in the antiques trade with two friends from Balliol College, Oxford: Philip Morrell, from a family of solicitors, and writer Logan Pearsall Smith, an American from a wealthy Quaker family. After Oxford, Percy went on to train in architect Reginald Blomfield's office. Philip began working for his family's law firm. Logan concentrated on writing his first book, *The Youth of Parnassus and Other Stories*.

The three friends, however, were in need of extra money and on the advice of Mary Berenson, Logan's sister, they teamed up to open a curiosity shop in Pimlico, London which opened in 1898. Called Miss Toplady, it sold 'antique furniture, China, Silks, and Brocades she collected in Italy and other Countries'. They also undertook the furnishing and decoration of houses. The men hired Grace Thomas Worthington, Logan's cousin to run the day-to-day operations. Philip was the silent partner, and together Logan and Percy would make trips to Italy where Mary lived with her husband, the art historian Bernard Berenson, to hunt for items to sell at the shop.

The most controversial items for sale were Italian Renaissance paintings of dubious origins furnished by Mary with Bernard's approval. The shop was not well thought of in some circles, perhaps because Berenson was mixing scholarship with selling paintings – a clear conflict of interest and something which bothered Berenson as well.[12]

In a letter to her daughter, Mary wrote,

> We have been to hundreds of shops, and found only a few things, but these very pretty, for Miss Toplady. However, I have thought of a way by which perhaps Miss Toplady can make a great deal of money, and I make some, too, and Uncle Logan and I are planning on it. There is more to be made in pictures than anything else, and as I know about pictures I can find them for Miss Toplady, and they can enter into relations with the art dealers.[13]

It never did make the money that Mary imagined and it closed its doors in early 1906.[14] Percy's experience though was useful in the Feilding's new venture at Beckley.

Clotilde wanted to use Cripps Cottage as a showroom for selling Italian art, antiques and rustic furniture which they imported from Italy with the help of Christopher, '. . . we will work up a clientele à la Bardini only personally recommended people admitted no public – later on we can have an annex in Bond Street or Park Lane'. Stefano Bardini was a famous Florentine art and antique dealer who specialized in Renaissance and Cinquecento-era artifacts many of which were fakes.

Clotilde invited dealers to give her advice. One told her to age the pieces to look older than they actually were. She instructed Christopher to have his carpenter do the work.

> The thing to be aimed at is a piece of furniture which has been lying in a shed or a loft for 200 years – an old newspaper stuck in a drawer has a great effect dated (17--). The polish must be subdued by 200 years of mildew and spider webs. Go to the Palazzo Davanzati and look at the furniture – it is all sham but looks old. Tell Montelatici not to stain the inside of chests or drawers of cupboards, brown, anything and better rub them over with ashes.[15]

In early 1921, a Mr. Jonedis arrived to photograph Beckley Park for 'his paper *House and Garden*'.[16] Clotilde showed him the cottage and the furniture; he was enthusiastic but by May, Clotilde decided that Cripps Cottage wasn't attracting enough people and Beckley Park itself would be a better setting. 'If I fail and only sell [the furniture] at a very small profit we must try another means of making money but I am full of hope and confidence . . . one has to find ones clientele – it is there – but one has to discover it. Once the store begins to roll there will be no stopping it.'[17] Clotilde and Percy took plum items for themselves one of which was a large chandelier Clotilde wanted for the hall. In all probability, this was the same extraordinary chandelier shown in the magazine photographs; it was hand forged metal with leaf and floral motifs.

With Clotilde's own collection of furniture and artwork, along with the items for sale, Clotilde and Percy decorated Beckley like an Italian palazzo. The rough was displayed next to the fine. The walls were hung with Venetian mirrors, ornamental plates and valuable paintings. The selection and placement of the furnishings were carefully thought out: robust dark Italian furniture including a refectory table in the dining room, chests and commodes, unusual *objets d'art* such as an architectural model in giltwood, classical columns used as stands for candelabras, porcelain jars, a Renaissance clock and an Adolf Hildebrand sculpture of Clotilde's grandmother, the Baroness von Stockhausen, placed on an inlaid chest in front of an ancient tapestry hanging on the wall. Laid on the floors were worn Persian, oriental and natural fiber carpets. *Country Life* thought the design of Beckley itself was influenced by Italian architecture,

> From the illustrations will be seen what a delightful home Mr. and Mrs. Feilding have made of Beckley, while preserving a rarely precious structure with admirable judgement. The simple Italian furniture fits perfectly into the rooms—which, it is allowable to believe, were built by one of the most prominent men of the Renaissance not without one eye on Italy.

The Feildings had a constant stream of visitors to see the house and furnishings. The socialite Nancy (Tree) Lancaster, decorator and owner of Colefax and Fowler fell in love with it. 'Called Beckley Park, this fairy-tale manor house, with its massive, peaked roof and thick walls, became one of Nancy's favorite houses in England – one she loved to take friends to see – so much so that when Lady Astor asked Mrs. Feilding if she ever opened Beckley to the public, she replied, "I don't, but Nancy Tree does."'[18]

There is no mention of the Feilding-Brewster antique import business after 1922. Strangely, no letters survive from Clotilde or Christopher from the year 1923 and it must be assumed that the venture was a failure and came to an end that year. Later, Christopher would open an antique shop in Florence, and less than a decade later Basil, Clotilde's and Percy's son, operated an antique shop in the Broad in Oxford.[19]

A brief description of the Feildings at this time comes from Ralph Brewster who was visiting in the summer of 1923:

> The discussions between her and Uncle Percy are amusing! Always as usual about possible improvements to be made on the house and the garden; and whether pink or red carnations would look better in a certain flower bed, and what sort of piers to build for the iron gates they mean to put up in front of the house. The only other topic of conversation between them is the question of their neighbour stopping up the water from running in the moat, and the lawsuit between them, which has been threatening since the last two or three years. The piano here is unfortunately quite rotten. They of course don't notice that, and think it all very good! In the evening we play cards or read, while Uncle Percy goes off to sleep in a chair.[20]

Improvements continued on the house, some more successful than others. In 1924 the kitchen was converted into a dining room and the new kitchen was relocated in the basement along with Clotilde's and Percy's office.[21] Unfortunately, after any period of rain the basement was prone to flooding. The writer Maurice Cardiff, a visitor at Beckley in the 1930s, later remembered that 'The dining room had been the original kitchen of the hunting lodge. It had a vast open fireplace with an ancient spit with weights for turning it. The present kitchen, a cross between basement and cellar, was beneath the hall. When it flooded, as it frequently did in winter, the maid would emerge from it in white cap and apron and wearing Wellington boots which left wet footprints on the floor [fig.101]. Only colleens from the Irish bogs could be induced to put up with such conditions.'[22] But even Irish colleens had their limits. After one suddenly quit, Clotilde is reputed to have said, 'And I only just built her a raft!'[23]

Outbuildings were repurposed as well. The brewhouse became two bedrooms and a sitting room for the servants 'a butler to wait at table and his wife to cook'. The stables were turned into the children's sitting room.[24]

In 1925, Christopher experienced a serious neurological impairment due to what was later diagnosed as an inoperable brain tumor. Clotilde contacted numerous doctors on his behalf and even wrote of a new cure-all device called the Abraham Box suggesting Christopher come to England and undergo treatment. She also wanted Percy to try it 'as his temper is something unimaginable'.[25] Geoffrey Feilding had been successfully cured using the Abraham Box:

> The treatment lasts 6 weeks 1 hour a day – you lie on a sofa with the magic box on you and you read a paper or write letters or do crossword puzzles – anything you like – the rest of the time you are free to do what you like. The fee is the same whether he [the doctor] does it (listens to the sound the box makes) or his assistant but he is interested in you – interested in you because of your case – and also because he is a great friend of Mrs. Boyd (Billy Boyd's wife) whom he is treating and who is a great friend of Percy. He is interested in Percy because he is the brother of his latest wonder cure

101 The old kitchen at Beckley Park, converted into the dining room. Originally published in *Country Life*, 23 March 1929. Future Publishing Ltd

'Geoffrey'. Geoffrey is not the same man – from being incapable of moving, melancholy, depressed about himself – felt stupid – unable to do anything or take an interest in anything.[26]

Obviously, it was a hoax, but as practitioners were making large sums of money from desperate and gullible people, some continued to promote the device long after scientists had debunked it as a fake. It is unknown if Christopher or Percy undertook this treatment.

Percy's temper did not improve and in fact was worsened by Basil who was accident-prone. There were motorcycle and car collisions, injuries sustained on trains plus more unusual incidents. In 1926, Basil was setting off fireworks in celebration of New Year's Eve when the gunpowder exploded in his face, burning hair, eyelashes and brows. 'Percy took him to the doctor who said he would be alright in a week and bandaged him so that he looked like a knight Templar with only a chink for his eyes and his mouth. Percy brought him back in his car and left him near the bridge. Basil walked straight ahead thinking it was the bridge and fell into the moat. He came out quite black.'[27] Percy took to his bed while Clotilde removed the bandages and cleaned up Basil.

That same year, Basil was saved from drowning by his future wife and second cousin Peggy. He was seized by a cramp while bathing in the Thames and the 19-year-old Peggy, at great danger to herself, swam out to rescue him. When they became engaged three years later, the *Daily Mail* ran the

166 CLOTILDE BREWSTER

headline 'River Bathing Romance, girl who saved her fiancé'.[28]

As remembered by his daughter Amanda, there was a constant fear that the diabetic Basil would faint while high up on a ladder clipping the overgrown topiaries – something that had happened more than once. Unwisely, he would put off gardening till night-time, using a candle as his only source of light.[29]

Susan too was a source of grief. She had become religious, provoking Clotilde to write to Christopher:

> She has two passions, dress and religion. What is that going to lead to? Religion is the worst. She wants to go to confession every week and tells <u>awful lies</u> to get us to take her to Oxford, the nearest High Church of the highest. She wears a cross round her neck but it must be on a black velvet ribbon! I think she thinks us fools, dowdy and wrinkled! because we don't believe in facts, or in clothes or in holy water. If you know of a book which <u>reasonably</u> refutes religion or sensibly upholds irreligion I wish you would let me know of it.[30]

102   Percy Henry Feilding at Beckley Park, 1920. This photograph was taken just before the purchase of Beckley Park. Photographer: Ottoline Morrell. The National Portrait Gallery, London.

THE GARDENS

The topiaries at Beckley Park are described in the Pevsner Architectural Guides, The Buildings of England series, *Oxfordshire: North and West*, published in 2017, 'Atmospheric GARDENS within the triple moats, N. Their medieval substructure is overlaid by three great "outdoor rooms" of box and yew topiary, planned in 1919 by Bertie Moore, a Buddhist monk, for his friend Percy Feilding.'[31] Unfortunately, the entry contains some errors. Bertie Moore (1905–60) was not a friend to Percy but to Basil Feilding who met him when they both attended Oxford University. Moore studied at Exeter College for only a year between 1928 and 1929, well after the gardens were designed and planted.[32] Moore, in addition, only

became a monk after the Second World War in 1949. As to what exactly Moore's contribution was, can be gleaned from Maurice Cardiff's book, *Friends Abroad*, describing a visit to Beckley in the 1930s:

> Almost the whole garden was topiary, architectural or geometric in design except for the bear, which was certainly its masterpiece. It stood twelve feet high, settled in a comfortable bell-shape on its haunches, its head, with ears pricked, convincingly modelled, its forepaws indicated by deftly clipped protuberances emerging from its body.
> 'My husband planted all the yew and box,' Mrs. Feilding said, 'when we first came to live here. My

103 (ABOVE) and 104 (BELOW)
Beckley Park, Oxfordshire, the box garden, c.1940–41, black and white negative.
Photographer: Paul Nash, collection of the Tate, presented by the Paul Nash Trust, 1970

son, Basil, and Mr. Moore have clipped them into shapes following my husband's intentions. Mr. Moore, however, is wholly responsible for the bear.'[33]

In the 1929 *Country Life* article, one photograph shows the topiary rose garden fully matured. Another unpublished photograph located in their archives shows immature boxwoods which eventually became the third garden section populated by fanciful topiaries and Moore's bear.[34]

In fact, Basil records that it was in the spring of 1921, that Percy planted American boxwoods measuring eighteen inches in height.[35] They were first clipped about two or three years after planting. Some shrubs were clipped into cones, others into cubes, spheres and pyramids. This was the mathematical style of topiary which had been first introduced into England in the 1700s. The effect was more architectural in character than the natural gardens found elsewhere on the property (figs 103 and 104).

168   CLOTILDE BREWSTER

105 Small pavilion at corner of moat with new garden wall and thatched barns *c.*1929. Future Publishing Ltd

106 View of Beckley Park moat in present day. Author's collection

The rose garden had box edgings that were diamond-shaped enclosing the roses. The edgings were 2 feet high, 14 inches wide with pyramids rising from them every 5 feet. The backdrop to this garden was a high yew surround. The roses were gifts to Clotilde from Countess Sophie Benckendorff who was a grower of antique roses. Clotilde had advised her on her own walled gardens at her house in Lime Kiln in Claydon, Ipswich. The Countess also provided the climbing roses which still grow with profusion along the garden walls and outbuildings.

Another garden element attributed to Clotilde were the walls and the romantic pyramid-roofed stone pavilion located on a corner of the moat (figs 105 and 106). It is very reminiscent in design to a similarly placed pavilion at the Château de Longpra very near to Avignonet, the Brewster's own château which was destroyed by fire when Clotilde was a child. In designing the moat pavilion, Clotilde –knowingly or unknowingly – left a tribute to that time in her life when, after tragedy struck, her passion for architecture first emerged.

DEATHS OF CHRISTOPHER BREWSTER AND PERCY FEILDING

Christopher Brewster died in late 1928. He had developed dementia and wandered out alone and underdressed in winter and had contracted pneumonia. Clotilde had been asked by her sister-in-law Lisl to design his gravestone but she did not in the end, perhaps because she was too overwhelmed by grief or was upset with Lisl.[36] Lisl, who had converted to Catholicism many years before, wanted her husband to receive a Catholic death though Christopher, like Clotilde, was non-religious. This was something that Christopher would have fought against had he been able. Clotilde wrote with some untruthfulness.

I have been wanting to write to you for ages and I could not. I wanted to thank you for your letter – which gave me such happiness and at the same time I was so miserable that I could not write to you 'Grief makes one silent', so you wrote to Arthur and you were right. I want to tell you how happy I was to hear that Christopher had been buried in a Catholic churchyard – that you had given him a crucifix to hold and that he had died holding it and loving you – poor darling Christopher, I can't write to you about him.[37]

Six months later, Percy would die of heart failure at Beckley on the 29 June 1929, at the age of 61. He is buried with his ancestors in the churchyard at St Edith's, Monks Kirby, Warwickshire. He had been thinking about his own death for over ten years. In August 1916, he had experienced symptoms of angina and glumly wrote to Christopher that 'when doctors use long names and make long faces and speak solemnly of the 'serious state of one's health' it is only natural that one should go and choose one's place of burial and write one's epitaph'.[38]

Given Clotilde's experience designing grave monuments not only with Adolf Hildebrand for his illustrious clients, but for her own parents as well as cousins Alfred and Ellen Hearn, there is no doubt that Clotilde designed Percy's tomb. In the style of a classically molded chest tomb, the vertical surfaces are formed from concave and convex curves. Centered on each are flat tablets which feature carvings and inscriptions. Now worn with age, the tomb's engravings are barely decipherable. One is a double-headed eagle, the emblem of the Habsburgs. On its opposite side is a stylized tree with spheres dangling from the tip of each bough which is a tribute to the topiary gardens at Beckley. On the third tablet is engraved Percy's name and the dates of his birth and death.

On the fourth side is an inscription taken from a scene in E.M. Forster's book *A Passage to India* published in 1924. The main character Dr Aziz sees writing on a tomb of a Deccan King and vows to have it on his own tomb placed in a small but perfect mosque that he himself would design:

> *Alas without me for thousands of years*
> *The rose will blossom and the spring will bloom,*
> *But those who have secretly understood my heart–*
> *They will approach and visit the grave where I lie.*

With those closest to her gone she became reclusive, prompting Ethel Smyth to remember that 'After her husband's premature death it was almost impossible to persuade this brilliant, sociable, amusing, and utterly original woman to move beyond her own park gates.'[39]

Visitors to Beckley thereafter were mostly of the younger generation. A Beckley neighbor and friend, William Buchan brought fellow writers Elizabeth Bowen and Maurice Cardiff to visit as they were intrigued by his descriptions. Upon arriving they were immediately caught up in its spell. Cardiff wrote that Beckley,

> The interior, owing to the windows being small for the size of the rooms, was shadowy and mysterious. It contained some beautiful furniture and fine pictures and tapestries. Mrs. Feilding was an eccentric old lady and mixed the splendid with the primitive, so that if you were a fortunate guest you might sleep in a plumed four-poster or if less fortunate, in a narrow iron bed with sagging springs.[40]

On this visit they would meet Clotilde's longtime guest, Osbert 'Bertie' Moore, who would later become the renowned Buddhist monk called Ñanamoli Thera. At Oxford, Bertie had been hired to tutor Basil in Italian and they had become fast friends. After discovering their mutual passion for antiques, old furniture and paintings, they opened an antique shop together in Oxford upon leaving university. It was at this point that Bertie moved into Beckley. When Basil married in 1930 and moved to The Park, Bertie stayed on as Clotilde's guest until sometime after her death in 1937 when Basil, who had inherited Beckley from his mother, moved back in the house. He described this time in his life as a 'very pleasant and mainly graceful rock-pool'. As recorded by Maurice Cardiff, the introverted Bertie got on well with Clotilde, who had him play the harpsichord for guests and put him to work on various house projects.

> When I first visited Beckley, Bertie seemed to belong very much to the shadows in that remote and peaceful house. He would come into a room so quietly and remain so silent that one hardly realised that he was there. With his pale rather ascetic face he looked like a figure which had walked out of one of the tapestries, but his presence was wholly benign and once he was drawn into conversation his intelligence, good nature and quiet sense of humour at once became apparent. Mrs. Feilding liked to bully him and this was, perhaps, one of the reasons why he stayed so much in the background. Although he had already lived in the house for two years, she always addressed him as Mr. Moore and her usual opening was, 'Mr. Moore will do this'. Or 'Mr. Moore will do that'. Whatever she announced that Mr. Moore would do, he always did without showing the smallest resentment at her dictatorial manner. He was in fact very fond of the old lady and one of the tasks which he undertook for her exemplified what was perhaps the most unusual aspect of his many talents, his ability to teach himself almost any skill within a very short period and to carry it out to the highest degree of perfection. She had a set of Jacobean chairs of which the embroidered covers on the backs and seats had become threadbare. Although he had

never done any embroidery before Bertie set out to recover them and completed the set in six months. The work was so perfect that it might have been by the hand of an expert with years of experience.[41]

Harry Brewster came to know his Aunt Clotilde in the 1930s when he was a student at Oxford.

> Whether she sat or went about she was constantly holding a great mug of beer and whenever she laughed the old Elizabethan house would shake heartily in consonant rhythm. Her conversation had a rousing, stimulating, provocative quality, for she loved paradoxes – maddening sometimes, because she liked to lead you on into argument for the sake of argument, even if she held the opposite view, her contrary stance being taken for the fun of it all.[42]

Her passion for French literature remained undiminished as well as her dislike of Shakespeare. She 'worshipped Voltaire, Flaubert, Stendhal, Maupassant and other French writers mainly of the nineteenth century'.[43]

In her last years she continued successfully to play the stock market and took care of her many animals. When she had moved into Beckley she brought along dogs, pigeons, seven cats, a guinea pig and a mare. Her time was taken up caring for the old house and garden by herself as she was usually short staffed.

DEATH OF CLOTILDE

In late 1936, Clotilde developed pneumonia and had not fully recovered before she got up from her bed and resumed her daily activities. This action directly led to her falling severely ill on the 23 February when Basil found she was not herself and was running a fever. A doctor was called who mistakenly said it was nothing serious and that she must rest. Two days later she took turn a turn for the worse as recorded her nephew, Harry.

> On Thursday afternoon Basil was alone with her reading to her, when suddenly she went blue in the face and complained of being cold. Basil was awfully scared, rushed to the telephone and called for the doctor. The ordinary doctor was not at home, so he tried to get in touch with his colleague and as this one was doubtful of his being able to come, he got hold of a third doctor who promised to come straight away. At the time there was at Beckley only Basil, Susan's little daughter and her nanny. Cloto by now had fallen in a sort of semi-conscious state, and could only utter incongruous words. It must have been terrible for Basil. Then at last both doctors arrived at the same time.[44]

In short order, the doctors started quarrelling in the very room where Clotilde lay dying. 'Each said to Basil, "How dare you call me, when you have another doctor?"' By the time they had finished their dispute, doing nothing for their patient, ten minutes had passed and death quickly followed. It was 25 February 1937 – eight years and four months after Percy's death.

Clotilde Brewster Feilding's funeral was held two days later at Monks Kirby and attended by her son Basil, his wife Peggy and her parents, nephew Harry Brewster, Bertie Moore and two unnamed friends. She lies in an unmarked grave next to Percy Feilding's tomb.

16

CATALOG OF WORK

Partial list of projects by Clotilde Brewster, including: 1) original designs before marriage; 2) original designs after marriage in partnership with Percy Feilding. Some projects are mentioned in letters only.

I have inserted 'Built' or 'Unbuilt' when this information is known.

Abbreviations: C: client, L: location, D: date

ORIGINAL DESIGNS AND CONSULTING (1885–1904)

1. CHATEAU AVIGNONET – C: Clotilde Brewster. L: Avignonet, France. D: 1885–87. Unbuilt
2. DOVECOTE – C: H.B. Brewster. D: 1888–90. Built.
3. ENGLISH COTTAGE – D.1890. Unbuilt.
4. BOOKCASE – C: H.B. Brewster. D: 1890. Built.
5. TOMB OF HEINRICH EMIL HOMBERGER, Adolf Hildebrand Studio – L: Allori Cemetery, Florence, Italy. D: 1890. Built.
6. HOUSE ON SPECULATION – C: H.B. Brewster. L: Aix-les-Bains, France. D: 1891.
7. RASPONI PRIORY HOUSE AND CHAPEL, Adolf Hildebrand Studio – C: Giuseppe Rasponi. D: 1892.
8. VILLA FOR WORLD'S COLUMBIAN EXPOSITION, Design and working drawings – D: 1892–93.
9. ROCOCCO HOUSE – C: Eva Hildebrand. D: 1893. Unbuilt.
10. TOWNHOUSE – D: 1895.
11. CHAPEL – D: 1895. Unbuilt.
12. REMODEL OF BALFOUR HOUSE, Adolf Hildebrand Studio – C: Gerald Balfour. D: 1894.
13. COUNTRY HOUSE – C: Ernest von Stockhausen. L: Löwenhagen, Germany. D: 1896. Unbuilt.
14. COTTAGE: THE RUSHES – C: Clotilde Brewster. L: Farnborough, Hampshire. D: 1896–98. Built.
15. TOWNHOUSE – D: 1896.
16. ALTAR – C: Canon friend of Baroness Emily Halkett. L: Church in Exeter. D: 1896
17. HERMANN LEVI VILLA, Adolf Hildebrand Studio – L: Garmisch-Partenkirchen, Bavaria, Germany. D: 1896. Built.
18. ST PAUL'S SCHOOL FOR GIRLS, Reginald Blomfield's office – C: St Paul's School Board. L: Hammersmith, London. D: 1896. Competition entry. Unbuilt. Collaborators: Philip Bauhof, Harold Falkner and Mr. James.
19. SEASIDE HOUSE – C: Mary C.D. Hamilton. L: West Sussex, England. D: 1896. Unbuilt.

20 HOUSE, Adolf Hildebrand Studio – D: 1896.
21 FOUNTAIN, Adolf Hildebrand Studio – D: 1896.
22 MAUSOLEUM, Adolf Hildebrand Studio – L: Munich, Bavaria, Germany. D: 1896.
23 TRELLISES – D: 1896.
24 WELL INSCRIPTION, Reginald Blomfield office – D: 1897.
25 MANTELPIECE – C: H.B. Brewster. L: Living room, Palazzo Antici Mattei, Rome, Italy. D: 1897. Built.
26 MANTELPIECES – D: 1897.
27 OPEN AIR FESTIVAL THEATRE – C: Eleanora Duse. L: Albano, Italy. D: 1897. Unbuilt.
28 COUNTRY HOUSE – C: Mary C.D. Hamilton. L: Rustington, West Sussex, England. D: 1897.
29 SIEGFRIED FOUNTAIN BASE, Adolf Hildebrand Studio – L: Worms, Rhineland-Palatinate, Germany. D: 1898. Built.
30 MANTELPIECE – C: Friend of Louis de Glehn. D: 1897. Unbuilt.
31 GARDENS – C: Clotilde Brewster. L: The Rushes, Farnborough, Hampshire. D: 1898. Built.
32 OVERMANTEL MIRROR – C: Arthur Cohen. L: Highfield, Shoreham Sevenoaks, Kent, UK. D: 1898. Built.
33 TOWNHOUSE RENOVATION – C: Clotilde Brewster. L: 1 Barton Street, Westminster, London, UK. D: 1898. Built.
34 TOPIARY GARDEN LAYOUT AND STRUCTURES – C: Clotilde Brewster. L: 1 Barton Street, Westminster, London, UK. D: 1898–9. Built.
35 TOBACCO WAREHOUSE, Adolf Hildebrand Studio – C: Giuseppe Rasponi. L: Barbialla, Florence, Italy. D: 1898. Built.
36 EXTERIOR STAIRCASE – C: Giuseppe Rasponi. L: Tobacco Warehouse, Barbialla, Florence, Italy. D: 1898.
37 ROOF LANTERN – C: H.B. Brewster. L: Library, Palazzo Mattei, Rome, Italy. D: 1898. Unbuilt.
38 KING ALFRED MONUMENT, Collaborator: Feo Gleichen – D: 1898. Unbuilt.
39 TOMB OF JULIA BREWSTER – C: H.B. Brewster. L: Freiburg-im-Breisgau, Germany. D: 1898–9. Built.
40 RENOVATION OF OLD MILL COTTAGE – C: Mary C.D. Hamilton. L: Rustington, West Sussex, UK. D: 1899. Built.
41 HUBERTUSBRUNNEN, Adolf Hildebrand Studio – L: Munich. Germany. D: 1899. Clotilde's version of this fountain was not built.
42 GARDEN SHED – C: Clotilde Brewster. L: The Rushes, Farnborough, Hampshire, UK. D: 1899. Built.
43 MANTELPIECE AND SMALL ALTERATIONS – C: Charles and Agnes Anstruther-Thomson. L: possibly Rutland House, Knightsbridge, London, UK. D: 1899.
44 LIBRARY BOOKCASES – C: H.B. Brewster. L: Palazzo Antici Mattei, Rome, Italy. D: 1899. Built.
45 MANTELPIECE – C: H.B. Brewster. L: Living room, Palazzo Mattei, Rome, Italy. D: 1897 and 1899. Built.
46 FOUNTAIN OF MOTHER AND CHILD, n.d. – L: Drawings at Beckley Park, Oxon.
47 COUNTRY HOUSE ALTERATIONS – L: France. D: 1900.
48 NURSING HOME – C: Dr Lillias Hamilton. L: 29 Queen Anne St, London, UK. D: 1900. Built.
49 GARDENER'S COTTAGE – C: Lady Kenmare. L: Killarney, Ireland. D: 1900. Unbuilt.
50 UNSPECIFIED PROJECT – C: Alice Feilding. D: 1900.
51 SELABY HALL ADDITION – C: Charles and Mary Hunter. L: County Durham, UK. D: possibly 1898. Built.
52 SELABY HALL SOUTH LODGE – C: Charles and Mary Hunter. L: County Durham, UK. D: 1901. Built.
53 SELABY HALL RACKET COURT, BOTHY AND STABLES – C: Charles and Mary Hunter. L: County Durham, UK. D: 1900.

54 GAMEKEEPER'S HOUSE – C: Charles and Mary Hunter. L: Selaby Hall, County Durham, UK. D: *c*.1898.

55 DESIGN OF COLONNADE – C: Countess Feo Gleichen. L: Paris, France. D: 1900.

56 MONUMENTS AND ARCHITECTURAL DECORATION, Adolf Hildebrand Studio – D: 1901.

57 PALAZZO SODERINI – C: Marianna Soderini. L: Rome, Italy. D: 1901–3. Built.

58 PALAZZO FRANKENSTEIN – C: Alessandra de Frankenstein. L: Rome, Italy. D: 1901–3. Built.

59 TRELLIS – C: Mary Crawshay (born Leslie). D: 1901.

60 BENSON FOUNTAIN, Adolf Hildebrand Studio – D: 1902.

61 STABLES – C: Clotilde Brewster. L: Farnborough, Hampshire, UK. D: 1902. Built.

62 SPECULATION COTTAGE – C: Mary C.D. Hamilton. L: Rustington, West Sussex, UK. D: 1902. Built.

63 BOER WAR MEMORIAL FOUNTAIN – C: Violet Hippisley. L: Farnborough, Hampshire, UK. D: 1902–3. Built.

64 CHURCH FARM BUNGALOW – C: Mary C.D. Hamilton. L: Rustington, West Sussex, UK. D: 1902. Built.

65 SIEMENS HELMHOLTZ TOMB, Adolf Hildebrand Studio – L: Berlin. D: 1902. Built.

66 GLASS DISPLAY CASE – D: 1903.

67 HEARN MAUSOLEUM – C: Ellen Hearn. L: Menton, France. D: 1903–5. Built.

68 TOWNHOUSE RENOVATION – C: Ellen Hearn. L: London, UK. D: 1903–5. Built.

69 CASTELLO DELL'OSCANO – C: Ada Telfener. L: Cenerente, Perugia, Italy. D: 1903–5. Built.

70 HOUSE ADDITION – C: Sophie Benckendorff. L: Tambof, Sosnofka, Russia, 1903–4.

71 ROAD SIDE CHAPELS – C: Sophie Benckendorff. L: Tambof Sosnofka, Russia. D: 1903. Built.

72 HOUSE RENOVATION – C: Margaret Brooke, The Ranee of Sarawak. L: Greyfriars, Ascot, UK. D: 1904. Built.

73 HOUSE RENOVATION AND ADDITIONS – C: Charles and Mary Hunter. L: Wemmergill Hall, Middle-in-Teesdale. D: 1904. Built, 1904.

74 TOWNHOUSE RENOVATION – C: Clotilde Brewster. L: 40 Grosvenor Road, London, UK. D: Built.

75 COUNTRY HOUSE – C: sister-in-law of Countess Sophie Benckendorff. L: Russia. D: 1904.

76 SUCCURSALE [chapel] – C: Lady Mary Ponsonby. L: Gilmuire, Ascot, Berkshire, UK. D: 1904. Built.

PROJECTS AFTER MARRIAGE –
C & P FEILDING, ARCHITECTS

1 VILLINO FRANKENSTEIN – C: Henri and Anne Frankenstein. L: Rome, Italy. D: 1905. Clotilde project. Built.

2 FACADE FOR LABORATORIO SANTA CATERINA – C: Alessandra de Frankenstein. L: Rome, Italy. D: 1905. Clotilde project. Built.

3 RENOVATIONS FOR TWO CHURCHES, Percy project – D: 1905.

4 SUNDIAL, Percy project – D: 1905. Built.

5 HOSPITAL, Percy project – D: 1905.

6 CHAPEL – C: friend of Ellen Hearn. L: Moscow, Russia. D: 1905.

7 FREDERICK HAMLYN FUNERARY MONUMENT – C: Christine Hamlyn Fane. L: All Saints Churchyard, Clovelly, Devon, UK. D: 1905. Built.

8 COUNTRY HOUSE, Percy project – D: 1906.

9 COUNTRY HOUSE RENOVATION, Percy project – L: Newbury. D: 1906.

10 GARAGE AND CHAUFFEUR HOUSE – C: Arthur Merton Cohen. L: Highfield, Shoreham Sevenoaks, Kent, UK. D: 1906. Clotilde project. Built.

11 SIX-ACRE PARK AT THE RUSH HOUSE (formerly known as The Rushes) – L: Farnborough, Hampshire, UK, after expansion of property, constructing terraces, steps, hedgerows,

CATALOG OF WORK 175

transplanting trees, laying out of paths and avenues, seeding of lawns, etc. D: 1906. Built.

12 SPECULATION HOUSES – C: Clotilde and Percy Feilding. L: Farnborough, Hampshire, UK. D: 1907. Unbuilt.

13 LIBRARY ADDITION – C: Lady Mary Ponsonby. L: Gilmuire, Ascot, Berkshire, UK. Clotilde project. D: 1907. Built.

14 BUNGALOW AND SHOPS, additions and alternations, conversion into single family residence – C: Mary C.D. Hamilton. L: Rustington, West Sussex, UK. Clotilde project. D: 1907. Built.

15 ALTERATION OF STABLES – C: Clotilde and Percy Feilding. L: Rush House, Farnborough, Hampshire, UK. D: 1907. Built.

16 HOUSE RENOVATION – C: Mrs. Reginald Halsey Laye. L: Lees Court, Sheldwich, Kent, UK. Percy project. D: 1907–8. Built.

17 NEW PORCH – C: Mrs. Reginald Halsey Laye. L: Lees Court, Sheldwich, Kent, UK. Drawings by Clotilde. D: 1908. Unbuilt.

18 BATH TOWER – C: Mrs. Reginald Halsey Laye. L: Lees Court, Sheldwich, Kent, UK. Drawings by Clotilde. D: 1908. Unbuilt.

19 GATEHOUSE – C: Frederick and Grace North. L: Rougham Hall, Norfolk, UK. Percy project. D: 1907. Built.

20 SIX COTTAGES – D: 1908.

21 RENOVATION AND ADDITIONS TO HOUSE – C: Terence Bourke. L: Pekes Manor House, Chiddingly, East Sussex, UK. D: 1908. Built.

22 CONVERSION OF OAST HOUSE – C: Terence Bourke. L: Pekes Manor House estate, Chiddingly, East Sussex, UK. D: 1908. Built.

23 LODGE AND ENTRY GATES – C: Terence Bourke. L: Pekes Manor House estate, Chiddingly, East Sussex, UK. D: 1908. Built.

24 GARDENS – C: Terence Bourke. L: Pekes Manor House estate, Chiddingly, East Sussex, UK. D: 1908. Built.

25 TWO COUNTRY HOUSES, Percy Feilding project – D: 1908.

26 TOMBSTONE OF HENRY BENNET BREWSTER – C: Christopher Brewster and Clotilde Feilding. L: Non-Catholic Cemetery for Foreigners in Rome, Rome, Italy. D: 1908. Built.

27 HOUSE ADDITION – C: Percy and Clotilde Feilding. L: Rush House, Farnborough, Hampshire, UK. D: 1908–10. Built.

28 ORANGERY – C: Percy and Clotilde Feilding. L: Rush House, Farnborough, Hampshire, UK. D: 1909. Percy design. Built.

29 CONSULTING ON CONNECTOR PIECE BETWEEN TWO HOUSES – C: Sophie Benckendorff. L: Tambof, Sosnofka, Russia. Clotilde project. D: 1909.

30 COIGN COTTAGE – C: Ethel Smyth. L: Woking, Surrey, UK. Clotilde project. D: 1910.

31 ROOD SCREEN – C: St Mary's Church. L: Colkirk, Norfolk, UK. D: 1912. Built.

32 HOME DECORATION: C: Auberon Thomas Herbert and Nan Herbert. L: (?) 7 Cleveland Row, London. D: Pre-1912. Built.

33 COTTAGE ADDITION TO HOUSE – C: Col. Charles Needham. L: Tylehurst, Forest Row, East Sussex. Percy project. D: 1912. Built.

34 HOUSE RENOVATION AND ADDITION – C: Clotilde and Percy Feilding. L: Stonehill House, Chiddingly, East Sussex, UK. D: 1913–19. Built.

35 GARDENS – C: Clotilde and Percy Feilding. L: Stonehill House, Chiddingly, East Sussex, UK. D: 1913–19. Built.

36 COTTAGES – L: Stonehill House estate, Chiddingly, East Sussex. D: 1913. Built.

37 FARM BUILDINGS – C: Clotilde and Percy Feilding. L: Stonehill House estate, Chiddingly, East Sussex, UK. D: 1913–19. Built.

38 FARM HOUSE – C: Clotilde and Percy Feilding. L: Carter's Farm, Chiddingly, East Sussex. Sale particulars state 'Well-built Modern Farm House containing Four Bedrooms, Sitting Room,

Kitchen, Scullery, Dairy and Bakehouse.' The term 'Modern' indicates new construction.

39 FORECOURT AND TERRACE – C: Lady Alice (Thynne) Shaw Stewart. L: Ardgowan House, Greenock, Scotland. D: Pre-1918. Built.

40 TWO MODERN COTTAGES – C: Lady Louisa Feilding. L: Broome Park located in Betchworth, Surrey. The sale particulars of 1920 mention cottages. In 1905 writing from Broome, Clotilde stated they were doing work there.

41 CONSULTING ON HOUSE RENOVATION – C: Sophie Benckendorff. L: Lime Kiln House, Claydon, Ipswich, Suffolk, UK. D: 1918–19.

42 WAR MEMORIAL – C: Church of Chiddingly. L: Chiddingly, East Sussex, UK. D: 1919.

43 CONSULTING ON GARDEN WALLS AND STRUCTURES – C: Sophie Benckendorff. L: Lime Kiln House, Claydon, Ipswich, Suffolk, UK. Clotilde project. D: 1920 and 1927.

44 HOUSE RESTORATION – C: Clotilde and Percy Feilding. L: Beckley Park, Beckley, Oxon, UK. D: 1920–25.

45 MOAT PAVILION AND GARDEN WALLS – C: Clotilde and Percy Feilding. L: Beckley Park, Beckley, Oxon, UK. D: 1920–25.

46 CONVERSION OF BREW HOUSE INTO SERVANT'S QUARTERS – C: Clotilde and Percy Feilding. L: Beckley Park, Beckley, Oxon, UK. D: 1927.

47 CONVERSION OF STABLES INTO CHILDREN'S SITTING ROOM – C: Clotilde and Percy Feilding. L: Beckley Park, Beckley, Oxon, UK. D: 1927.

48 NEW BUILD BARN – C: Clotilde and Percy Feilding. L: Beckley Park, Beckley, Oxon, UK. D: 1922.

49 CRIPPS COTTAGE and WHEELWRIGHT SHOP RENOVATION – C: Clotilde and Percy Feilding. L: Beckley village, Oxon, UK. D: 1920. Built.

50 RENOVATION OF COTTAGES – C: Clotilde and Percy Feilding. L: Beckley village, Oxon, UK. D: 1920 and 1927.

51 GATE – C: Clotilde and Percy Feilding. L: Beckley Park, Beckley, Oxon, UK. Clotilde's project. D: 1925.

52 RENOVATION OF MIDDLE PARK, 'THE FARM' – C: Clotilde and Percy Feilding. L: Beckley, Oxon, UK. D: 1925.

53 TOMB OF PERCY HENRY FEILDING – C: Clotilde and Percy Feilding. L: St Edith's Church cemetery, Monks Kirby, Warwickshire, UK.

NOTES

ABBREVIATIONS

BASFP   The Brewster Archives at San Francesco di Paola
CHB   Christopher Henry Brewster
CKB   Clotilde Kate Brewster
ES   Ethel Smyth
HBB   Henry Bennet Brewster
JB   Julia Brewster
PHF   Percy Henry Feilding

INTRODUCTION

1. Student registers, Royal Academy Library, Collections Department.
2. Dame Ethel Smyth, 'Mrs. Percy Feilding, An Appreciation', *The Times*, Thursday, 4 March 1937, iss.47624, p.16.
3. Robert Weir Schultz, 'Here and There', *The Architectural Review*, vol.24, no.142, 1908, p.154.
4. BASFP, CKB to HBB, 16 January 1901.
5. Clotilde used the male term 'Architetto' on the Palazzo Soderini permit drawings with the spelling of Brewster Italianized to 'Bruster'.
6. BASFP, CKB to HBB, 20 June 1901.
7. Robert Becker, *Nancy Lancaster: Her Life, Her World, Her Art* (New York: A.A. Knopf, 1996), p.198.
8. Smyth, 'Mrs. Percy Feilding'.
9. Viscountess Wolseley, 'Historic Houses of Sussex – Stonehill, Chiddingly', *Sussex County Magazine*, vol.11, no.3, 1937, pp 142–7.
10. Nicholas Antram and Nikolaus Pevsner, *Sussex: East, with Brighton and Hove*, Pevsner Architectural Guides: Buildings of England (New Haven: Yale University Press, 2013), p.311.
11. 'Beckley Park', *Vogue* (London), vol.66 no.5, 1925 (Early September) – vol.66, no.12, 1925 (Late December). Article is specifically in the Early November issue of 1925, pp 61–3.
12. 'A Little Portfolio of Good Interiors', *House & Garden* (New York), vol.51, January 1927, pp 89–91.
13. Christopher Hussey, 'Beckley Park, Oxfordshire: The Residence of Mr. Percy Feilding', *Country Life*, vol.65, iss.1679, 1929, pp 407–8.
14. Alan Brooks and Jennifer Sherwood, *Oxfordshire: North and West*. Pevsner Architectural Guides: Buildings of England (New Haven: Yale University Press, 2017), p.136.
15. Oliver Wainwright, *Snubbed, Cheated, Erased: The Scandal of Architecture's Invisible Women*, 16 October 2016, https://www.theguardian.com/artanddesign/2018/oct/16/the-scandal-of-architecture-invisible-women-denise-scott-brown.

I   FAMILY BACKGROUND

1. *Hof-und Staats-Handbuch für das Königreich Hannover, auf das Jahr 1846* (Hannover, 1846).

2. *The Correspondence of John Lothrop Motley, Vol. II*, ed. George William Curtis (New York: Harper & Brothers, 1889), p.329.
3. Ethel Smyth, *Impressions That Remained: Memoirs* (New York: Alfred A. Knopf, 1946), p.64.
4. BASFP, CKB to Eva Hildebrand, 4 October 1892.
5. *Norwich Aurora* (Norwich, Connecticut), 1 November 1871, p.3.
6. The *Southern Dental Journal and Luminary* (Atlanta, Georgia), vol.5, May 1886, p.140.
7. Apolloni Pierre Préterre, 'Biographie Le docteur Brewster', *L'Art Dentaire*, 1857, p.28.
8. *Medical Times*, vol.15 (London: J. Angerstein Carfrae, 1839–51), p.345.
9. *The Southern Dental Journal and Luminary*, p.141.
10. The 'Adressbuch der Deutschen in Paris' of 1854 lists Baron de Stockhausen having a residence at 18, rue de Miroménil, https://adressbuch1854.dhi-paris.fr/search/results?type=simp&text=stockhausen.
11. Harry Brewster, *The Cosmopolites: A Nineteenth Century Family Drama* (Norwich: Michael Russell Publishing, 1994), p.57.
12. Brewster, *The Cosmopolites*, p.48.
13. Obituary, 'Dr. Christopher Starr Brewster', *The Dental Cosmos: A Monthly Record of Dental Science*, vol.13, February 1871, pp 95–6.
14. 'The Cholera', *The Times* (London), 1 July 1873, p.12.
15. Smyth, *Impressions That Remained*, p.63.

2 *GENIUS LOCI* – FLORENCE

1. Henry James, *Travelling Companions* (New York: Boni and Liveright, 1919), p.144.
2. Paul R. Baker, *The Fortunate Pilgrims: Americans in Italy, 1800–1860* (Cambridge, MA: Harvard University Press, 1964).
3. 'Nota mondana', *La Vita Italiana, Rivista Illustrata*, ed. Angelo de Guernatis, vol.6, February–April 1896, pp 191–2.
4. Leonardo Ginori Lisci, *The Palazzi of Florence: History and Art, Vol. II*, trans. Jennifer Grillo (Florence: Giunti, 1985), p.673.
5. The street number of the palazzo changed in the 20th century from no.22 via de' Bardi to no.28.
6. Harry Brewster, 'Henry James and the Gallo-American', *Botteghe Oscure*, Vol. XIX (Rome: Botteghe Oscure, 1957), p.173.
7. BASFP, letter to CKB to HBB, 23 September 1885.
8. BASFP, letter to CKB to HBB, 6 January 1886.
9. BASFP, letter to CKB to HBB, 29 January 1886.
10. BASFP, letter to CKB to HBB, 7 June 1886.
11. BASFP, letter to CKB to HBB, 29 November 1886.
12. BASFP, letter to CKB to HBB, 1 April 1888.
13. BASFP, letter to CKB to HBB, 4 April 1887.
14. BASFP, letter to CKB to HBB, 20 April 1886.
15. BASFP, letter to CKB to HBB, 4 April 1887.
16. BASFP, letter to CKB to HBB, 2 June 1887.
17. BASFP, letter to CKB to HBB, 19 May 1887.
18. Aurello Gotti, *Narrazione delle feste fatte in Firenze nel maggio 1887 per lo scoprimento della facciata di S. Maria del Fiore e del V centenario dalla nascita di Donatello. [A spese del comune di Firenze]* (Florence: Salvadore Landi, 1890), p.120.
19. William Warren Vernon, *Recollections of Seventy-two Years* (London: John Murray, 1917), p.336.
20. Joseph Garrow, Esq. A.M., *The Early Life of Dante Alighieri: Together with the Original in Parallel Pages* (Florence: Felix Le Monnier, 1846), p.118.
21. BASFP, CKB to HBB, 22 November 1890.
22. Letter from Truman Seymour to Emma [Weir Casey], 29 June 1891, Historic New England, Casey family papers, MS008, https://www.historicnewengland.org/explore/collections-access/gusn/351693.
23. BASFP, Truman Seymour to CHB, 18 August 1891.

3 TWO CHILDHOOD TRAUMAS

1. Emanuel La Roche, correspondence to his mother, 13 November 1888, Staatsarchiv Basel-Stadt, Switzerland.
2. J.C. Michel, 'Le Château d'Avignonet, Pour Ne Pas Oublier', *Revue d'histoire des Amis de la Vallée de la Gresse et des environs*, no.36, December 1995, pp 29–32.
3. Ethel Smyth, *The Memoirs of Ethel Smyth*, abridged by Ronald Crichton (Harmondsworth: Viking, 1987) p.120.
4. Smyth, *Memoirs*, pp 121–2.
5. Smyth, *Memoirs*, p.130.
6. Ethel Smyth, *What Happened Next* (London: Longmans, Green and Co., 1940), pp 12–13.
7. Amanda Harris, 'The Smyth-Brewster Correspondence: A Fresh Look at the Hidden Romantic World of Ethel Smyth', *Women and Music: A Journal of Gender and Culture*, vol.14, 2010, pp 72–94.
8. BASFP, HBB to ES, 26 May 1905.
9. BASFP, CKB to HBB, 30 July 1885.
10. BASFP, CKB to HBB, 23 October 1886.

11 BASFP, CKB to HBB, 25 May 1887.
12 BASFP, CKB to HBB, 1 April 1887.
13 BASFP, CKB to HBB, 18 October 1887.
14 BASFP, CKB to HBB, 19 October 1887.
15 Harry Brewster, *The Cosmopolites: A Nineteenth Century Family Drama* (Norwich: Michael Russell Publishing, 1994), p.91.
16 Brewster, *The Cosmopolites*, p.25.
17 Regine Steffani, 'Der Bildhauer Theodor Georgii 1883–1963. Biografie und Werkverzeichnis', PhD diss., Ludwig-Maximilians-Universität, Munich, 2013.
18 *Offizieller Katalog der Internationalen Kunst-Ausstellung*, Munich, 1902, p.31 and fig.50.
19 Steffani, 'Der Bildhauer Theodor Georgii 1883–1963'.
20 'Ein Leben für die Kunst. Zum 70. Geburtstag von Frau Irene Georgii' [A Life in Art: On the 70th Birthday of Frau Irene Georgii], *Mangfall-bote*, 21 January 1950.
21 BASFP, CKB to HBB, 9 December 1890.
22 BASFP, CKB to HBB, 19 April 1891.
23 BASFP, CKB to HBB, 17 December 1896.
24 Susanna Ragionieri and Francesca Centurione Scotto Boschieri, *Natura E Bellezza: Elisabeth Brewster Hildebrand*, exh.cat. (Lucca: Maria Pacini Fazzi Editore, 2007), pp 5–6.

4 LESSONS WITH EMANUEL LA ROCHE AND MOTHER'S HEALTH

1 Rose Marie Schulz-Rehberg, *Architekten des Fin De Siecle Bauen in Basel um 1900* (Basel: Christoph Merian Verlag, 2012).
2 Emil Rudolf Seiler-La Roche, *Chronik der Familie Hebdenstreit genannt La Roche* (Munich: C. Wolf and Sohn, 1920).
3 R. Wackernagel and E. La Roche, *Beiträge zur Geschichte des Basler Münsters* (Basel: Schwabe, 1881–85).
4 Hans Georg Oeri, 'Die Bronzetüren an der Galluspforte des Basler Münsters: ein Werk des Architekten Emanuel La Roche (1892)', *Basler Zeitschrift für Geschichte und Altertumskunde*, vol.100, 2000, p.194.
5 Letter, 7 March 1889, Staatsarchiv Basel-Stadt, Switzerland.
6 Jacob Burckhardt, *Briefwechsel mit Heinrich von Geymüller* (Munich: Georg Müller and Eugen Rentsch, 1914), pp 115–16. Letter, January 1888.
7 Emanuel La Roche, *Indische Baukunst, Vol. I* (Munich, 1921), p.XI.
8 BASFP, CKB to HBB, 16 March 1889.
9 BASFP, CKB to HBB, 9 December 1890.
10 BASFP, CKB to HBB, 22 December 1890.
11 BASFP, CKB to HBB, 14 March 1891.
12 Letter from Emanuel La Roche to his mother, 30 December 1890, Staatsarchiv Basel-Stadt, Switzerland.
13 Ethel Smyth, *Impressions that Remained* (New York: Alfred A. Knopf, 1946), p.246.
14 Smyth, *Impressions*, p.307.
15 Smyth, *Impressions*, p.317.
16 BASFP, CKB to Eva Hildebrand, 17 December 1891.
17 Excerpt from *Midi* by Charles-Marie Leconte de Lisle (1818–94), translated from the French in *Fables of the Self* by Rosanne Warren (New York: W.W. Norton & Company, 2008).
18 BASFP, CKB to HBB, 17 February 1891.
19 BASFP, CKB to HBB, 14 March 1891.
20 BASFP, CKB to HBB, 12 April 1891.
21 BASFP, CKB to HBB, 19 April 1891.
22 BASFP, CKB to HBB, 28 April 1891.
23 BASFP, CKB to HBB, 28 April 1891.
24 BASFP, Emanuel La Roche to Irene Hildebrand, 1 April 1891.
25 BASFP, Emanuel La Roche to Baroness Clothilde von Stockhausen, early December 1891.
26 BASFP, CKB to HBB, 27 December 1891.
27 Smyth, *Impressions*, p.302.
28 BASFP, CKB to Eva Hildebrand, 14 March 1892.
29 BASFP, CKB to Eva Hildebrand, 16 February 1892.
30 BASFP, CKB to HBB, 16 May 1892.
31 Emanuel La Roche, *Indische Baukunst, Vol. I* (Munich, 1922), preface.
32 Letter from La Roche's widow, Elisabeth, to Emil Gratzl, librarian at the Munich State Library, 20 September 1922, in archive material related to the publication of La Roche's *Indische Baukunst*, Universität Basel.
33 Zivilstandsamt der Stadt Basel; Aktenzeichen: 1928 A 1301.

5 ROME AND THE WORLD'S FAIR

1 BASFP, CKB to Eva Hildebrand, 13 February 1893.
2 BASFP, CKB to Eva Hildebrand, 2 February 1892.
3 'Nota mondana', *La Vita Italiana, Rivista Illustrata*, ed. Angelo de Guernatis, 6, February–April 1896, pp 191–2.
4 BASFP, CKB to Adolf Hildebrand, 1 February 1893.

5 BASFP, CKB to Eva Hildebrand, 18 March 1892.
6 Countess Cini was born Adele Piacentini, and the widow of Count Giuseppe Cini who died c.1885–6.
7 Ethel Smyth, *As Time Went On* (London: Longmans, Green and Co., 1936), p.233.
8 Clementine C. Hugo, *Rome en 1886: Les choses et les gens*, 2nd edn (Rome: Imprimerie Nationale, 1886) p.259.
9 *Frank Leslie's Popular Monthly*, vol.27 (New York, 1889), p.736.
10 BASFP, CKB to Eva Hildebrand, 28 February 1892.
11 BASFP, CKB to Eva Hildebrand, 5 March 1892.
12 Letter from Herzogenberg to Brahms, *Johannes Brahms: The Herzogenberg Correspondence*, ed. Max Kalbeck, trans. Hannah Bryant (New York: E.P. Dutton and Company, 1909), p.407.
13 BASFP, CKB to Eva Hildebrand, 14 March 1892.
14 Carlo Marchese Guerrieri Gonzaga and his wife Emma Marchesa Guerrieri Gonzaga (née Hohenemser). Guglielmo Mengarini and his wife, Margarete Traube; though married to the brilliant Mengarini (a famous electrical engineer), Traube was a force in her own right; she was a feminist and an activist for women's rights who hosted an influential cultural salon in Rome.
15 BASFP, Kate de Terrouenne to HBB, n.d., early 1890.
16 BASFP, HBB TO CKB, 19 December 1890.
17 Lisa Daniels, 'Houses as they might be': Rediscovering Rhoda and Agnes Garrett and their Influence on the Victorian Middle-Class Home', *Journal of the Decorative Arts Society 1850–the Present*, Omnium Gatherum, no.35, 2011, pp 82–101.
18 Elizabeth Crawford, *Enterprising Women: The Garretts and their Circle* (London: Francis Boutle Publishers, 2002) p.170.
19 BASFP, HBB to CKB, 15 May 1892.
20 BASFP, CKB to Eva Hildebrand, 15 July 1892.
21 BASFP, ES to HBB, 14 August 1892.
22 Clotilde is listed in the official catalog of the World's Columbian Exposition of 1893 as being from New York.
23 Beverly Willis Foundation, Dynamic National Archive of Women in Architecture, http://dna.bwaf.org/.
24 Laura Fitzmaurice, *Annie M. Cobb: A Remarkable Woman*, Boston Society of Architects, Research Grant 2010 Report.
25 'Chicago: The Architect of the Woman's Building', *American Architect and Building News*, vol.38, no.885, 10 December 1892, p.158.
26 BASFP, CKB to Eva Hildebrand, 14 October 1892.

6 NEWNHAM COLLEGE

1 BASFP, CKB to Eva Hildebrand, 14 October 1892.
2 BASFP, CKB to JB, 30 June 1893.
3 Margaret Birney Vickery, *Buildings for Bluestockings, The Architecture and Social History of Women's Colleges in Late Victorian England* (Newark: University of Delaware Press, 2000).
4 Eleanor Field, 'Women at an English University, Newnham College, Cambridge', *The Century*, vol.42, 1891, p.294.
5 BASFP, CBK to JB, 23 January 1894.
6 BASFP, CKB to JB, 22 April 1894.

7 LADY PUPIL IN REGINALD BLOMFIELD'S OFFICE

1 BASFP, CKB to JB, 29 June 1894.
2 'Architecture – A Profession or an Art?', *The British Architect*, 13 November 1891, pp 355–6.
3 CPI Inflation Calculator, https://www.officialdata.org/uk/inflation/1894?amount=145.
4 Richard A. Fellows, *Sir Reginald Blomfield, An Edwardian Architect* (London: A. Zwemmer, 1985).
5 BASFP, CKB to JB, 13 July 1894.
6 BASFP, CKB to HBB, 9 December 1894.
7 Harry Brewster, *The Cosmopolites: A Nineteenth-Century Family Drama* (Norwich: Michael Russell Publishing, 1994), p.250. The letter to Julia Brewster is dated October 1894.
8 BASFP, CKB to HBB, 27 October 1894.
9 Letter from Logan Pearsall Smith to his mother, 6 May 1902. Correspondence of Logan Pearsall Smith, Houghton Library, Harvard University.
10 BASFP, CKB to HBB, 27 October 1894.
11 Sir Reginald Blomfield, *Memoirs of an Architect* (London: Macmillan and Co., 1932), p.36.
12 BASFP, CKB to HBB, 27 October 1894.
13 BASFP, CKB to HBB, 2 December 1895.
14 BASFP, CKB to HBB, 21 December 1895.
15 BASFP, CKB to HBB, 13 December 1895.
16 Fellows, *Sir Reginald Blomfield*, p.73.
17 Loggia del Mercato Nuovo, a building in located in Piazza Della Repubblica, Florence, Italy.
18 BASFP, letter from Richard Norman Shaw to Clotilde Brewster, 27 October 1895.
19 BASFP, CKB to HBB, 13 January 1896.
20 *Proceedings of the Royal Institute of British Architects, 1881–82*, August 1882, p.44.

21 BASFP, CKB to HBB, 13 January 1896.
22 BASFP, CKB to HBB, 6 March 1896.
23 BASFP, CKB to HBB, 6 March 1896.
24 Blomfield, *Memoirs of an Architect*, p.38.
25 BASFP, CKB to HBB, 17 March 1896.
26 BASFP, letters from CKB to HBB, 12 December 1896, 17 December 1896 and 22 December 1896.
27 Sir Reginald Blomfield, *Richard Norman Shaw, R.A., Architect, 1831–1912: A Study* (London: B.T. Batsford, 1940), p.73.
28 Blomfield, *Memoirs of an Architect*, p.65.
29 BASFP, CKB to HBB 3 April 1897.
30 BASFP, CKB to HBB, 16 April 1897.

8 THE NEW WOMAN AND THE PROBLEM WITH DUENNAS

1 The Countess of Aberdeen (ed.), *International Congress of Women of 1899*, History of Women, Vol. 3 (London: T. Fisher Unwin, 1900), p.78.
2 'Architecture as a Profession for Women', *The Lady's Pictorial*, 13 April 1901, p.706.
3 Agnes Garrett, 'Home Decoration for Women', *The Decorator and Furnisher*, vol.19, no.3, December 1891, pp 89–91.
4 BASFP, CKB to HBB, 20 October 1897.
5 BASFP, CKB to HBB, 1 February 1898.
6 BASFP, CKB to HBB, 2 March 1898.
7 BASFP, CKB to HBB, 4 April 1898.
8 BASFP, Kate Terrouenne to HBB, 16 September 1900.
9 BASFP, CKB to HBB, 12 January 1904.
10 BASFP, The Hibbert-Hingston Collection, Margaret Sarawak to CKB, early 1904.
11 BASFP, CKB to HBB, 26 September 1902.
12 Harry Brewster, *The Cosmopolites: A Nineteenth Century Family Drama* (Norwich: Michael Russell Publishing, 1994), pp 295–6.
13 BASFP, CKB to HBB, 8 June 1900.
14 BASFP, CKB to HBB, 13 September 1903.
15 BASFP, CKB to HBB, 25 January 1904.
16 William Buchan, *The Rags of Time: A Fragment of Autobiography* (Southampton: Ashford, Buchan & Enright, 1990), p.225.
17 BASFP, HBB to ES, February 1897, quoted in Brewster, *The Cosmopolites*, p.297.
18 BASFP, CKB TO HBB, 4 November 1902.
19 BASFP, CKB to JB, 5 February 1895.
20 BASFP, CKB to HBB, 8 June 1897.
21 '200 Millions – 70 Titles: List Of American Girls Who Married Foreign Noblemen', *Washington Times* Newspaper Archives, 24 March 1895, p.6.
22 CPI Inflation Calculator, https://www.in2013dollars.com/us/inflation/.
23 Dorothy Erskine Muir, *Lift the Curtain* (London: Cape, 1955).
24 BASFP, CKB to HBB, 12 November 1898.
25 BASFP, CKB to HBB, 12 November 1898.
26 BASFP, CKB to HBB, 28 November 1898.
27 BASFP, CKB to HBB, 28 November 1897.
28 Sibyl Oldfield, 'Mary Sheepshanks Edits an Internationalist Suffrage Monthly in Wartime: *Jus Suffragii* 1914–19', *Women's History Review*, vol.12, no.1, 2003, pp 119–134.
29 Unpublished memoirs of Mary Sheepshanks, Women's Library Archives, The London School of Economics and Political Science, pp 56–8.
30 Unpublished memoirs of Mary Sheepshanks, p.6. Women's Library Archives, The London School of Economics and Political Science.
31 Unpublished memoirs of Mary Sheepshanks, p.29.
32 Unpublished memoirs of Mary Sheepshanks, p.37.
33 Letter from Thomas Hardy to Florence Henniker, 10 June 1893, in Richard Little Purdy and Michael Millgate (eds), *The Collected Letters of Thomas Hardy, Vol. Two* (Oxford: Oxford University Press, 1977).
34 BASFP, The Hibbert-Hingston Collection, HBB to CKB, 2 April 1898.
35 BASFP, CKB to CHB, 2 August 1900.
36 Unpublished memoirs of Mary Sheepshanks, p.40.
37 Unpublished memoirs of Mary Sheepshanks, p.37.
38 BASFP, ES TO HBB, 11 March 1900.
39 BASFP, CKB to Feodora Gleichen, copy of which was enclosed in a letter to her father dated 11 December 1900.
40 BASFP, CKB to CHB, 22 August 1902.
41 BASFP, CKB to HBB, 17 December 1901.
42 BASFP, Mary Sheepshanks to CHB, 2 February 1902.
43 BASFP, CKB to CHB, 6 May 1902.
44 BASFP, CKB to HBB, 16 February 1901.
45 BASFP, HBB to ES, Last Sunday in March 1901.
46 BASFP, CKB to HBB, 20 June 1901.
47 BASFP, PHF to HBB, 1 March 1904.
48 BASFP, CHB to Elisabeth Hildebrand Brewster, 30 April 1904.
49 BASFP, CKB to HBB, 15 February 1905.
50 CPI Inflation Calculator, https://www.officialdata.org/uk/inflation/1904?amount=6500
51 BASFP, CKB to HBB, 7 November 1925.

52 BASFP, CKB to Elisabeth Hildebrand Brewster, 5 April 1904.
53 Unpublished memoirs of Mary Sheepshanks, p.40.

9 BETWEEN SPIRITUALISTS AND PHYSICIANS – PROJECTS FOR THE HAMILTONS

1 BASFP, HBB to CKB, The Hibbert-Hingston Collection, 14 April 1906.
2 Pemberton Valley Estate, https://www.ucl.ac.uk/lbs/claim/view/16948.
3 Dane Love, *Scottish Ghosts* (Stroud: Amberley Publishing, 2009), pp 1–2.
4 BASFP, CKB to HBB, 27 February 1894.
5 Knut Holtsträter (ed.), *Jahrbuch des Zentrums für Populäre Kultur und Musik, Vol. 63*, 'Musik und Krieg', 2018, pp 168, 183.
6 Mary C.D. Hamilton, on behalf of a Meeting held in the Lecture Hall of the Somerville Club, on 2 May 1882. (1882), UK Parliament.
7 BASFP, CKB to HBB, 8 June 1897.
8 CKB to HBB, 10 March 1899.
9 CKB to HBB, 17 September 1902.
10 CKB to HBB, 24 November 1902.
11 In the Bev and Mary Taylor collection, courtesy of Graham Taylor, there are two photographs. They are not dated but appear to be from *c*.1915 and show the same workmen in front of a partial view of Church Farm Bungalow. The same tree to the right of the building is in both images. The earlier or 'before' photograph shows the building in brick, the second shows it covered in pebbledash.
12 Clayre Percy and Jane Ridley (eds), *The Letters of Edwin Lutyens to His Wife Lady Emily* (London: Collins, 1985), p.139.
13 Mary Taylor, *This was Rustington*, published by the author.
14 Multiple classified advertisements, *Morning Post* (London), Monday 25 April 1898, no.39277.
15 Christopher Timmis, 'Lillias Hamilton: Personal Physician to the Amir of Afghanistan', *Journal of Medical Biography*, vol.29, no.4, pp 236–45.
16 BASFP, CKB to HBB, 22 March 1900.
17 George Frederick Wright, a builder whose addresses included 17 Cowley Street and 25 Wood Street, Westminster.
18 BASFP, CKB to HBB, 5 February 1900.
19 BASFP, CKB to HBB, 1 June 1900.
20 BASFP, CKB to HBB, 13 July 1901.
21 Dion Fortune, *Psychic Self-Defense* (Newburyport, MA: Red Wheel/Weiser, 2020[1930]), pp xxvii–xxxiv.

10 SOCIALITES AND SUFFRAGETTES – PROJECTS FOR THE SMYTHS

1 Jacques-Émile Blanche, *Portraits of a Lifetime*, trans., ed. Walter Clement (London: J.M. Dent & Sons Ltd, 1937), p.121.
2 Ethel Smyth, *What Happened Next* (London: Longmans, Green and Co., 1940), p.219.
3 Ethel Smyth, *As Time Went On* (London: Longmans, Green and Co., 1936), p.177.
4 BASFP, CKB to HBB, 10 March 1899.
5 BASFP, CKB to HBB, 10 February 1910.
6 BASFP, CKB to HBB, 11 September 1911.
7 'Small Talk', *The Sketch*, 21 October 1914; 88; 1134; ProQuest p.58.
8 Hermione Lee, *Edith Wharton* (London: Chatto & Windus, 2007), pp 237–8.
9 'The Police Raid Hill Hall', *The Essex County Chronicle*, 9 February 1918, p.2.
10 Smyth, *What Happened Next*, p.97.
11 Selaby Hall, Gainford, investigative work in the west wings. ASUD Report 995, May 2003, Archaeological Services University of Durham.
12 Selaby Hall, Gainford, historic building report, by Peter Lawson-Smith Associates, December 1993.
13 BASFP, CKB to HBB, 2 January 1900.
14 BASFP, CKB to HBB, 30 December 1900.
15 BASFP, CKB to HBB, 20 January 1900.
16 BASFP, CKB to HBB, 6 January 1901.
17 BASFP, CKB to HBB, 23 November 1903.
18 'Modernised Wemmergill Hall, Motoring Through the Lune Valley, the Exquisite Taste of a Lady', *The Teesdale Mercury*, Wednesday, 27 July 1904.
19 'Entertaining in Yorkshire for "The Twelfth"', *The Gentlewoman and Modern Life*, vol.35, no.892, 10 August 1907, p.184.
20 Ethel Smyth, *The Memoirs of Ethel Smyth*, abridged by Ronald Crichton (Harmondsworth: Viking, 1987), p.161.
21 Smyth, *Memoirs*, p.226.
22 Smyth, *Memoirs*, p.271–2.
23 BASFP, CKB to HBB, 28 December 1895.
24 BASFP, 6 December 1902.
25 BASFP, 28 August 1904.
26 BASFP, 17 September 1902.

27 BASFP, 27 October 1902.
28 BASFP, 4 November 1902.
29 BASFP, 21 May 1903.
30 Maria Theresa Earle, *Letters to Young and Old* (London: Smith, Elder, 1906) pp 199–20.
31 BASFP, CKB to CHB, 29 March 1910.
32 Transcription by Surrey History Centre of an incomplete and unpublished memoir, the original manuscript held in the Ethel Smyth Collection, University of Michigan, 1910–62.
33 Census accessed through https://www.ancestrylibrary.com.

II ROMAN HIGH SOCIETY MEETS THE LADY ARCHITECT – PROJECTS FOR THE FRANKENSTEINS

1 Mrs. Winthrop Chanler, *Roman Spring* (Boston: Little, Brown, 1934), p.280 and Rogers Memorial Collection, Harvard Library.
2 Letter to Margaret Chanler from Edith Wharton, 8 March 1903, Yale University.
3 Kazimierz Reychmann, *Szkice genealogiczne, Serja 1* [Genealogical Sketches, Series 1](Warsaw: F. Hoesick, 1936).
4 The Kronenberg Family, The YIVO Encyclopedia of Jews in Eastern Europe, online edition. https://yivoencyclopedia.org/article.aspx/Kronenberg_Family.
5 Andrzej S. Ciechanowiecki, 'Remarks on, and a Supplement to the 'Genealogical Sketches' of Kazimierz Reychmann', in Antony Polonsky (ed.), *Polin: Studies in Polish Jewry Volume 5: New Research, New Views*, (Liverpool University Press/Littman Library of Jewish Civilization, 2008), pp 372–84.
6 Teodor Jeske-Choiński, *Neofici polscy; materyały historyczne* [Polish Neophytes: Historical Materials], (Warsaw: Druk P. Laskauera, 1904), p.190.
7 Albert Sowiński, *Les musiciens polonais et slaves, anciens et modernes* [Polish and Slavic musicians, ancient and modern] (Paris: Adrien Le Clere et cie, 1857), pp 198, 199.
8 *Le Mémorial diplomatique*, 1 January 1876 (Paris), p.220.
9 Paris, France, Births, Marriages and Deaths, 1555–1928 for Edouard de Frankenstein, 08e arrondissement, 1888, Décès [Death], All, 0001-1042. Image 122 of 146, accessed through https://www.ancestrylibrary.com
10 Brianna Carafa, *Gli angeli personali* (Rome: Cliquot, 2021), p.21.
11 Carafa, *Gli angeli personali*, p.23.
12 Carafa, *Gli angeli personali*, p.24.
13 Maria Franca Mellano, *I salesiani nel quartiere romano del Testaccio: primo ventennio del '900* (Rome: LAS, 2002), p.97.
14 *The Westminster Gazette*, 'The Pope Yields to the Marquise', *The New York Times*, 15 March 1895, p.13.
15 *Rivista internazionale di scienze sociali e discipline ausiliarie: pubblicazione periodica dell'Unione cattolica per gli studi sociale in Italia*, vol.14, pt.2, 1906 (Rome: A. Befani), p.570.
16 *Il voto alle donne: le donne dall'elettorato alla partecipazione politica* (Rome: Camera dei Deputati, 1965), pp 108–14.
17 Marianna Soderini, 'Pauperismo – Caratteri e rimedi', *Nuova Antologia di Lettere, Scienze ed Arti*, vol.228, no.912, 1909, p.647.
18 Stefania Bartoloni, *Italiane alla guerra: l'assistenza ai feriti 1915–1918* (Venice: Marsilio, 2003), p.70.
19 BASFP, HBB to CKB, 16 February 1894.
20 BASFP, CKB to HBB, 27 February 1897.
21 BASFP, HBB to ES, 27 December 1897.
22 BASFP, HBB to ES, Last Sunday in March 1901.
23 Guida Monaci, 'Guida Commerciale di Roma e Provincia, Direzione ed Amministrazione' (Rome, 1905) pp 523, 1613.
24 BASFP, The Hibbert-Hingston Collection, Marianna Soderini to CKB, 3 September 1901.
25 BASFP, CKB to CHB, 6 February 1902.
26 BASFP, HBB to ES, 5 June 1901.
27 BASFP, CKB to HBB, 14 March 1905.
28 *Bollettino della Società geografica italiana*, year 4, no.3–4, 1891 (Palermo: Tipografia Editrice, 1891), pp 12–36.
29 'Notes et Impressions sur l'Afrique Australe', *La Revue Générale*, vol.54 (Brussels, 1891), pp 425–48.
30 'Italian Somaliland – Agricultural Economy in General – Land Tenure and Colonization', *International Review of Agricultural Economics* (Monthly Bulletin of Economic and Social Intelligence), vol.75, no.3, 1917, p.107.
31 Henri de Frankenstein, *Lettres de Somalie de Henri de Frankenstein et sa femme Anne Seabury Brewster, 1908–1937* (Dijon: Darantiere, 1968), p.144.
32 De Frankenstein, *Lettres de Somalie*, p.13.
33 BASFP, The Hibbert-Hingston Collection, HBB to CKB, 13 March 1905.
34 BASFP, The Hibbert-Hingston Collection, HBB to CKB, 2 December 1905.
35 BASFP, The Hibbert-Hingston Collection, HBB to CKB, 17 May 1905.
36 BASFP, The Hibbert-Hingston Collection, HBB to CKB, 2 December 1905.

12 THE HEIRESS AND THE CASTLE – PROJECT FOR CONTESSA ADA TELFENER

1. Lady Harriet J. Jephson, *Notes of a Nomad* (London: Hutchinson and Co., 1918), p.130.
2. Berlin, *Silver Platter*. The mansion was purchased in 1876.
3. 'Milestones', *Time Magazine*, 17 September 1928 (Obituary of Louise Mackay).
4. Giulia Ajmone Marsan, *Giuseppe Telfener: precursore degli imprenditori globali* [Giuseppe Telfener: precursor of global entrepreneurs] (Milan: Archinto, 2018), p.70 (quoting article 'Carnet d'un mondain', *Le Figaro*, 2 March 1881).
5. Paul Lambeth, 'Title Not All: Miss Reid Is Not Anxious To Marry A Foreign Nobleman Merely For The Rank. No Chance For Brooke Rumor That She Will Wed Heir Of Warwick Doubted', *Detroit Free Press* (1858–1922), 15 October 1905.
6. Ajmone Marsan, *Giuseppe Telfener*.
7. Lily Theodoli, *Under Pressure* (New York: Macmillan, 1892), p.217.
8. *La Stampa*, Sunday 21 April 1878, p.3.
9. Berlin, *Silver Platter*, p.268.
10. 'Count Joseph Telfener: Something About The Gentleman Now Building Railroads In Texas A Friend Of King Humbert, Of Italy, Who Prefers A Busy Life In America To One Of Ease And Luxury In Europe', *Daily American* (1875–94), 14 December 1882.
11. 'Espèces Chevaline', *Exposition Universelle Internationale de 1878, à Paris. Catalogue officiel Tome VII, Concours d'Animaux Vivants* (Paris: Imprimerie Nationale, 1878), pp 35, 37.
12. Telesforo Sarti, *I Rappresentanti del Piemonte e d'Italia nelle tredici legislature del regno* (Rome: Paolini, 1880), pp 826–7.
13. 'Paris: The Ball at M. Henri de Cernuschi's: A Dream of Light and Flowers', *Chicago Daily Tribune*, 11 June 1878.
14. 'The Marriage of Count Telfener to Miss Ada Hungerford', *Boston Daily Advertiser*, 4 April 1879, p.2; Ajmone Marsan, *Giuseppe Telfener*, p.72.
15. *The American Register for Paris and the Continent*, 4 October 1879.
16. Berlin, *Silver Platter*, p.281.
17. Ajmone Marsan, *Giuseppe Telfener*, pp 95–6.
18. Elena Carpi, Carolina Flinz and Annick Farina, eds, *Le guide touristique: lieu de rencontre entre lexique et images du patrimoine culturel*, vol. I (Florence: Firenze University Press, 2018), pp 71–3.
19. *Guida Commerciale di Roma e Provincia*, 1905, p.781. Ajmone Marsan, *Giuseppe Telfener*.
20. Jephson, *Notes of a Nomad*, p.131.
21. The purchase of the property was carried out by Countess Ada on 30 July 1901, deed Vannisanti Pietro Notary in Rome registered in Rome on 12 August 1901 at no.828, and transferred to the land registry on 29 August 1901 at number 3309. Information located at the State Archives of Perugia, the registers of the Gregorian Land Registry.
22. Ajmone Marsan, *Giuseppe Telfener*, pp 104–7.
23. The retaining wall appears on an 1895 Cadastral Map located at the Land Registry of the Municipality of Perugia. Strangely, the map does not show the ancient tower.
24. BASFP, CKB to HBB, 19 December 1903.
25. BASFP, CKB to HBB, 12 January 1904.
26. BASFP, The Hibbert-Hingston Collection, HBB to CKB, 3 February 1904.
27. BASFP, CKB to HBB, 23 February 1905.
28. BASFP, CKB to HBB, 8 March 1894.
29. Ajmone Marsan, *Giuseppe Telfener*, p.105.
30. Christopher Hussey, 'Beckley Park, Oxfordshire: The Residence of Mr. Percy Feilding', *Country Life*, vol.65, no.1679, 1929, pp 407–8.
31. 'Court and Society', *Sunday Times*, 13 August 1905, p.4. The Sunday Times Historical Archive (accessed 13 February 2022).
32. 'A Wonderful Operation', *The Phrenological Journal and Science of Health*, vol.118, no.9, 1905, p.300.

13 EDWARDIAN PROSPERITY AND PEKES MANOR AND ESTATE

1. BASFP, CKB to HBB, 1 March 1904.
2. BASFP, PHF to CHB, 29 March 1904.
3. BASFP, PHF to CHB, 15 February 1905.
4. BASFP, PHF to CHB, 15 February 1905.
5. BASFP, CKB to HBB, 18 August 1907.
6. Paul Rutledge, *History of Colkirk Church* (Colkirk, 1960), p.16.
7. BASFP, CKB to HBB, 17 January 1908.
8. Olive Risley Seward, *Around the World Stories* (Boston: D. Lothrop & Co., 1889), p.166.
9. 'P.F.', 'Mr. Terence Bourke', *The Times*, 22 May 1923, p.14.
10. Sir Harry Johnston, *The Story of My Life* (London: Chatto & Windus, 1923), pp 86–7.
11. Wilfrid Scawen Blunt, *My Diaries, Being a Personal Narrative of Events, 1888–1914* (London: Martin Secker, 1919).
12. Letter from Logan Pearsall Smith to his sister, 19 February 1913, Houghton Library, Harvard University.

13 H.A. Bryden (ed.), *Great and Small Game of Africa; an Account of the Distribution, Habits, and Natural History of the Sporting Mammals, with Personal Hunting Experiences* (London: Roland Ward Ltd, 1899), p.513.
14 Philip Mainwaring Johnston, 'Ancient Paintings at Pekes, Chiddingly', *Sussex Archaeological Collections Relating to the History and Antiquities of the County*, vol.53, 1910, pp 38–142.
15 Frances Garnet Wolseley, *Some of the Smaller Manor Houses of Sussex* (London and Boston: The Medici Society, 1925), p.180.
16 *The Gardeners' Chronicle: A Weekly Illustrated Journal of Horticulture and Allied Subjects*, vol.33 (third series), London, 1903, p.280.
17 'To-day's Gossip', *Nottingham Evening Post*, 14 September 1906, p.4.
18 H. Avray Tipping, 'A Bothy at Godinton', *Country Life*, vol.22, no.557, 1907, pp 335–7.
19 'Oast House Fatality', *London Standard*, Newspaper Archives, 31 August 1909, p.7.
20 J.H. Elder-Duncan, *Country Cottages and Week-End Homes, with Numerous Illustrations and Plans of Cottages by Well-Known Architects* (London: Cassell and Co., Ltd., 1912), pp 81, 91, 92.
21 *The Times*, Tuesday, 22 May 1923, no.43347, p.14.

14 HOME SWEET HOME: STONEHILL, CHIDDINGLY, EAST SUSSEX

1 Letter to Lady Ottoline Morrell, located at the Harry Ransom Humanities Research Center, The University of Texas at Austin.
2 BASFP, CKB to CHB, 7 July 1913.
3 Logan Pearsall Smith to his sister Mary Berenson, 20 November 1912, Houghton Library, Harvard University.
4 BASFP, PHF to CHB, 17 January 1913.
5 BASFP, PHF to CKB, The Hibbert-Hingston Collection, 23 April 1912.
6 BASFP, CKB to CHB, 25 March 1916.
7 BASFP, CKB to CHB, 13 November 1913.
8 Sale particulars, 'The Stonehill and Gatehouse Estates, Chiddlingly Sussex', 18 May 1920, Historic England Archive, Swindon, England.
9 BASFP, PHF to CHB, 15 August 1919.
10 BASFP, CKB to CHB, 31 January 1913.
11 BASFP, CKB to CHB, 11 September 1911.
12 BASFP, CKB TO CHB, 10 April 1913.

13 BASFP, CKB TO CHB, 10 April 1913.
14 *Country Life*, 5 May 1923, p.625.
15 Sir Lawrence Weaver, *Small Country Houses: Their Repair and Enlargement; Forty Examples Chosen from Five Centuries* (London: Country Life and George Newnes Ltd; New York: Charles Scribner's Sons, 1914), pp 53–6.
16 BASFP, CKB to CHB, 10 April 1913.
17 BASFP, CKB to CHB, 29 March 1915.
18 BASFP, CKB to CHB, 25 November 1918.
19 BASFP, CKB to CHB, 15 February 1919.
20 BASFP, CKB to CHB, 19 October 1919.
21 BASFP, CKB to CHB, 24 December 1919.
22 BASFP, CKB to CHB, 24 December 1919
23 BASFP, CKB to CHB, 3 February 1920.
24 Denis Mackail, *The Story of J.M.B.* (London: Peter Davies, 1941), p.550.

15 MOATED GRANDEUR AND SHABBY CHIC: BECKLEY PARK

1 BASFP, CKB to CHB, 16 May 1921.
2 HM Land Registry, Gloucester Office. Title Number ON145383. Clotilde is listed as the sole purchaser.
3 Ottoline Morrell, *Ottoline at Garsington: Memoirs of Lady Ottoline Morrell, 1915–1918*, ed. with Introduction by Robert Gathorne-Hardy (London: Faber and Faber, 1974), p.217.
4 Ray McKenzie, *The Flower and the Green Leaf: Glasgow School of Art in the Time of Charles Rennie Mackintosh* (Edinburgh: Luath Press Limited, 2009), p.24.
5 Margaret Moran, 'Bertrand Russell as Scogan in Aldous Huxley's *Crome Yellow*', *Mosaic: An Interdisciplinary Critical Journal*, vol.17, no.3, 1984, pp 117–32.
6 BASFP, CKB to CHB, 11 November 1920.
7 BASFP, CKB to CHB, 12 December 1920.
8 BASFP, PHF to CHB, 8 October 1921.
9 BASFP, PHF to CHB.
10 BASFP, PHF to CHB, 18 February 1927.
11 BASFP, CKB to CHB, 12 April 1920. KCB – Knight Commander of the Bath; KCVO – Knight Commander of the Royal Victorian Order; CMG – Companion of the Order of St Michael and St George.
12 Machtelt Brüggen Israëls, 'Mrs. Berenson, Mrs. Gardner and Miss Toplady: Connoisseurship, Collecting and Commerce in London (1898–1905)', *Visual Resources*, vol.33, no.1/2, 2017, pp 158–81.
13 Brüggen Israëls, 'Connoisseurship, Collecting and Commerce'.

14 Letter from Logan Pearsall Smith to Mary Berenson, 26 March 1906, Houghton Library, Harvard University.
15 BASFP, CKB to CHB, 4 March 1921.
16 BASFP, CKB to CHB, 16 March 1921.
17 BASFP, CKB to CHB, 16 May 1921.
18 Robert Becker, *Nancy Lancaster: Her Life, Her World, Her Art* (New York: Alfred A. Knopf, 1996), p.198.
19 Harry Brewster, *Memoirs, Part 2, 1930–1956*. Unpublished.
20 BASFP, letter from Ralph Brewster to CHB, 30 July 1923.
21 Letter, CKB to Sophie Benckendorff, 13 February 1924, Columbia University.
22 Maurice Cardiff, *The Life of Osbert Moore Also Known As Ñanamoli Thera* (The Netherlands: Path Press).
23 Author's conversation with Clotilde's grandchildren, Jocelyn Feilding and Valerie Hibbert-Hingston.
24 BASFP, CKB to CHB, 6 May 1927.
25 BASFP, CKB to CHB, 28 May 1925.
26 BASFP, CKB to CHB, 18 June 1925.
27 BASFP, CKB to CHB, 1 January 1927.
28 'River Bathing Romance', *Daily Mail*, 4 September 1930, p.7.
29 Tiffany Daneff, 'As Old as Time', *Country Life*, 25 December 2019, pp 46–50.
30 BASFP, CKB to CHB, 6 June 1921.
31 Alan Brooks and Jennifer Sherwood, *Oxfordshire: North and West*, Pevsner Architectural Guides: Buildings of England (New Haven: Yale University Press, 2017), p.136.
32 Matriculation card for Osbert John Salvin Moore, Exeter College Archives.
33 Maurice Cardiff, *Friends Abroad: Memories of Lawrence Durrell, Freya Stark, Patrick Leigh-Fermor, Peggy Guggenheim, and Others* (London and New York: Radcliffe Press, 1997), p.145.
34 'Beckley Park', *Country Life*, Future Publishing Ltd, ID: 1000681886.
35 'A Garden of Topiary Box at Beckley Park In England', *The Boxwood Bulletin*, American Boxwood Society, vol.6, no.1, July 1966.
36 BASFP, Elisabeth Hildebrand Brewster to CBF, 15 June 1929.
37 BASFP, CKB to Elisabeth Hildebrand Brewster, 8 February 1929.
38 BASFP, PHF to CHB, 17 August 1916.
39 Dame Ethel Smyth, 'Mrs. Percy Feilding, An Appreciation', *The Times*, 4 March 1937, p.16, no.47624.
40 Maurice Cardiff, 'Osbert Moore, A Character Sketch', in *Visakha Puja* (Bangkok: The Buddhist Association of Thailand, 1967).
41 Cardiff, 'Osbert Moore'.
42 Harry Brewster, 'Reflections on Clotilde', 22 April 1980. Unpublished.
43 Brewster, 'Reflections'.
44 BASFP, Harry Brewster to Elisabeth Brewster, 3 March 1937.

INDEX

Numbers in *italics* refer both to illustrations and/or captions

Aalto, Aino (née Marsio) 10
Aalto, Alvar 10
Abbé Constantin, L' 119
Abraham Box 165–6
Aldershot, Hampshire 89, 99, 100
Anderson, Dr Elizabeth Garrett 48
Architecture, A Profession or an Art 55
Around the World Stories 132
Art Workers Guild 55
Arts and Crafts movement 54, 85
Asquith, Margaret 151

Baillie Scott, M.H. 80
Balfour, Gerald 31–2, *33*, 173
Balliol College, Oxford University 57, 163
Baltus, Georges-Marie 156
Baltus, Silvie 'Vivi' (née Hildebrand) 156
Barberini, Princess Henrietta (née Frankenstein) 114
Barbialla, Italy 42, 69, 174
Bardini, Stefano 164
Bargello Museum 23
Barrie, James Matthew 154
Barton Street, Westminster, London 74–8, 174
Baudissin, Wolf Graf 12
Bauhof, Philip 57–9, 61, 63, 66, 173
Benckendorff, Countess Maria Sergeievna von (Princess Dolgorukova) 72, 175
Benckendorff, Countess Sophie von (née Shuvalov) 72, 98, 121, 145, 152, 170, 175–7

Berenson, Bernard 163
Berenson, Mary (née Pearsall Smith) 133, 144, 163
Bertrand, Russell 159
Blanche, Jacques-Émile 89
Blomfield, Sir Reginald 8–9, 54–63, *63*, 66, 68, 140, 173–4
Blunt, Wilfred Scawen 133
Bourke, Blanche (née Wyndham), Lady Mayo 132–3, 137, 140–41
Bourke, Evelyn (née Haines) 133, 141
Bourke, Richard, the 6th Earl of Mayo 130, 132
Bourke, the Hon. Terence 130, 132–4, 140–41
Brewster, Anna Maria (née Bennet) 14–15, 17
Brewster, Christopher Henry 19, 24–5, 32, 66, 74, 76–8, 115–16, 127, 152, 163–5, 170
Brewster, Dr Christopher Starr 13–17, 20, 42,
Brewster, Clotilde (later Feilding) 8–10, *19, 27, 34, 45, 51, 55,* 68
    career 42–43, 67–74, 128–30
    childhood 22–5
    death 172
    education 22, 30, 32, 37–8, 48, 51, 54–6, 59–61, 63, *64, 65,* 66
    influences on design styles 80, 85, 123, 138, 140, 151
    marriage 77–8, 127
    personality 9, 11, 13–15
    as described by Harry Brewster 172
    as described by Maurice Cardiff 171

    as described by Ethel Smyth 9, 171
    projects 173–7
        Beckley Park, Beckley, Oxfordshire 123, 155–6, *156, 157, 158,* 159–67, *60, 61, 62, 66, 67,* 177
        – Gardens 167–8, 170, *168, 169,* 177
        Boer War Memorial Fountain, Farnborough, Hampshire *100,* 98–101
        Castello dell'Oscano, Cenerente, Perugia, Italy 121, *122,* 123, *124, 125, 126,* 126, 175
        Church Farm Bungalow, Rustington, West Sussex 85, *86, 87,* 175–6
        Coign Cottage, Woking, Surrey 101, 176
        Country House for Miss Hamilton, Rustington, West Sussex 80–82, *81, 82,* 174
        Funerary monument of Frederick Hamlyn, All Saints Churchyard, Clovelly, Devon *128, 129,* 175
        Hearn mausoleum 70, *71,* 175
        Nursing home, Cavendish Square, London 79, 87–8, 174
        Old Mill Cottage buildings, Rustington, West Sussex 80, 82, *83, 84,* 174
        Palazzo Frankenstein, Rome, Italy 102, *112,* 113, 175
        Palazzo Soderini, Rome, Italy 8, 73, 102, 105–6, 109–10, 113, *106, 107, 108, 109, 110, 111,* 175

Pekes Manor and Estate, Chiddingly, East Sussex (house) 134, *135*, *136*, *137*, 176
 – Colonnade Garden *139*, 176
 – Edwardian Wing 137–8, *138*, 176
 – Entry gate and lodge 134, 176
 – Oast House 21, 138, *139*, *140*, 140–41, 176
Overmantel mirror, Highfield, Shoreham Oaks, Kent *70*, 71, 174
Rood Screen, St. Mary's Church Colkirk, Norfolk 129, *129*, 176
Selaby Hall, Gainford, Darlington 91, *91*, *92*, *93*, *94*, 93, *95*, 95,
Selaby Lodge, Gainford, Darlington 95–7, *96*
Siegfried Fountain 68–9, *68*, 174
Stonehill, Chiddingly, East Sussex (house) 142, *143*, 144–5, *145*, *146*, *147*, 147, *148*
 – barn 150–51
 – cottages 152, *152*
 – farm buildings 151, *151*
 – garden walls 149–50, *150*
 – landscaping 149
Villino Frankenstein, Rome, Italy 102, 115–16, *116*, *117*, 175
Wemmergill Hall *97*, 97–8, 175
Speech on architecture as a profession for women 67–8
Brewster, Harry 13, 17, 172
Brewster, Henry Bennet 'H.B.' 13–17, *15*, 19, 21–2, 29, 39–41, 44, 51, 72, 75–6, 80, 91, 97–8, 102–3, 106, 113, 115–16, 121, 123, 192
 advising Clotilde on architectural training 47–8, 50
 romance with Ethel Smyth 26–9
Brewster, Julia (née Stockhausen) 12–13, *13*, 17, 19, 21–2, 24, 26, 28–30, 39–42, 47, 50–52
Brewster, 'Kate' Mary Catherine (later Baronne de Terrouenne) 14, 47, 71
Brewster, Louis Seabury 14, 16
Brewster, Ralph 43, 163, 165
Brewster, William (Elder Brewster, Mayflower passenger) 11
Brewster, William Cullen 115

Brewster-Hildebrand, Elisabeth 'Lisl' 31–2, *33*, 35, 78, 170,
Brittain-Catlin, Timothy 151, 159
Brooke, Lady Margaret, Ranee of Sarawak 71, 175
Brydon, John MacKean 48
Buchan, William 72, 171

Cardiff, Maurice 165, 167, 171,
Cave, Walter 151
Cernuschi, Henri 119–20
Certosa di Firenze (Chartreuse) 23
Champneys, Basil 48, 85
Chanler, Margaret 102
Charles, Bessie Ada 8, 60
Charles, Ethel Mary 8, 60
Château Ben Negro 133–4, 141, *133*
Château d'Avignonet 26, 28–9, 30, 170, 173
Chicago World's Fair (*see* the World's Columbian Exposition)
Chiostro dello Scalzo 38
Chopin, Frédéric 11–12
Cini, Countess Adele (née Piacentini) 45, 181n6
Cobb, Anna 'Annie' (née Raeburn) 49
Cole, Henrietta 'Henny' 73
Cole, Letitia 'Tishy' 73
Colonna di Stigliano, Princess Evelyne 'Eva' (née Bryant-Mackay) 119
Colonna di Stigliano, Prince Ferdinando 119
Cohen, Arthur Merton 71, 145, 170, 174–5
Cottier, Daniel 48
Country Life 10, 123, 140, 145, *146*, *148*, 150, 154, 156, *158*, 160, 160–61, *161*, *162*, 164, *166*, 168
Crane, Lionel 57, 58–61
Crawshay, Mary (née Leslie) 77, 175
Cripps Cottage 156, 164, 177

Dante (Dante Alighieri) 24
Davies, Michael Llewelyn 154
Della Robbia workshop 20–21, *141*, 141
Devey, George 80
Dial House, Farnham, Surrey 140
Dick, Captain H.P. 154
Dodge, Mary 98–9
Donatello (sculptor) 23, 31

Douglas, Lord Alfred 152
Duse, Eleonora 31, 73, 175

Earle, Maria Theresa 100
Edwardians and Their Houses (Timothy Brittain-Catlin) 151, 159
Eugénie, Empress 76, 99

Falkner, Harold 58–61, 63, 140, 173
Farnborough, Hampshire, UK 62, 76, 90, 98–100, 128–9, 144, 173–6
Fawcett, Millicent Garrett 48
Fawcett, Philippa Garrett 48
Feilding, Amanda 167
Feilding, Basil 78, 128, 155, 162, 165–8, 171–2
Feilding, Clotilde Kate (*see* Brewster, Clotilde Kate)
Feilding, Major General Sir Geoffrey 153, 163, 165–6
Feilding, Percy Henry 9–10, 57, *57*–61, 63, 90, 132, 140–41, 144–5, 147, 152–4, 156, 161–8, *167*
 career 128–30, *130*
 death 170
 marriage 77–8, 127
 projects 175–7
 Beckley Park, Beckley, Oxfordshire 123, 155–6, *158*, 159–67, *160*, *161*, *162*, *166*, *167*, 177
 – gardens *157*, 167–8, 170, *168*, *169*, 177
 Funerary monument of Frederick Hamlyn, All Saints Churchyard, Clovelly, Devon 129, *129*, 175
 Pekes Manor and Estate, Chiddingly, East Sussex (house) 134, *135*, *136*, *137*, 176
 – Colonnade Garden *139*, 176
 – Edwardian Wing 137–8, *138*, 176
 – Entry gate and lodge 134, 176
 – Oast House 21, 138, *139*, *140*, 140–41, 176
 Rood Screen, St Mary's Church Colkirk, Norfolk 129, *129*, 176
 Stonehill, Chiddingly, East Sussex (house) 142, *143*, 144–5, *145*, *146*, *147*, 147, *148*
 – barn 150–51

INDEX 189

– cottages 152, *152*
– farm buildings 151, *151*
– garden walls 149–50, *150*
– landscaping 149
Feilding, Susan 128, 152, 167
Forster, Edward Morgan 170
Fortune, Dion 88
Franco-Prussian War 16
Frankenstein, Alessandra (née Aleksandra Kronenberg) 72–3, 102–3, 106, 113–14, 121, 175
Frankenstein, Edward 103
Frankenstein, Henri 73, 102, 114–15, 121, 130, 175
Frankenstein, Anne Seabury (née Brewster) 71, 106, 114–15, 175

Garrett, Agnes 47–8, 68, 80
Garrett, Rhoda 48, 80
Gentlewoman and Modern Life, The 98
George & Peto 60–61
Georgii, Theodor 31, *32*
Girton College, Cambridge University 53
Giovannoni, Gustavo 106
Giuliani, Carlo 123
Gladstone, Helen 53
Glehn, Louis de 68, 74
Glehn, Wilfrid de 74, 90
Gleichen, Lady Feodora 71, 74, 76, 90, 174–5
Greyfriars, Ascot 71, 175
Godinton Park, Ashford, Kent 55, 140
Gothic revival style 61, 80
Graves, Margaret 53
Grenoble, Switzerland 26, 28

Halkett, Baroness Emily 73–5, 173
Halkett, Baron Hugh Colin 73, 74
Halkett, Baroness Sarah (née Phelps Stokes) 73
Halevy, Ludovic 119
Hamilton, Dr Lillias 72, 79, 87–8, 174
Hamilton, Mary Christian Dundas 79–80, 82, 85, 87
Hammond, John 144
Hammond, Mr. (builder) 100
Hamlyn, Frederick *128*, 129, 175
Hamlyn Fane, Christine 128–9, 175
Hardy, Thomas 75

Hayden, Sophia 49–50
Hearn, Ellen (née Joubert de la Ferté) 71, 128, 170, 175
Heiden, Switzerland 76–7
Hertz, Henriette 73
Herzogenberg, Elisabeth 'Lisl' von (née Stockhausen) 12, 23, 39
Herzogenberg, Henrich Freiherr von 12, 23, 26, 47, 76
Hildebrand, Adolf 22, 26, 30–32, *34*, 35–6, 38, 40, 42–3, 45, 61–2, 66, 68–9, *69*, 71, 73, 77, 100, 109, 144, 164, 170, 173–5
Hildebrand, Eva 'Nini' 39, 42, 48, 50, 59, 116
Hildebrand, Irene (née Schäuffelen) 26, 30–31, 40, 42, 77
Hildebrand-Georgii, Irene 'Zusi' 31–2, *32*, 35
Hippisley, Honoria Violet (née Smyth) 89, 98–100, 175
Hippisley, Richard Lionel 98–9
Hollings, Nina 99
Homberger, Heinrich Emil 32, 173
Hopkins, Michael John 10
Hopkins, Patty 10
Horsley, Gerald 62
Horsley, Sir Victor 126
House and Garden (New York) 161, 164
Howe, Lois Lilley 49
Hungerford, Daniel Elihu 118
Hungerford, Eveline (née Visera) 118, 121
Hunter, Mary (née Smyth) 89–91, 95–6, 98–9
Hunter, Charles 89–91, 96–8
Hussey, Christopher 123
Huxley, Aldous 156, 159
Huxley, Maria (née Nys) 156, 159

Indische Baukunst (Emanuel La Roche) 43
International Congress of Women 8, 67
International Suffrage Alliance 74
Italian National Theatre 73, 174

Jacobean Revival style 85
James, Henry 19, 31, 67, 75, 90
James, Mr. (clerk of works) 57–9, 61, 63, 66

Jephson, Lady Harriet 118, 121
Johnston, Sir Harry 133
Johnston, Philip Mainwaring 134
Jones, Inigo 130

Kaufhaus, Freiburg-im-Breisgau, Germany 56
Karo, Georg Heinrich 47
King Alfred Monument 74, 174
Koch, Gaetano 106
Kronenberg, Henryk Andrzej 103
Kronenberg, Leopold 103
Kronenberg, Samuel Eleazer 103
Kurz, Isolde 31

La Roche, Emanuel 26, 30, 36–9, *37*, 40–43, 47–9
Lady's Pictorial 8, 68
Lancaster, Nancy (formerly Tree) 9, 164
Lees Court, Sheldwich, near Faversham, Kent 130, *131*
Lepri, Marchese Carlo 114
Lee, Vernon (née Violet Paget) 89, 99
Leighton, Sir Frederic 60
Levi, Hermann 31, *62*, 62, *63*, 173
Lutyens, Edwin 80, 85
Lytton, Lady Constance 100

Mackay, John William 118–20
Mackay, Louise (née Hungerford) 118–19, 121
MacNamara, Lady Sophia 71
Magnanelli, Candida 22, 40, 41
Marsan, Giulia Ajmone 119
Melvill, Alice 79
Memorialists 54
Messer, Arthur 101
Middle Park, Beckley, Oxfordshire 156, 177
Milman, Angelina Frances 'Lena' 75–6, 99
Milman, Gen. Sir George Bryan 75–6
Miss Toplady, Pimlico, London 163
Moore, George 75, 89
Moore, Osbert 'Bertie' (later Ñanamoli Thera) 167–8, 171–2
Morrell, Lady Ottoline 128, 142, 154, 156, 159, *167*

190   CLOTILDE BREWSTER

Morrell, Philip 154, 156, 163
Motley, John Lothrop 12–13
Murat, Princess Eugène 89, 99

Newnham College, Cambridge University 48, 50–54, 79, 85
Nichols, Minerva Parker 49
Niven, Wigglesworth, & Falkner 140
Nyon, Switzerland 47–8, 51

Old Cottages and Farmhouses in Kent and Sussex (Edward Guy Dawber) *143*
Ospedale degli Innocenti 21

Palazzo Ferrini Cini 45
Palazzo Guicciardini 38
Palazzo Mattei *25*, 102, 174
Palazzo Vecchio 23–4
Parry, Sir Hubert 80
Parry, Maud 80
Passage to India, A (E.M. Forster) 170–71
Pazzi Chapel 38
Pearsall Smith, Logan 133, 144, 163
Pearson, Frank Loughborough 56
Pevsner, Sir Nikolaus 10, 167
Piazza del Popolo, Rome 8, *104*, *105*, 106, 110,
Phantasms of the Living 80
Polignac, Princess Edmond de 89, 99
Ponsonby, Lady Mary (née Bulteel) 72, 76, 175, 176
Ponte Sant'Angelo, Rome 44
Porto di Ripetta, Rome 45, *46*

Rasponi dalle Teste, Count Giuseppe 31, 42–3, 69, 71, 173–4
Rasponi, Countess Angelica (née Pasolini) 31, 42
Rasponi, Lucrezia 'Rezia' 69, 42
Rod, Édouard 76
Rodin, Auguste 36, 90
Roman Spring (Margaret Chanler) 102
Rossi, Miss 22, 39
Royal Academy of Arts 8, 56, 59–62, 66
Royal Institute of British Architects (RIBA) 54
Rushes, Farnborough, Hampshire 62, 128–9, 173–5

St Paul's Girls' School competition 55, 62, *64–5*, 173
San Francesco di Paola, Florence, Italy 31–2, 35, 42
Sargent, John Singer 8, 90, 106, 128
Schumann, Clara (née Wieck) 12, 31
Schultz, Robert Weir 8
Scott Brown, Denise 10
Seitz, Rudolf 38
Selaby, racket court 96, 174
Selaby, stables 97
Seward, Olive Risley 132
Seymour, Louisa (née Weir) 24
Seymour, Brigadier General Truman 24–5
Shaw, Richard Norman 48, 54–6, 59, 60, 62, 66, 80, 85
Shaw-Stewart, Lady Alice (née Thynne) 177
Sheepshanks, John, Bishop of Norwich 74
Sheepshanks, Mary 74–8
Smyth, Ethel Mary 12–13, 17, *28*, 39, 45, 49, 74, 75, 76, 89–91, 98–9, 101, 171, 176
  romance with H.B. Brewster 26–9
Smyth, Robert Napier 76
Società romana di colonizzazione 114
Society for Psychical Research 79
Soderini, Count Edoardo 103, 106
Soderini, Countess Emilia 'Marianna' (née Frankenstein) 72, 102–6, 109, 113, 175
South Kensington Museum (later the Victoria and Albert Museum) 56, 58
Spiers, Richard Phené 60–61
Stockhausen, Baron Bodo Albrecht von 11–12, 12, 15
Stockhausen, Baroness Clothilde von (née Baudissin) 12, 15, 22–3, 39–41, 164
Stockhausen, Elisabeth (*see* Herzogenberg)
Stockhausen, Ernst von 12
Stockhausen, Julia (*see* Brewster)
Strong, Eugénie (née Sellers) 73, 75
Studio Moretti Caselli 123
Studley Horticultural and Agricultural College for Women, Warwickshire 87

Sundrum Castle, Ayrshire, Scotland 79
Swynnerton, Annie 90

Telfener, Countess Ada (née Hungerford) 118–21, 123, 126
Telfener, Count Guiseppe di Carlo 'Joseph' 119–21
Temple-Leader, Sir John 123
Terrouenne, Kate de (*see* Brewster, 'Kate' Mary Catherine)
Theodoli, Marchesa Lily (née Conrad) 106, 119
Theosophical Society 79
Thomas, Inigo 56, 66
Tobacco Depot (warehouse) 69, 71, 174
Tricca, Angiolo 24
Tricca, Fosco 23–4
Troubetzkoy, Prince Paul 90
Tudor style 80
Tylehurst, Forest Row, East Sussex 130, *130*, 176

Venturi, Robert 10
Vernon, William Warren 24
Vickery, Margaret Birney 52
Villa Ada (Cenerente) 121
Villa Ada (Rome) 120–21
Vitetti, Count Leonardo 126
Vitetti, Countess Natalie Mai (née Coe) 126
Viti de Marco, Marchesa Etta de (née Lathrop Dunham) 152
Vogue magazine 10
Voysey, C.F.A. 80

Wainwright, Oliver 10
Warren, Edward Prioleau 56
Waterhouse, Alfred 61
Wealden hall house 134, 144
Wharton, Edith 102
Wharton, Edward 'Teddy' 102
Wolkoff, Madame 71–2
Wolseley, Frances Garnet, 2nd Viscountess Wolseley 10, *135*, 137, 149
World's Columbian Exposition 8, 48–50, 173
Wren, Christopher 55, 75
'Wrenaissance' style 55, 62
Writer's Club, London 56–7
Wright, George F. 87–8

INDEX 191

PICTURE CREDITS

1, 2 courtesy of The Brewster Archives at San Francesco di Paola; 3 United States Library of Congress; 4 courtesy of The Brewster Archives at San Francesco di Paola; 5 Harvard Fine Arts Library, Digital Images and Slides Collection d2015.01580; 6 courtesy of Architekturmuseum der TUM, Sign. hild-491-1001; 7 courtesy of The Brewster Archives at San Francesco di Paola; 8 courtesy of Dr Johannes Wetzel; 9 courtesy of The Brewster Archives at San Francesco di Paola; 10 courtesy of Architekturmuseum der TUM, Sign. hild-238-3; 11 Photo © Museum Associates/LACMA; 12 The Eduard Wölfflin Thesaurus Foundation; 13 courtesy of The Brewster Archives at San Francesco di Paola; 14 The Royal Danish Library – Art Library; 15 courtesy of The Brewster Archives at San Francesco di Paola; 16 Photographer: Mary C.D. Hamilton, courtesy of The Brewster Archives at San Francesco di Paola; 17 courtesy of The Brewster Archives at San Francesco di Paola; 18 courtesy of Architekturmuseum der TUM, Sign. hild-208-43; 19 courtesy of Architekturmuseum der TUM, Sign. hild-208-42; 20 courtesy of RIBA Collections; 21 courtesy of The Brewster Archives at San Francesco di Paola; 22 Author; 23 courtesy of Amanda Feilding; 24, 25 courtesy of The Brewster Archives at San Francesco di Paola; 26, 27, 28 courtesy of Amanda Feilding; 29, 30, 31, 32, 33, 34 courtesy of Graeme Taylor; 35 © Raby Estates, courtesy of Lord Barnard; 36 courtesy of The Story, Durham D/Ad 1/1/1554; 37 courtesy of The Story, Durham D/Ad 1/1/1552; 38 courtesy of The Bowes Museum, Barnard Castle, County Durham; 39 courtesy of The Story, Durham D/Ad 1/1/1569; 40 courtesy of The Story, Durham D/Ad 1/1/1570; 41 courtesy of The Story, Durham D/Ad 1/1/1583; 42 courtesy of Mick Collinson; 43 Author; 44 United States Library of Congress; 45 Author; 46 courtesy of the Carena-Ricotti family; 47 Centro di Studi per la Storia dell'Architettura; 48 courtesy of the Carena-Ricotti family; 49 Author; 50, 51 courtesy of the Carena-Ricotti family; 52, 53 courtesy of the Centro di Studi per la Storia dell'Architettura; 54 courtesy of the Archivio Storico Capitolino di Roma Capitale; 55, 56, 57, 58 courtesy of Amanda Feilding; 59 courtesy of Pierfrancesco and Lory de Martino; 60 Author; 61, 62, 63, 64 courtesy of Fabrizio Temperini; 65 courtesy of Umberta Telfener; 66 courtesy of photographer Janice Dennis; 67 courtesy of photographer Paul Brittain; 68, 69, 70 courtesy of Amanda Feilding; 71 courtesy of Kildare Bourke-Borrowes; 72 courtesy of Brighton and Hove City Council; 73 Photographer: Candida Lacey, courtesy of The Brewster Archives at San Francesco di Paola; 74 Author; 75 courtesy of Kildare Bourke-Borrowes; 76, 77, 78, 79 Author; 80 courtesy of Pamela Berry; 81 Author; 82 Photographer: Christopher Brewster, courtesy of The Brewster Archives at San Francesco di Paola; 83 Author; 84, 85 Future Publishing Ltd; 86 Author; 87 Future Publishing Ltd; 88 Author; 89 Photographer: Christopher Brewster, courtesy of The Brewster Archives at San Francesco di Paola; 90 Author; 91, 92 Photographer: Christopher Brewster, courtesy of The Brewster Archives at San Francesco di Paola; 93, 94 Photographer: Norman Taylor, Author; 95 Author; 96 Future Publishing Ltd; 97, 98 Author; 99, 100, 101 Future Publishing Ltd; 102 Photographer: Ottoline Morrell, courtesy of The National Portrait Gallery, London; 103, 104 Photographer: Paul Nash, © Tate; 105 Future Publishing Ltd; 106 Author